Entrepreneurship and Organised Crime

Entrepreneurship and Organised Crime

Entrepreneurs in Illegal Business

Petter Gottschalk

Professor of Information Systems and Knowledge Management, Department of Organisation and Leadership, Norwegian School of Management, Norway. He also Lectures on Entrepreneurship and Organised Crime, Norwegian Police University College, Oslo, Norway

Edward Elgar

Cheltenham, UK • Northampton, MA, USA

Published by
Edward Elgar Publishing Limited
The Lypiatts
15 Lansdown Road
Cheltenham
Glos GL50 2JA
UK

Edward Elgar Publishing, Inc.
William Pratt House
9 Dewey Court
Northampton
Massachusetts 01060
USA

A catalogue record for this book
is available from the British Library

Library of Congress Control Number: 2009921835

ISBN 978 1 84844 316 7

Printed and bound by MPG Books Group Ltd, UK

Contents

Introduction		1
1.	Entrepreneurship in organised crime	4
	Organised crime	4
	Illegal business	7
	Criminal entrepreneurship	10
	Entrepreneurial capital	15
	The case of Terrence 'Terry' Adams	17
2.	Stage models for criminal entrepreneurs	19
	Stages of growth models	19
	Stages of criminal career	22
	The case of Willem 'The Nose' Holleeder	25
	Stages of growth for criminal organisations	25
	Alternative stage model for criminal organisations	30
	The case of Italian mafia Cosa Nostra	34
	Stages of organised crime by business organisations	38
	The case of diamonds by De Beers in Antwerp	43
	Stages of financial crime by business organisations	43
	The case of shipowner Anders Jahre	49
	Stages of business criminal interactions	50
3.	Entrepreneurial leadership and management	54
	Entrepreneurial judgment in decision making	54
	Entrepreneurial management	56
	Chief executive officers	57
	Leadership roles	61
	Managing criminal projects	66
	The case of Curtis 'Cocky' Warren	72
	The case of eco-crime: the tropical timber trade	76
4.	Value configurations in criminal entrepreneurship	78
	The value chain	79
	The value shop	81
	The value network	84
	Comparison of value configurations	86
	The case of illegal alcohol in Norway (value chain)	87
	The case of the Russian mafia (value shop)	88
	The case of Marzola Paedophile Services (value network)	90

5.	Entrepreneurial structure and culture	92
	Characteristics of organised crime groups	92
	Organisational structure	99
	Occupational culture	106
	Management structures	108
	Entrepreneurial education	109
	The case of London's first organised crime lord	111
	The case of the vehicle theft market in Bulgaria	115
6.	Entrepreneurial growth in illegal business	117
	Entrepreneurial strategy	118
	Expanding crime business	120
	Managing resources for crime	123
	Improving business processes	127
	How successful leaders think	129
	Women entrepreneurs in organised crime	131
	Interoperability in organised crime	133
	The case of Thomas 'The Licensee' McGraw	135
	The case of new players in an old game	139
7.	Strategic planning for criminal entrepreneurship	140
	Strategy levels and elements	141
	The Y model for IS/IT strategy work	145
	Describing the current IS/IT situation	148
	Describing the current and desired business situation	150
	Strategic alignment	153
	Crime strategy	160
	The case of Sam Goodman	161
	The case of strategic adaption by the Bedouin	162
8.	Knowledge management in criminal entrepreneurship	164
	Characteristics of knowledge	165
	Knowledge value level	169
	Identification of knowledge needs	170
	Knowledge categories	172
	Crime knowledge	180
	The case of terrorist networks	181
	The case of interviewing Finnish criminal entrepreneurs	182
	The case of interviewing Norwegian alcohol smugglers	183
	Conclusion	185
	References	190
	Index	201

Introduction

Organised crime has received increased attention in recent years. To fight organised crime, there is a need to understand criminal organisations in terms of criminal business enterprises. In this book, terminology from the business and management literature is applied to the growing area of organised crime. Rather than thinking of organised crimes as acts of criminals, this book suggests an understanding of criminal entrepreneurship similar to non-criminal entrepreneurship.

Most of the entrepreneurship literature seems to engage in a positive enthusiasm about the role of the entrepreneur. There is a need to take a neutral look at how some entrepreneurs engage in illegal business and how entrepreneurship is not always a wholesome and clean endeavour. This book makes a contribution by linking entrepreneurship to organised crime and by revealing criminal aspects of entrepreneurial endeavour.

It is expected that this book will appeal to a readership interested in entrepreneurialism as well as criminology. What is unique about this book is its contribution to the entrepreneurship literature. This book investigates and describes how organised crime is often entrepreneurial in character and how entrepreneurship is often the basis for illegal business.

This book has been written with the interested reader in mind, who would like to explore new perspectives on entrepreneurship. The text has a clear logical structure, which systematically develops the reader's deeper comprehension of the basics of organised crime as an entrepreneurial business enterprise.

This book has been designed to provide the reader with a realistic concept and understanding of the problem of organised crime activity and the role of entrepreneurs in illegal business. The material is presented from an organisational, sociological, managerial, historical, theoretical and practical perspective so that the reader might appreciate insights into all aspects of organised crime activity.

Chapter 1 introduces and defines the basic concepts in this book: entrepreneurship, organised crime, entrepreneurs and illegal business. A criminal entrepreneur is a person who takes the risks involved in initiating and developing an illegal business enterprise. Potential business opportunities can be found in human trafficking, money laundering, the narcotics trade, slavery, piracy, smuggling, 'protection' and other illegal markets.

Chapter 2 introduces the concept of stages of growth. Several 'stages of growth' models for organised crime are presented. The idea is to understand illegal business as dynamic enterprises changing character over time. For example, a start-up enterprise might be classified as an opportunity-based criminal organisation. Later, it changes character to an activity-based criminal organisation, before moving on to a knowledge-based and later strategy-based criminal organisation.

Chapter 3 focuses on the leadership and management roles of criminal entrepreneurs. The emergence of criminal business enterprises is strongly associated with entrepreneurial innovation rather than an extension of managerial routine. While the entrepreneur is the agent of development, the criminal business enterprise is the means of coordination and the object of growth. As the means of coordination, the enterprise allows deployment of resources according to market opportunities. Entrepreneurial management manifests itself in a regime in the organisation. A regime is the set of rules, both formal and informal, that regulate the operation of organised crime and its interaction with society. It is dependent on both organisational structure and culture, where many criminal organisations choose a network structure rather than a hierarchical structure.

Both legal and illegal business entrepreneurs have the choice between three alternative value configurations, as presented in Chapter 4. A value configuration is the set of primary activities performed in the organisation to create value. Traditionally, many legal enterprises were value chains, where they transformed physical input through manufacturing to physical output. Value chains were the dominant value configuration in the industrial age. In the knowledge economy, more and more organisations have the value configuration of value shop and value network. Since few criminal entrepreneurs have involved themselves in manufacturing, criminal organisations have typically for centuries been value shops and value networks.

Entrepreneurial structure and culture in illegal business are discussed in Chapter 5. An occupational culture can be found among criminals, who tend to share the same values in successful enterprises. Some criminal organisations only employ relatives to secure loyalty and common values. Other businesses have only employees with the same ethnic background. In knowledge-intensive crimes, entrepreneurs tend to employ and organise knowledge workers who remain unknown to each other.

Chapter 6 presents a number of topics related to entrepreneurial growth in illegal business enterprises. A key element in entrepreneurship is managing resources, as resources are enablers of business development. Entrepreneurship can be perceived as a resource-based process, where entrepreneurial innovation is the carrying out of new combinations of available resources. It is such a process of recombination that leads to the innovation on which an organisation can build its competitive advantage over other illegal business enterprises. To manage resources successfully, there is a need to understand how resources promote corporate entrepreneurship and how different kinds of resources contribute to the enterprise's competitive advantage.

The final chapters, 7 and 8, take a broader view and introduce the general topics of strategic planning and knowledge management in organisations such as criminal organisations. While the topics are general and applicable to all business enterprises, they are important to entrepreneurship in criminal business development as well.

Upon completion of this book, readers will be able to define organised crime, discuss the role of entrepreneurs in illegal business and identify major entrepreneurial activities that are criminal in nature. Also, the reader should be able to identify different types of entrepreneurship by applying stages of growth for organised crime.

1. Entrepreneurship in organised crime

Organised crime by criminal entrepreneurs is not a new phenomenon. Felsen and Kalaitzidis (2005) describe historical cases such as piracy, slavery and opium smuggling. The most famous and far-reaching pirates in medieval Europe were the Vikings – warriors and looters from Scandinavia. They raided the coasts, rivers and inland cities of all Western Europe as far as Seville. While being admired as entrepreneurial heroes at home, they were the most feared enemy abroad.

ORGANISED CRIME

There are numerous definitions in the literature about what constitutes organised crime; however, many are confusing, puzzling or simply contradictory. As Abadinsky (2007) states, there is no generally accepted definition of organised crime. To further emphasize this point with regard to European attempts to define organised crime, von Lampe (2005) notes that the overall picture is murky, fragmented and often contradictory because of culturally induced differences in perceptions and conceptualizations. Lyman and Potter (2007) sum up the definitional problem when they comment that the greatest problem in understanding organised crime is not the word *crime* but the word *organised*.

Furthermore, part of the definitional problem is the idiosyncratic use of a range of different terms such as mafia, mob, gang, syndicate, outfit, network, cell, club, cartel and so forth, which are often used to characterize organised crime. In an attempt to somewhat overcome the definitional and theoretical challenge surrounding the meaning, nature and conceptualization of organised crime, we have drawn on Albanese's (2004) work in which he produced a definition of organised crime based on a consensus of writers, scholars and researchers over the past 35 years regarding organised criminal activity. Albanese's (2004: 4) definition is as follows:

> Organised crime is a continuing criminal enterprise that rationally works to profit from illicit activities that are often in great public demand. Its continuing existence is maintained through the use of force, threats, monopoly control, and/or the corruption of public officials.

This consensus definition of organised crime while not perfect is at least adequate for our purposes. It captures the essence very clearly of our thesis in this work, which is that first and foremost organised crime is an entrepreneurial business enterprise, regardless of what else it may be and/ or involve. For our purposes the central dynamic we are interested in exploring in this book is the notion of organised crime as entrepreneurship. Entrepreneurship involves risk-taking individuals who undertake industrial and commercial activities (businesses) with a view to making a profit. In the case of organised crime such entrepreneurial risk taking focuses on illegal activities as the core business strategy for profit making by those involved in the enterprise.

An organised crime is any crime committed by persons occupying, in an established division of labour, positions designed for commission of crime. Organised crime is crime committed by criminal organisations whose existence has continuity over time and across crimes, and that may use systematic violence and corruption to facilitate their criminal activities. These criminal organisations have varying capacities to inflict economic, physical, psychological and societal harm. The greater their capacity to harm, the greater the danger they pose to society. Organised crime involves a continuing enterprise in a rational fashion, geared towards profit achieved through illegal activities (van Duyne et al., 2003, 2005; Wright, 2006). It is an ongoing criminal conspiracy, with a structure greater than any single member, and the potential for corruption and/or violence to facilitate the criminal process.

When the Federal Bureau of Investigation (FBI, 2008) adds the word 'international' in its new law enforcement strategy to combat the increasing threat of international organised crime, it defines international organised crime as those self-perpetuating associations of individuals who operate internationally for the purpose of obtaining power, influence, monetary and commercial gains, wholly or in part by illegal means, while protecting their activities through a pattern of corruption and violence.

In order to speak about organised crime, according to the European Union, at least 6 out of a set of 11 characteristics need to be present, 4 of which must be those numbered 1, 3, 5 and 11 out of the following list (Elvins, 2003):

1. *Collaboration of more than two people*;
2. Each with their own appointed tasks;
3. *For a prolonged or indefinite period of time*;
4. Using some form of discipline or control;
5. *Suspected of the commission of serious criminal offences*;
6. Operating at an international level;

7. Using violence or other means suitable for intimidation;
8. Using commercial or businesslike structures;
9. Engaged in money laundering;
10. Exerting influence on politics, the media, public administration, judicial authorities or the economy;
11. *Determined by the pursuit of profit and/or power.*

Characteristic 8 suggests commercial or businesslike structures, as assumed and explored in terms of managing organisations in this book. Several other characteristics are similar to characteristics of traditional projects. For example, a project is normally a collaboration of more than two people (1), each with his or her own appointed tasks (2), and for a prolonged or indefinite period of time (3). While an organised crime seldom will be for an indefinite period of time, the criminal organisation might very well be. Compared with legal business projects, we suggest that criminal projects have a tighter control structure.

A typical criminal organisation is the Russian mafia group that was discovered by law enforcement on Mallorca in 2008. The Russian criminal entrepreneur is Gennadijus Petrov, who set up a criminal enterprise on the Spanish island several years before the police discovered the group. The organisation was a collaboration of 20 Russian criminals. The criminal organisation on Mallorca was set up to launder money from criminal activities in the Russian Federation. After some time, the criminal enterprise expanded its business activities into other kinds of organised crime.

Symeonidou-Kastanidou (2007) argues that there is a need for a new definition of organised crime, where entrepreneurial structure is included as an important element. An entrepreneur is a person who operates a new enterprise or venture and assumes some accountability for the inherent risks. The view on entrepreneurial talent is a person who takes the risks involved to undertake a business venture. Entrepreneurship is often difficult and tricky, as many new ventures fail. In the context of the creation of for-profit enterprises, entrepreneur is often synonymous with founder. Business entrepreneurs often have strong beliefs about a market opportunity and are willing to accept a high level of personal, professional or financial risk to pursue that opportunity.

An organisation is considered to have an entrepreneurial structure when the following elements cumulate: (1) allocation of roles, (2) hierarchy and (3) concrete structure. Allocation of roles within an organisation occurs when a group of members is exclusively tasked with planning and preparation activities, a second one is tasked with the implementation and execution of the plan, while a third one is responsible for securing the proceeds. Hierarchy occurs when a predetermined superior–inferior relationship exists among members of the organisation. Concrete structure is considered to exist when a group possesses its own assets (Symeonidou-Kastanidou, 2007).

It is primarily the first and third of the above criteria that are perceived as harmful to society. These two ensure the organisation's continuity and survival. Criminal organisations invest money and other resources so as to achieve power at a political level and to intervene in emerging markets (Symeonidou-Kastanidou, 2007).

ILLEGAL BUSINESS

As indicated by our definition of organised crime drawn from Albanese (2004) above, this book is based on the enterprise paradigm of organised crime (Liddick, 1999: 404):

> The enterprise paradigm is really an approach to studying the problem of organised crime, grounded in the structural–functional school of sociology, general systems theory, and the theories of formal legal organisations.

Currently, a considerable number of academics and practitioners exist that perceive organised crime as networks, rather than structured and rational hierarchies. In that school of thought, criminal activities are often driven by rational choice or entrepreneurship. This does not automatically lead to a rational organisation of the criminal activities according to a rational business model. However, in our view, it is not at all the case that legal businesses are rational organisations. On the contrary, corporations are social systems filled with political and other non-rational activities. Hence, we argue that to apply the business enterprise paradigm, there is no need to assume neither rationality nor hierarchy in the criminal organisation. We agree with Albanese (2004), who argues that the enterprise model of organised crime grew out of dissatisfaction with both the hierarchical and ethnic models that have dominated the criminological literature about how organised crime is structured.

A common view in the literature according to Albanese (2004) is that research should focus on the factors that cause illicit relationships and hence criminal gangs to form. It is the conspiratorial gang-like nature of organised crime that sets it apart from individual criminal behaviour. It is not the individual drug dealer and illegal casino operator or money lender that is the primary concern but rather how these individuals entrepreneurially form an enterprise to organise links to customers and suppliers as well as their foot soldiers to provide illicit goods and services for profit.

Since many criminal organisations operate according to the network model rather than the hierarchical model, functions such as marketing, logistics and finance may be spread to several places in the network. For example in the American mafia, a place might be a family (Abadinsky, 2007: 8):

> The member of the American Mafia, acting as a patron, controls certain resources as well as strategic contacts with people who control other resources directly or who have access to such persons. The member-as-patron can put a client 'in touch with the right people'. He can bridge communication gaps between the police and criminals, between businessmen and syndicate-connected union leaders; he can transcend the world of business and the world of the illegitimate entrepreneur. He is able to perform important favours and be rewarded in return with money or power. There is a network surrounding the patron, a circle of dyadic relationships orbiting the OC (Organised Crime) member in which most clients have no relations with another except through the patron.

Albanese (2004) argues that the realization that organised crime operates as a business spurred a series of studies in an effort to isolate those factors that contribute most significantly to the formation of criminal enterprises. For example, when applying general organisation theory to criminal activity, it was found that organised crime stems from the same fundamental assumptions that govern entrepreneurship in the legitimate marketplace: a necessity to maintain and extends one's share of the market. According to this finding, organised crime groups form and thrive in the same way that legitimate businesses do: they respond to the needs and demands of suppliers, customers, regulators and competitors. The only difference between organised crime and legitimate business is that organised criminals deal in illegal products, whereas legitimate businesses generally do not.

The supply of illegal goods and services does not seem to be marked by a tendency towards the development of large-scale criminal enterprises, due to the illegal nature of the product. Instead, smaller, more flexible and efficient enterprises characterize this type of organised crime. While criminal entrepreneurship is focused on both establishing and developing the business over time, a decentralized structure may be chosen to avoid law enforcement, thereby creating more competition and economic rivalry.

We assume there is an evolutionary nature in criminal business enterprises. An entrepreneurial account of the nature of organised crime is inherently dynamic, in that it encourages the future to intrude on the explanation of the enterprise. The explanation of the enterprise lies not, or at least not solely, in forces that are visible today; it lies instead in how criminals organise to deal with an uncertain future.

Evolution in criminal business enterprise might be exemplified by Marzola's Studio. As a paedophile, Sergio Marzola discovered there was money to be made in the market. As an entrepreneur, he set up a secret Internet service for trading in images of children being raped by adults. The typical supplier of new images was a father raping his daughter. Marzola paid 250 euro for a daughter filmed in lingerie, 500 euro filmed naked and subsequently 750 euro filmed when raped. Marzola was selling the images through Internet bulletin boards whose existence was known only to paedophiles. They spend only minutes or even seconds on these boards before making contact and then disappearing into private chat rooms to conduct business. Marzola is an Italian but he moved to Ukraine, where he had bought a house and a studio in the city of Karkov. Young Ukrainian girls were raped and filmed in Marzola's Studio.

Evolution might be defined as change in the characteristics of an organisation over time. Evolution is a process that happens to an organisation. An organisation is not a stable entity, as it changes because of internal dynamics and reactions to the environment. Evolution is not a random process; it has a certain direction.

Langlois (2007: 1115) identified three factors that determine organisational change and development in firms:

1) *The pattern of existing capabilities in the firm and market*. Are existing capabilities distributed widely among many distinct organisations or are they contained importantly within the boundaries of large firms?
2) *The extent of the market and the level of development of market-supporting institutions*. To what extent can the needed capabilities be tapped through existing arrangements and to what extent must they be created from scratch? To what extent are there relevant standards and other market-supporting institutions?
3) *The nature of the economic change called for*. When technological change or changes in relative prices generate a profit opportunity, does seizing that opportunity require a systemic reorganisation of capabilities (including the learning of new capabilities) or can change proceed in autonomous fashion along the lines of an existing division of labour?

Evolution will occur in several combinations of these factors. For example, when an entrepreneurial opportunity arises, a systemic rearrangement of capabilities and development of new capabilities will occur, especially when existing capabilities are dispersed and market-supporting institutions are weak.

The entrepreneurial theory of the criminal firm argues that entrepreneurship is a crucial element in explaining the nature and boundaries of the criminal enterprise. According to this theory, a criminal enterprise exists because of entrepreneurship. Here, entrepreneurship is the professional examination of how, by whom and with what effects opportunities to create future profit are discovered, evaluated and exploited. Entrepreneurship involves the study of sources of opportunities; the processes of discovery, evaluation and exploitation of opportunities; and the set of individuals who discover, evaluate and exploit them (Langlois, 2007).

The entrepreneurial theory of the criminal firm suggests that the criminal enterprise represents a realization of entrepreneurial vision. Setting up a firm organisation means hiring staff whose services are not completely specified in advance by the employment or network arrangement. This incompleteness is compensated by entrepreneurial vision. An essential contribution from entrepreneurial vision to firm organising of resources is the provision of a cognitive input in the form of a business conception. A business conception consists of subjective, sometimes highly idiosyncratic imaginings in the mind of an entrepreneur of what business is to be created, and how to do it. Like a business frame, Witt (2007: 1127) argues that 'a business conception is the basis for the entrepreneur's interpretation of incoming information with respect to its relevance and meaning for the imagined business venture'.

An entrepreneurship perspective on the nature of the firm rests on two fundamental assumptions about the nature of business activity: profit-seeking individuals and asymmetrically dispersed knowledge across economic actors. The quest for profit, wealth and power plays an important motivational role in the criminal entrepreneur's pursuit of new criminal business opportunities. Asymmetrically dispersed knowledge implies differentiated sets of knowledge held by decision makers, which in the business context causes variation in the ability to identify and assimilate new information and events. Individual decision makers tend to notice new information that relates to and can be combined with knowledge they already have (Zander, 2007).

When criminal entrepreneurs engage in knowledge-intensive ventures, the need for human and social capital exceeds the need for physical assets. Human capital might be defined as the abilities individuals possess and their demographic characteristics. Social capital might be defined as a network contributing to entrepreneurial goals, where resources are obtained through the social network of actors (Madsen et al., 2008).

CRIMINAL ENTREPRENEURSHIP

As already mentioned, an entrepreneur is a person who operates a new enterprise or venture and assumes some accountability for the inherent risk (Symeonidou-Kastanidou, 2007). The newly and modern view on entrepreneurial talent is a person who takes the risks involved to undertake a business venture. Entrepreneurship is often difficult and tricky, as many new ventures fail. In the context of the creation of for-profit enterprises, entrepreneur is often synonymous with founder. Most commonly, the term entrepreneur applies to someone who creates value by offering a product or service in order to obtain certain profit.

Except for criminal entrepreneurs' readiness to use personal violence and the ability to shield oneself from it, other social or individual constrictions and qualities do not seem to differ that much from those encountered in successful legal businessmen among successful drug entrepreneurs in Colombia, according to Zaitch (2002: 49):

> Opportunities to become a successful drug entrepreneur in Colombia have remained, of course, unequally distributed. Except for the readiness to use personal violence and the ability to shield oneself from it, other social or individual constrictions and qualities do not seem to differ that much from those encountered in successful legal businessmen: sex, age, personal or family contacts, entrepreneurial skills of all sorts, personal attributes such as creativity, alertness or charisma, skills to both exercise power and deal with existing power pressures, and luck.
>
> However, access to the entrepreneurial levels of [the] cocaine business has been remarkably open to a wide and heterogeneous range of people. The social origins of cocaine entrepreneurs can not be traced to one social, economic or ethnically specific group. Although some backgrounds and patterns can be observed according to regional differences and historic events, they far from constitute general trends.

Entrepreneurship is the practice of starting new organisations or revitalizing mature organisations, particularly new businesses generally in response to identified opportunities. Entrepreneurship is sometimes labelled entrepreneurialism. Entrepreneurship is often a difficult undertaking, as a vast majority of new businesses fail. Entrepreneurial activity is substantially different from operational activity as it is mainly concerned with creativity and innovation. Entrepreneurship ranges from small individual initiatives to major undertakings creating many job opportunities.

The majority of recent theories in the business and managerial economic literature assume that the economic performance of small and medium-sized firms depends largely on the entrepreneurs' (or team's) capacities. Even so, economists still do not fully understand the relationship between entrepreneurs and firm performance. The entrepreneurial process is the result of a complex interaction between individual, social and environmental factors. Taken separately, neither the personality of the entrepreneur nor the structural characteristics of the environment can, on its own, determine an organisation's performance (Thomas and Mancino, 2007).

In order to provide an example of the relationship between entrepreneurs' subjective characteristics/traits and organisational performance, Thomas and Mancino (2007) carried out an empirical study. The study aimed to explain how the presence of entrepreneurs' specific subjective characteristics can influence an organisation's strategic orientation and, as a consequence, local development. By analysing several subjective characteristics taken from a sample of 101 successful entrepreneurs from southern Italy, certain issues emerge regarding the link between the economic performance of the ventures launched in this area and the weak level of growth. Successful entrepreneurs' behaviour and decisions are heavily influenced by family support. The entrepreneurial culture of the family also tends to substitute the protective role played by public institutions. The entrepreneurial decisions of local entrepreneurs are triggered both by their need to rid themselves of poverty and their feeling that they are destined to continue the family business, the majority of them being the children of entrepreneurs. Most of the interviewees were classified as necessity rather than opportunity entrepreneurs.

An entrepreneur might be driven by a compulsive need to find new ways of allocating resources. He or she might be searching for profit-making opportunities and engineer incremental changes in products and processes. While strongly innovative entrepreneurs tend to champion radical changes in resource allocation by making new product markets and pioneering new processes, weakly innovative entrepreneurs tend to seek small changes in resource allocation to explore profit-making opportunities between already established activities (Markovski and Hall, 2007).

Founders of new legal firms tend to be experienced professionals who pursue opportunities closely related to their previous employment. Entrepreneurs often have several years of work experience in the same industry as their own start-up enterprises. This suggests that entrepreneurs do not come from out of the blue, but build their human intellectual capital through work experience in established firms. Similarly, criminal entrepreneurs might be experienced professionals before establishing their own criminal business enterprise.

Jacobides and Winter (2007) phrased the question: How do entrepreneurs choose the boundaries of their own ventures? To answer this question, they started from the premise that while entrepreneurs believe themselves to have superior ideas in one or multiple parts of value creation arenas, they are characteristically short of cash, and of the ability to convince others to provide it. This premise motivates a simple model in which the entrepreneur has a value-adding set of ideas for parts of a value creation arena (e.g. smuggling of cocaine from Colombia to Germany via the Netherlands). Assuming that the entrepreneur's objective is to maximize criminal wealth, it might be observed that initial scope depends not only on available cash, but also on how much value the entrepreneur's ideas add to each participant in the organised crime. Entrepreneurs will focus on the areas that provide the maximum profit and minimum risk per available cash.

Audretsch and Keilbach (2007) operationalized entrepreneurship in terms of entrepreneurial behaviour that involves the activities of individuals who are associated with creating new organisations rather than the activities of individuals who are involved with maintaining or changing the operations of ongoing established organisations. Accordingly, entrepreneurial thinking and the cognitive process associated with the identification of an opportunity can be viewed in conjunction with the decision to engage in entrepreneurial action.

Motivation and personality traits are part of an entrepreneurial initiative. Motivational needs of entrepreneurs typically include needs for achievement, affiliation, dominance and autonomy. Personality traits of entrepreneurs typically include sociable, decisive, authoritative, goal oriented, self-confident, anxious, risk taker, intuitive, internal locus of control and leader (Seet et al., 2008).

Since motivation and personality traits often are important parts of an entrepreneurial initiative, Jayasinghe et al. (2008: 250) deem rationality and bounded rationality approaches as inappropriate for a comprehensive analysis of the entrepreneur:

> Such approaches marginalise the influence of emotions and the entrepreneur's private life and assume that entrepreneurial behaviour is conditioned to rational and calculative self-interest. Treating the entrepreneur as an 'integrated self', characterised by rationality and bounded rationality in her/his behaviour, disguises the 'unconscious motivations' of agential actions, while viewing emotions as operating outside her/his consciousness disregards their contribution to the entrepreneur's 'practical consciousness'.

Jayasinghe et al. (2008) argue that a framework is needed to define the entrepreneur as a socially situated agent exercising his or her own agency. In fact, entrepreneurs have many of the same characteristics as leaders, where social aspects are more focused than rational decision making. Entrepreneurship is a kind of leadership focusing on creativity and innovation. As leaders are sometimes contrasted with managers, so also are entrepreneurs. Managers tend to be administrators who are more methodical and less prone to risk taking. The entrepreneur has an enthusiastic vision, the driving force of an enterprise. The entrepreneur's vision tends to be supported by a set of related ideas not spelled out before. The overall blueprint to realize the vision is clear; however specific, actions may be incomplete, flexible and evolving.

Similarly, Williams (2006) argues that even if there are frequent debates whether specific individuals admired in the media should be included as entrepreneurs or not, the widespread agreement is that what is being defined and delineated is essentially a wholesome and virtuous subject. Entrepreneurs typically have several of the following characteristics: a need for independence, a need for achievement, internal locus of control, ability to live with uncertainty and take measured risks; they are opportunistic, innovative, self-confident, proactive and decisive with higher energy, self-motivation, and vision and flair.

Von Lampe (2007) made some observations on the social microcosm of illegal entrepreneurs. He examined the patterns of interaction of offenders involved in the importation and wholesale distribution of contraband cigarettes in Germany. He assumed that under normal circumstances offenders would prefer to operate alone and in complete isolation, but found that smugglers and wholesale distributors of contraband cigarettes came into contact with a number of individuals in the course of their illegal activities.

The social microcosm of an illegal entrepreneur includes all those individuals he or she encounters in the course of his or her criminal activities who are in a position to influence the success or failure of that particular criminal enterprise (von Lampe, 2007: 132):

> The concept of the 'social microcosm of illegal entrepreneurs' encompasses three aspects that have variously been addressed in the criminological and organised crime literature: co-offending, the social embeddedness of criminal networks, and the interaction between illegal and legal spheres of society.

Co-offending includes the joint execution of criminal activity. Social embeddedness includes relatives, friends and others in the personal network that participate in social transactions that do not have a criminal connotation as such, but do nevertheless have some bearing on the criminal activity. Interaction between illegal and legal institutional environments is typically visible in terms of corruption and infiltration.

Von Lampe (2007) found that cigarette smugglers, like any other offender, do not operate in a social vacuum. As the stakes increase, cigarette smugglers increasingly rely on actors from outside their immediate social milieu. Contacts with legitimate third parties are established ad hoc.

Entrepreneurial orientation varies among criminal entrepreneurs as among legal entrepreneurs. Entrepreneurial orientation refers to the processes, practices and decision-making activities used by entrepreneurs that lead to the initiation of an entrepreneurial enterprise. Proactiveness, risk taking and innovativeness are typical conceptualizations of entrepreneurial orientation. Proactiveness refers to an opportunity-seeking, forward-looking initiative that involves introducing new methods ahead of the competition. Risk taking represents a behaviour of taking bold actions with uncertain outcomes. Innovativeness refers to an ability to identify and stimulate creativity and experimentation in introducing new methods (Kropp et al., 2008).

ENTREPRENEURIAL CAPITAL

When a criminal entrepreneur decides to set up a criminal enterprise, he or she will need capital to do so. Capital, in the financial sense, is the money which gives the business the power to buy goods and services to be used in the production of other goods or the offering of a service. For example, if the enterprise is starting up in smuggling drugs, there will be a need for capital to buy drugs, because smugglers have to pay their suppliers before they get paid by their customers.

In the legal sector of the economy, corporate finance is the task of providing the funds for a corporation's activities. It generally involves balancing risk and profitability while attempting to maximize an entity's wealth and the value for its stakeholders. Long-term funds are provided by ownership equity and long-term credit. Short-term funding in terms of working capital is mostly provided by banks that are extending a line of credit. The balance between these forms the company's capital structure.

To start up a criminal business enterprise, some of these options are not available to a criminal entrepreneur. Typically, the entrepreneur will need to search for funding from crime money. Crime money will be available if the potential profit is high and the potential risk is low. According to van Duyne (2007), in many cases the money handled is cash and is carried around personally by criminals, in clothes, suitcases, on or in the body, boot of the car or some other hiding place. Banking transactions are much less frequent. Dealing with crime money is different from dealing with clean money.

Van Duyne (2007: 87) studied what wealthy criminals do with their ill-gotten money: their criminal money management as well as what they actually did with their money in economic terms:

> The criminal money-management (or laundering in common parlance) was carried out with a sophistication geared to the available acumen as well as what was required in the given circumstances. In general the sophistication hardly mirrored the imagery of criminals-getting-smarter and always-'ahead-of-us'. Ethnic minority crime-entrepreneurs with a social-economic home elsewhere used to take their money cash out of the country, while indigenous

entrepreneurs faced always the requirement of justifying the acquired registered assets, like cars, boats, real estate and of course well-filled bank accounts. Apart from a few complicated and well thought-out exceptions, extensive chains of financial cross-border transactions had a low frequency.

Van Duyne (2007) found that the field of criminal finances and related activities (money laundering and the total set of countermeasures) is far from clear. The range and reach of crime markets are so large that no law enforcement agency seems capable of identifying all kinds of crime money transactions. Both origin and destination are hard to determine. In many official presentations crime money flows are projected from tax haven to tax haven and to unstable states, but the evidence is not clear.

An important part in criminal finances of start-up enterprises is corruption. To get into a market, corruption is often required. Markovska (2007) tells the story of how legal Western firms are able to start up in Ukraine if they bribe at different levels and in different sectors. For example, to get involved in the medical sector, the following actors need to be bribed by pharmaceutical companies:

- Pharmaceutical Committee in Kiev (the main absorbent of bribes, the first contact of Western pharma companies with Ukrainian reality). Most corrupt practice is tender purchase;
- major hospitals (paid for clinical trials);
- specialized hospitals (paid for research results and general publication);
- local surgeries (basic equipment, torches, pens and paper).

Markovska's (2007) study considered the systemic nature of corruption in Ukraine. The transition from Soviet rule and communism to independence and capitalism enabled many successful criminal enterprises to start up. Financing criminal enterprises became easy, as illegal privatization enabled criminals to quickly gain control over enormous wealth.

Corruption requires the presence of entrepreneurial capital. According to Pinto et al. (2008), corruption is a persistent feature of human societies, with the earliest references dating back to the fourth century BC. Receivers of the funds can be corrupt individuals and/or corrupt organisations. When an individual is the beneficiary of the corrupt activity, the individual behaves as an agent by favouring the source at the expense of a third party. By applying agency theory, we label the corrupt individual an agent and the corrupting individual a principal, and the principal achieves a favour from the agent because of the benefit. When an organisation is the beneficiary of the corrupt activity, the benefit causes unlawful organisational behaviour and corporate crime.

THE CASE OF TERRENCE 'TERRY' ADAMS

This case was written by David Amoruso and published on the Internet (Amoruso, 2007a).

Terrence 'Terry' Adams is the head of Britain's most enterprising, and feared, organised crime gang: the Adams family, otherwise known as the A-Team, or the Clerkenwell Crime Syndicate. Terry was the oldest of 11 children, born to a law abiding, working class, Irish Catholic family. He grew up in Islington, north London. Terry was the closest to his younger brothers Patrick (a.k.a. Patsy) and Sean (a.k.a. Tommy) with whom he would go into a life of crime. That life of crime began by extorting money from traders and stallholders at street markets close to their home in the Clerkenwell area, before moving on to armed robberies. Patrick served seven years in prison for armed robbery in the 1970s.

Terry was the brain behind their criminal operations, Sean dealt with financial matters and Patrick was the muscle. A former associate of the Adams brothers said the following: 'Terry was always the most levelheaded one out of the bunch. His brother Tommy was wild and the other brother, Patsy, could be very wild and crazy. A lot of the people involved in this kind of business don't have a lot going on up top. But Terry and his brothers were different. They were a real class act. Terry was always well dressed and in charge of whatever was going on. When he walked into a room, everyone stood up. He was like royalty.'

Terrence Adams was a criminal entrepreneur who initiated and operated a new enterprise and assumed some accountability for the inherent risks. As argued by Symeonidou-Kastanidou (2007), a criminal entrepreneur is a person who has the talent of taking risks involved in a new business venture. Terry was the founder who recruited his own brothers. As argued by Thomas and Mancino (2007), successful entrepreneurs' behaviour and decisions are heavily influenced by family support. The entrepreneurial culture of the family also tends to substitute the protective role played by public institutions. The criminal enterprise represented a realization of Terry's entrepreneurial vision.

By the 1980s the Adams family had moved into the drug trade. There was a huge demand for cocaine and cannabis in the 1980s, and ecstasy during the 1990s. They built up links with Yardie groups and the Colombian cocaine cartels. The money made was laundered through various corrupt financiers, accountants, lawyers and other professionals, and subsequently invested in property and other legitimate businesses.

Like most criminal groups (van Duyne et al., 2003, 2005; Wright, 2006), the Adams family ruled through intimidation and violence. They are rumoured to have been involved in 30 murders. An accountant, Terry

Gooderham, allegedly skimmed £250,000 of drug money from the Adams brothers. He was found dead, alongside his girlfriend, in Epping Forest in 1989.

A rival Irish family, the Reillys, challenged the Adams family's dominance of Islington. Patrick Adams and an associate went into a pub controlled by the Reillys. There the Adams associate insulted a Reillys member. The Reillys went away to arm themselves and returned to the pub. It was an ambush; their BMW was fired on repeatedly by members of the Adams gang. No one was killed but the incident sent out a clear message: the Adams family runs Islington.

By the late 1990s the heat was on. In 1998 Sean 'Tommy' Adams was convicted of organising an £8 million hashish smuggling operation, and was sentenced to seven years' imprisonment. When a judge ordered that he surrender some of his profits or face a further five years, his wife turned up twice to the court, carrying £500,000 in cash inside a briefcase on each occasion.

In May 2003 Terry Adams was arrested and charged with money laundering, tax evasion and handling stolen goods. He was released on £1 million bail. And in February 2007 he pleaded guilty to conspiracy to launder £1.1 million. The Judge said: 'Your plea demonstrates that you have a fertile, cunning and imaginative mind capable of sophisticated, complex and dishonest financial manipulation.' On 9 March 2007 Terry Adams at the age of 52 was sentenced to seven years in prison.

As a criminal entrepreneur, Terry is probably driven by a compulsive need to find new ways of allocating resources in organised crime while in prison. He has probably championed radical changes in resource allocation and pioneered new processes, as described by Markovski and Hall (2007).

2. Stage models for criminal entrepreneurs

'Stages of growth' models have been used widely in organisational research. These models describe the possible evolution of an organisation over time. In this book, several stage models for criminal organisations are developed. In one of the models, the stages are opportunity-based, activity-based, knowledge-based and strategy-based criminal organisations respectively. Such models may prove helpful to law enforcement agencies as they try to understand how entrepreneurs develop criminal organisations over time.

Finckenauer (2005) suggested a distinction between certain crimes that may be extremely complex and highly organised in their commission, but which are not committed by criminal organisations, and true organised crime. Hagan (2006) suggested that 'Organised Crime' be used to refer to crime organisations, while 'organised crime' should refer to activities – crimes that often require a degree of organisation on the part of those committing them. According to him, not all 'organised crime' is committed by 'Organised Crime' groups.

Both Finckenauer (2005) and Hagan (2006) have suggested that criminal organisations evolve over time. Building on their work as well as research by von Lampe (2005) and von Lampe and Johansen (2003), the first stages of growth model suggested for criminal organisations in this chapter is developed, which might be applied to determine the maturity level to which a criminal organisation is brought by the entrepreneur. Maturity is regarded as an indication of the efficiency and effectiveness with which a criminal organisation responds to environmental changes in a professional way.

STAGES OF GROWTH MODELS

Stages of growth models have been used widely in both organisational research and management research. According to King and Teo (1997), stages of growth models describe a wide variety of phenomena – the organisational life cycle, product life cycle, biological growth, and so on.

These models assume that predictable patterns (conceptualized in terms of stages) exist in the growth of organisations, the sales levels of products and the growth of living organisms. These stages are (1) sequential in nature, (2) occur as a hierarchical progression that is not easily reversed, and (3) evolve a broad range of organisational activities and structures.

Organisational stage models suggest that organisations follow certain steps into higher levels as they evolve and develop. The assumption is that organisational evolution is upward and sequential. In particular, these models suggest that the challenges and requirements for organisational success vary with different stages, and thus organisational actions must change as the stages change (Pfarrer et al., 2008).

Benchmark variables are often used to indicate characteristics in each stage of growth. A one-dimensional continuum is established for each benchmark variable. The measurement of benchmark variables can be carried out using Guttman scales (Frankfort-Nachmias and Nachmias, 2002). Guttman scaling is a cumulative scaling technique based on ordering theory that suggests a linear relationship between the elements of a domain and the items on a test.

Various multistage models have been proposed for organisational evolution over time. For example, Nolan (1979) introduced a model with six stages for information technology maturity in organisations, which later was expanded to nine stages. Earl (2000) suggested stages of growth model for evolving the e-business, consisting of the following six stages: external communication, internal communication, e-commerce, e-business, e-enterprise and transformation, while Rao and Metts (2003) describe a stage model for electronic commerce development in small and medium-sized enterprises. In the area of knowledge management, Housel and Bell (2001) developed a five-level model. In the area of knowledge management systems, Gottschalk (2007) developed a four-stage model applied to knowledge management in law enforcement. Gottschalk and Tolloczko (2007) developed a maturity model for mapping crime in law enforcement, while Gottschalk and Solli-Sæther (2006) developed a maturity model for IT outsourcing relationships. Each of these models identifies certain characteristics that typify firms in different stages of growth. Among these multistage models, models with four stages seem to have been proposed and tested most frequently (King and Teo, 1997).

A recent example is a stages of growth model for corrupt organisations, where the four-stage model proposed by Pfarrer et al. (2008) is concerned with organisational actions that potentially increase the speed and likelihood that an organisation will restore its legitimacy with stakeholders following a transgression. The four stages are labelled discovery, explanation, penance and rehabilitation respectively.

The concept of stages of growth has been widely employed for many years. Two decades ago, Kazanjian and Drazin (1989) found that a number of multistage models had been proposed, which assumed that predictable patterns exist in the growth of organisations, and that these patterns unfold as discrete time periods best thought of as stages. These models have different distinguishing characteristics. Stages can be driven by the search for new growth opportunities or as a response to internal crises. Some models suggest that organisations progress through stages while others argue that there may be multiple paths through the stages.

Kazanjian (1988) applied dominant problems to stages of growth. Dominant problems imply that there is a pattern of primary concerns that firms face for each theorized stage. In criminal organisations, for example, dominant problems can shift from lack of skills to lack of resources to lack of strategy associated with different stages of growth.

Kazanjian and Drazin (1989) argue that either implicitly or explicitly, stages of growth models share a common underlying logic. Organisations undergo transformations in their design characteristics which enable them to face the new tasks or problems that growth elicits. The problems, tasks or environments may differ from model to model, but almost all suggest that stages emerge in a well-defined sequence, so that the solution of one set of problems or tasks leads to the emergence of a new set of problems and tasks, that the organisation must address.

Rather than specific and discrete stages, Hagan (2006) suggested a revised 'Organised Crime Continuum' that features two tiers: one for primary characteristics and one for secondary characteristics of groups that might be labelled 'Organised Crime'. The higher these groups score on these characteristics, the better an example they are of 'Organised Crime' groups. The characteristics are as follows:

- Primary characteristics:
    - the extent of ideology in the organisation;
    - the extent of violence and threat of violence;
    - the extent of illicit services and criminal enterprises;
    - the extent of immunity, corruption and intimidation;
- Secondary characteristics:
    - the extent of structured hierarchy;
    - the extent of rules and codes of secrecy;
    - the extent of initiation and exclusion of membership.

Hagan (2006) provided some possible examples of 'Organised Crime' groups using this continuum. This might suggest the following levels of 'Organised Crime' groups: Level 1 (fully fledged groups such as the Cosa

Nostra), Level 2 (semi-Organised Crime groups that lack full development of some characteristics) and Level 3 (street gangs and others that are lower level in exhibiting full development).

Building on work by both Hagan (2006) and Finckenauer (2005), several new stage models for criminal entrepreneurship are presented in this chapter.

STAGES OF CRIMINAL CAREER

Criminal career in a gang often emerges out of something else, such as a playgroup, a clique of friends or a loose subculture. Entry factors in relation to criminal gangs might include attraction to join because of ideology and politics, provocation and anger, protection, thrill seeking, violence and weapons. Exit factors might include negative social sanctions, disillusionment with the activities of the group and loss of position in the group (White, 2007).

While a young entrepreneur often is the common hub initially in a gang, groups that persist over different generations of young people would appear to involve a transfer of some type of commonality within communities. The persistence of a gang identity can be explained in terms of sharing the same ethnic background or social experiences (White, 2007). For example, as the daughter of a Yakuza mafia-boss in Japan, Shoko Tendo (2007: 7) was a gang member by the age of 15:

> I was born in the winter of 1968, a yakuza's daughter. I was the third child of four born to my father Hiroyasu and mother Satomi [...] Besides being the boss of the local yakuza gang, my dad managed three other businesses [...] By the time I reached ninth grade, I was still running away from home and had stopped going to school altogether. I used to have fun hanging out with Yoshimi and her gang. We were heavily into sleeping pills, which we would crush between our teeth and then wash down with soda because we thought this would make them work faster. Then we'd fight off sleep by sniffing thinner, and enjoy the buzz it gave us.

The suggested stages of growth model for criminal career in gangs has four stages (Figure 2.1):

- *Stage 1: Gang of friends.* This is a group of persons who enjoy each others' company. When short of excitement, they may use violence or other tools to frighten or achieve power in the neighbourhood. When short of money, they may steal goods that they sell on the black market. The criminal activity is neither planned nor important

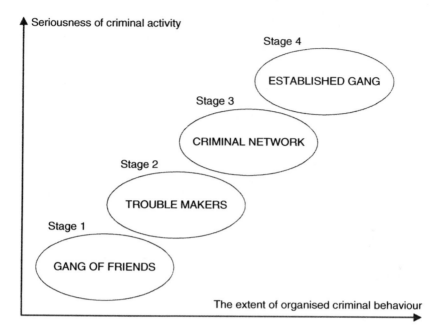

Figure 2.1   Stages of criminal career in gangs

to the social dynamics in the group. The role of the entrepreneur is to show initiative and courage by being the lead figure in both regular and criminal activities.

- *Stage 2: Trouble makers.* At this stage, the group is more conscious of its criminal activities and individual criminal behaviour. Personal identity and group identity are linked to criminal activities. Criminal projects such as retail drug commerce, prostitution rings and bank robbery are planned but not always carried out, and very often are not successful. The entrepreneur brings his or her gang to this stage by internal provocation, where gang members are challenged and requested to organise and commit more serious crimes.

- *Stage 3: Criminal network.* The gang changes from a group structure based on trust and identity to profit-seeking behaviour based on competence. While charismatic and later dominating entrepreneurs were successful at Stages 1 and 2, resourcing entrepreneurs enter the management level at Stage 3.

- *Stage 4: Established gang.* At this stage, the gang is concerned with weaknesses and strengths, opportunities and threats. Rival gangs have to be beaten and criminal opportunities have to be identified. Identity becomes important again at this stage, as an established gang tends to be a combination of both shared interests and professional crime. For example, Hells Angels has both the element of identity in Harley Davidson motorcycles, as well as trafficking and money laundering. Strategic entrepreneurship is needed to develop the gang into this maturity level.

On the other hand, historic criminology has described the underworld role of entrepreneurial Fagin – an adult who forces, seduces or teaches minors to commit crimes for him. In addition to a gang of friends, then, there are other ways of becoming a criminal. Well-known examples are the thief-takers of three centuries ago, who were running criminal businesses. Their role as control entrepreneurs gave them leverage to pressure and force thieves to commit crimes for them. The thief-takers were prepared to turn thieves in if they judged that to be in their interest (Kivivuori, 2007).

In their famous book *Freakonomics*, Levitt and Dubner (2005: 99) tell the story of a gang of friends called Black Disciples in a poor neighbourhood:

> So how *did* the gang work? An awful lot like most American businesses, actually, though perhaps none more so than McDonald's. In fact, if you were to hold a McDonald's organizational chart and a Black Disciples org chart side by side, you could hardly tell the difference.
>
> The gang that Venkatesh had fallen in with was one of about a hundred branches – franchises, really – of a larger Black Disciples organization. J.T., the college-educated leader of his franchise, reported to a central leadership of about twenty men that was called, without irony, the board of directors. J.T. paid the board of directors nearly 20 percent of his revenues for the right to sell crack in a designated twelve-square-block area. The rest of the money was his to distribute as he saw fit.

The rapper Jay-Z has become one of the most powerful celebrities in the United States. He was once a drug dealer on the street. He grew up in the Bedford-Stuyvesant area of Brooklyn, one of New York's toughest areas. Jay and his three siblings were brought up by a single mother. There was drug abuse in the family, and Jay often had to visit friends to get food. At home there was nothing. He started pushing drugs on the street to get money to buy food. He joined a gang of friends to make drug pushing more efficient. In 1988 a miracle happened. A rapper in the neighboorhood took Jay with him to record an album in London. In England the crack-dependent rappers met money in the music business. Among other things, they had full access to a car with a driver during the visit. In hindsight, Jay thinks this experience was an important turning point for him. According to Forbes magazine, Jay-Z earned 423 million US dollars in 2007 through music and real estate.

THE CASE OF WILLEM 'THE NOSE' HOLLEEDER

This case is based on an article in Wikipedia published on the Internet (www. wikipedia.org).

Willem Frederik Holleeder is a Dutch criminal born on 29 May 1958 in Amsterdam. He was one of the perpetrators of the kidnapping of brewery president, Freddy Heineken in 1983, for which Holleeder received a jail sentence of 11 years. He is assumed to be responsible for extortions of various real estate magnates, including Willem Endstra, who was murdered in 2004. A total of 24 people are suspected of being part of a crime ring controlled by Holleeder. The nickname of 'The Nose' is because of the size of Holleeder's nose.

The Dutch newspaper *De Telegraaf* reported on 16 July 2006 that Willem Holleeder and Cor van Hout had planned to kidnap Prince Bernhard instead of Freddy Heineken in the 1980s. Thomas van der Bilj, who was murdered in his bar in Amsterdam in April 2006, made these allegations in a deposition before the Dutch national police.

With companions Sam Klepper, John Mieremet and his later brother-in-law Cor van Hout, Holleeder was already, in the 1970s, a member of an opportunity-based criminal organisation. They carried out armed robberies more or less at random. At the age of 18 they already had enough money to drive around in expensive cars. The kidnapping of Heineken in 1983 gave them a ransom of 16 million euros.

After release from prison in 1992, Holleeder engaged in large-scale drug trafficking and extortion with his colleagues in their activity-based organisation, where drugs and extortions were the main criminal business activities. With van Hout and estate agent Rob Grifhorst, Holleeder bought in 1994 the erotic nightclub Casa Rosso in Amsterdam's red light district.

In 2002, Holleeder made the news when the monthly magazine *Quote* printed a photo of him with Endstra. Endstra was regarded as 'the banker' of the Dutch underworld. Endstra laundered drug money and invested it in property. Holleeder ordered the extortion of Endstra in 2004 after Endstra started to give information to the Dutch national police. Hells Angels carried out the extortion, because Holleeder enjoyed significant influence in the criminal motorcycle club.

STAGES OF GROWTH FOR CRIMINAL ORGANISATIONS

While our first model focused on the gang, we will here present a model of potential stages of growth for criminal organisations. The model consists

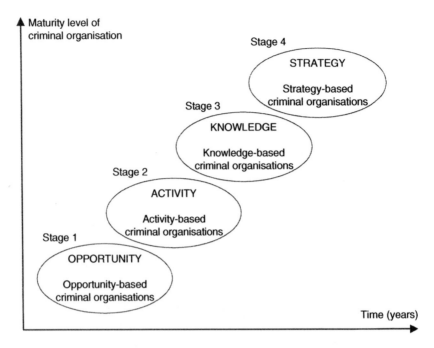

Figure 2.2　Stages of growth for criminal organisations

of four stages, as illustrated in Figure 2.2. Hagan's (2006) activity focus versus group focus might be recognized in the middle of the figure as levels 2 and 3 respectively, where group focus is concerned with knowledge management in the group.

Each level in the stages of growth model for criminal organisations can be described as follows:

- *Stage 1: Opportunity. An opportunity-based criminal organisation.* As criminal opportunities emerge, members of the criminal organisation will organise to benefit from them. The criminal entrepreneur will be the first to discover opportunities in areas such as the drug trade, smuggling, trafficking, theft or other illegal activities. Criminal business entrepreneurs often have strong beliefs about an illegal market opportunity and are willing to accept a high level of personal, professional or financial risk to pursue that opportunity (Symeonidou-Kastanidou, 2007). When changes in laws, demand, competition or trade generate a profit opportunity, then the entrepreneur organises resources and capabilities to seize that opportunity. Entrepreneurial thinking and the cognitive process associated with the identification of an opportunity lead to organised engagement in entrepreneurial action.

- *Stage 2: Activity. An activity-based criminal organisation.* The criminal organisation organises its criminal activities according to the business it is in. Activity-based theory conceives the organisation as a bundle of activities. The role of the production function in transforming inputs into end products is important here, where the entrepreneur is concerned with flows of resources in activities. Activity-based management emphasizes the impact of the organisation's production function on creating value, while giving little attention to differences in stocks of resources. Criminal organisations at this second stage are typically local or regional, while criminal organisations at higher stages are typically international and transnational in their operations (Klerks, 2007). The typical value configuration of an activity-based organisation is the value chain. In the value chain, value is created through efficient production of goods and services based on a variety of resources. The organisation is perceived as a series or chain of activities (Stabell and Fjeldstad, 1998).

- *Stage 3: Knowledge. A knowledge-based criminal organisation.* The criminal entrepreneur employs knowledge workers that accumulate organisational memory to learn from previous experience to improve efficiency and effectiveness in criminal performance. While activity-based theory conceives the organisation as a bundle of activities, resource-based theory conceives the organisation as a bundle of resources. The main resource is found in the knowledge belonging to organisation members. Knowledge as a resource is an enabler for criminal activities. The typical value configuration of a knowledge-based organisation is the value shop, which will be described more comprehensively in Chapter 4. In the value shop, activities are scheduled and resources are applied in a fashion that is dimensioned and appropriate to solve a problem, while a value chain performs a fixed set of activities that enables it to produce a standard product or service in large numbers. The value shop is an organisation that creates value by solving unique problems for customers and clients. Knowledge is the most important resource, and reputation is critical to organisational success (Stabell and Fjeldstad, 1998).

- *Stage 4: Strategy. A strategy-based criminal organisation.* Entrepreneurs in criminal organisations at this stage are concerned with strategic directions that position the organisation for the future. When the chief executive and top management team develop corporate strategy, they apply methods such as SWOT analysis (strengths, weaknesses, opportunities and threats), where avoiding law enforcement might be both an opportunity and a threat to be solved by corruption and other means. An interesting issue is how new chief executives are recruited to head a criminal organisation as compared with legal organisations (Zhang and Rajagopalan, 2003), since some criminal entrepreneurs may withdraw from daily operations and leave the executive role to a professional manager. While one might observe rather sophisticated market strategies and other functional strategies in areas such as drug markets brought forward by young entrepreneurs, Stage 4 is also characterized by corporate strategies involving finance as well as alliances and globalization, technology and reorganisation.

Many criminal organisations have grown over time as indicated by the stage model. For example, changes in the organisation of cocaine trafficking as well as heroin trafficking might be interpreted as a move from Stage 1 via Stage 2 to Stage 3 in this model. While the main trafficking route for cocaine is from Colombia to the US and Europe, the main trafficking route of opiates for heroin is from Afghanistan to Europe (Chawla and Pietschmann, 2005).

Another example is the evolution aspect of the Sicilian mafia that can be found in many history books about Cosa Nostra. While violent activity at Stage 2 was typical in 1870, running local communities at Stage 4 became the norm a few decades later. Steady improvements and revitalization of the mafia were carried out by criminal entrepreneurs such as Stefano Bontate, Tano Badalamentri, Michele Greco and Salvatore Riina in the 1990s (Dickie, 2006).

A third example is the Verhagen Group in the Netherlands, which was involved in trafficking hashish into cities such as Amsterdam, the Hague and Rotterdam. One of the leaders and the main entrepreneur had traded cars in Europe and the United States before he established the Verhagen Group. This provided him with extensive contacts in small-scale business activities in other countries. According to the stage model for criminal organisations, the Verhagen Group moved from Stage 1 to Stage 2. Key characteristics of this loosely organised group were the extensive use of transborder smuggling operations and the occasional use of violence and corruption. Apart from drug smuggling, the group engaged in a diversity of other illegal activities, according to the United Nations (2002).

Our fourth example is from Brazil. Since the late 1970s, there have been two contending criminal rings or organisations linking several towns (favelas) in Brazil, splitting their residents into friends and enemies: Comando Vermelho and Terceiro Comando (Zaluar, 2001). Again, this seems to be an example of evolution from Stage 1 to Stage 2 in the model.

A fifth example is the traditional smuggling of alcohol to Norway, where a state monopoly is in charge of the alcohol trade. The legal consumption of alcohol in Norway is relatively low compared with Europe in general. According to Johansen (2005), the illegal alcohol market in Norway is partly a replication economy, due to the taxes, restricted availability and the state of monopoly on the distribution and sale of wines and spirits. But it may be seen as a supplementary, an alternative or a criminal economy too, depending on the modus operandi and links to other networks. Criminal organisations handle most of the smuggling of alcohol to Norway. One of the entrepreneurs is Erik Fallo. After a case of alcohol containing Methanol was smuggled to Norway, causing the death of several consumers, smuggling organisations moved from Stage 2 to Stage 3.

Our sixth example is also from Norway, where the robbery of Norsk Kontantservice (NOKAS) took place. NOKAS is a Norwegian company offering solutions for management, control and distribution of cash to Norwegian banks. It is owned by several major Norwegian banks. The NOKAS central teller in the city of Stavanger was robbed on 5 April 2004. The outcome of the robbery was in Norwegian currency the equivalent of almost 10 million US dollars, which makes it the largest robbery in Norwegian history. A Norwegian police officer was killed in the line of duty, which had not happened for many years. The Norwegian Supreme Court confirmed the sentence of 11 men for organised crime on 28 June 2007. The mastermind and entrepreneur David Toska was given 18 years in prison, while his main partner, who fired the shots that killed the Stavanger police officer during the raid, was sentenced to 16 years in preventive detention. During the trial, David Toska was described as a typical entrepreneur, who was able to identify opportunities, mobilize relevant resources and implement criminal intentions with others. David Toska had been a notorious criminal since the mid-1990s in Norway before initiating the daring raid in Stavanger. From an evolutionary perspective it seems that the NOKAS robbers moved from Stage 1 to Stage 2. After imprisonment, it seems that David Toska is able to run his criminal organisation at Stage 3, where we find the knowledge-based criminal organisation. By distributing and sharing knowledge, David Toska as an entrepreneur is able to initiate organised crime and protect his criminal organisation.

A seventh and final example illustrates development all the way from Stage 1 to Stage 4 in five decades. When Lo Hsing Han started an opium trade in Burma in the late 1950s, he was running an opportunity-based criminal organisation. When he was arrested in 1973 and sentenced to death, he was running an activity-based criminal organisation. While in prison, he transformed it into a knowledge-based criminal organisation and established a network of contacts, enabling him to be released from prison after only seven years in 1980. In 1992, Han founded the Asia World Company in Singapore, based on the strategy of having a front-end legitimate organisation. Together with Tay Za, Lo Hsing Han is controlling the economy in Burma and financing the military junta, which is running Burma and keeping Nobel Peace Prize winner Aung San Suu Kyui under house arrest. Lo Hsing Han paid for the wedding of military dictator Than Shwe's daughter in 2006.

ALTERNATIVE STAGE MODEL FOR CRIMINAL ORGANISATIONS

To illustrate how further research might lead to a revision of the proposed model, an alternative model for criminal organisation stages is presented (Figure 2.3). While still having four stages, the stages have been relabelled activity based, knowledge based, strategy based and value based respectively:

- *Level 1: Activity. An activity-based criminal organisation.* The criminal organisation organises its criminal activities according to the

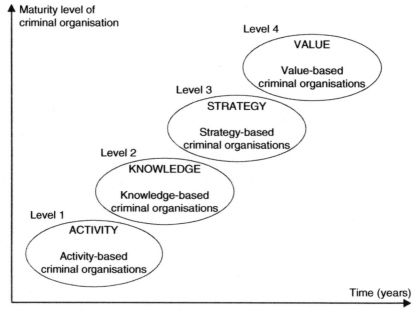

Figure 2.3   Alternative stages of growth for criminal organisations

business it is in. More or less random perceptions of opportunities govern the organisation. Rules determine roles and activities; it is a rule-based organisation. Breaking rules will have tough consequences. Activity-based criminal organisations are involved in a variety of organised crimes, such as drug trafficking. More than 14 million people worldwide, 0.3 per cent of the global population aged 15 and above, are estimated to use cocaine (Chawla and Pietschmann, 2005). The main change in the organisation of cocaine trafficking over the past decade has been the end of cartelization. This followed the dismantling of the Medellin and the Cali cartels. The operations of the cartels were increasingly taken over by a large number of decentralized trafficking groups. Production of coca leaf, which used to take place mainly in Peru, shifted to Colombia, which is closer to the cocaine laboratories, following successful operations to break the air bridge linking Peru and Colombia.

- *Level 2: Knowledge. A knowledge-based criminal organisation.* The criminal entrepreneur employs knowledge workers that accumulate organisational memory to learn from previous experience to improve efficiency and effectiveness in criminal performance. Knowledge as a resource is put to work in organised crime to avoid mistakes and complete crimes successfully. Criminal activities may require different knowledge categories. For example, money laundering requires knowledge of money transfer, while human trafficking requires knowledge of smuggling routes and manipulation techniques. Knowledge as a resource represents an enabler that enables criminal activities to be carried out by criminals. Knowledge is a renewable, reusable and accumulating resource of value to the organisation. Knowledge is what a knower knows; there is no knowledge without someone knowing it. Knowledge has the highest value, the most human contribution, the greatest relevance to decisions and actions, and the greatest dependence on a specific situation or context. Compared with data and information, knowledge is also the most difficult of content types to manage because it originates and is applied in the minds of human beings. Criminals who are knowledgeable not only have information, but also have the ability to integrate and frame the information within the context of their experience, expertise and judgment. In doing so, they can create new information that expands the state of possibilities, and in turn allows for further interaction with experience, expertise and judgment. Therefore, in an organisational context, all new knowledge stems from people. Some knowledge might be incorporated in organisational artefacts such as processes, structures and technology (Gottschalk, 2007).

- *Level 3: Strategy. A strategy-based criminal organisation.* Strategy is an ongoing process of evaluating purpose as well as questioning, verifying and redefining the manner of interaction with the competitive environment. Strategy is both a plan for the future and a pattern from the past; it is the match an entrepreneur makes between the organisation's internal resources and skills (sometimes collectively called competencies) and the opportunities and risks created by its external environments. Strategy is the long-term direction of an organisation as well as a course of action for achieving an organisation's purpose. Strategy is the direction and scope of an organisation over the long term, which achieves advantage for the organisation through its configuration of resources within a changing environment and to fulfil stakeholder expectations. Therefore, strategy as a plan is a direction, a guide or course of action into the future, a path to get from here to there. Strategy as a pattern is a consistency in behaviour over time. Strategy as a position is the determination of particular goods or services in particular markets. Strategy as a perspective is an organisation's way of doing things.
- *Level 4: Value. A value-based criminal organisation.* At this level, a strong organisational culture emerges that creates a strong common sense of shared values in the organisation. The entrepreneur envisages and communicates values. Organisational culture is a set of shared norms, values and perceptions that develop when the members of an organisation interact with each other and the surroundings. It is holistic, historically determined, socially constructed and difficult to change (Hofstede et al., 1990). Organisational culture might determine how the organisation thinks, feels and acts. Embedded in traditions and history, occupational culture, in terms of having a criminal occupation, contains accepted practices, rules and principles of conduct. These are applied to a variety of situations. In addition, occupational cultures contain generalized rationales and beliefs. It is often argued that mafia-type organisations and motorcycle gangs have strongly shared values that set them apart from society.

In the case of Terry Adams in the UK, the criminal entrepreneur ruled through intimidation and violence. He is rumoured to have been involved in 30 murders. Based on this account, the Adams brothers only reached Level 3 in the growth model, since they were unable to develop and share common values with member criminals, which is the requirement of the value-based criminal organisation at Level 4.

In analysing the culture of a particular group or organisation at Level 4, Schein (1990) finds it desirable to distinguish three fundamental levels at which culture manifests itself: (1) observable artefacts, (2) values and (3) basic underlying assumptions. When one enters an organisation one observes and feels its artefacts. This category includes everything from the physical layout, the dress code and the manner in which people address each other, to the more permanent archival manifestations such as company records, products, statements of philosophy and annual reports. These are all observable artefacts in the organisation. A typical example is artefacts found on jackets and tattoos found on bodies, such as A.F.F.A. (Angel. Forever. Forever. Angel.), which are manifestations of Hells Angels Motorcycle Club (HAMC) members.

Motorcycle clubs such as HAMC are fairly consistent in their modal organisation, consisting of national, regional/state and local tiers, which emerged after a formative period. Individual bikers, cliques and chapters answer to the national leadership, which controls their right to claim membership, but they also have sufficient autonomy to accommodate their extremely independent and rebellious personalities (Quinn and Koch, 2003).

This tension between intense loyalty and hierarchical control on the one hand, and autonomous masculinity on the other is perplexing to many outsiders. Loyalty to a singular national hierarchy reinforces deeply felt tribal solidarity and power. Autonomy permits local flexibility in promoting growth and hegemony and avoids instigating rebellion among individuals. It also functions to make their actions difficult to link directly to the group's formal leadership and keeps the relationship between the club and the actions of its members distant from each other (Quinn and Koch, 2003).

Values at the second level can be studied in terms of norms, ideologies, charters and philosophies. Strong values in HAMC include respect for other members. Basic underlying assumptions at the third and final level of organisational culture are concerned with perceptions, thought processes, feelings and behaviour.

While studies have shown that people within the same legal organisation have very different values, often measured in terms of deviation from the mean, we expect members of criminal organisations at Level 4 in our maturity model to have very similar values. Their values will not only be typical for criminal organisations, but they will also have much smaller deviations between members than in criminal organisations at lower levels.

In Figure 2.4, some potential values of criminal organisations are exemplified. On a value scale from security to challenge, one might expect a mature organisation to share the view that security is somewhat more important than challenge. Furthermore, one might expect a mature criminal organisation to be almost as much planning oriented as action oriented.

Figure 2.4   Organisational values for criminal organisations

The focus will be long term rather than short term, and there will be less task orientation and more relationship orientation.

Benchmark variables are needed to indicate characteristics of each stage as listed in Table 2.1. At Level 1, management is characterized by rules and regulations, as indicated in the table. Knowledge-based criminal organisations will typically have knowledge management, while strategy-based organisations will be concerned with establishing and achieving goals and objectives. At the highest level of value-based criminal organisations, there is consistency in organisational values as developed over time by entrepreneurial management.

In strategy-based criminal organisations, goals and objectives are set for the organisation. To achieve goals, strategies are implemented. One out of many strategies might be systematic corruption of politicians and other stakeholders in the society.

The stage hypothesis implicitly suggested by the maturity model for criminal organisations might be empirically tested in future research. By classifying known cases of criminal organisations, such as those listed by the United Nations (2002), it may be possible to validate benchmark variables.

Generally, stages of growth models enable the classification of criminal organisations into different maturity levels. In this alternative model, a four-stage model was proposed: activity-based, knowledge-based, strategy-based, and value-based criminal organisations.

THE CASE OF ITALIAN MAFIA COSA NOSTRA

The mafia in Sicily is often regarded as the typical criminal organisation. In terms of our alternative model for stages of growth for criminal organisations, the Italian mafia has developed from activity-based via knowledge-

Table 2.1   Benchmark variables for stages of growth in criminal organisations

Benchmark variables for maturity-level characteristics	Level 1 Activity-based criminal organisations	Level 2 Knowledge-based criminal organisations	Level 3 Strategy-based criminal organisations	Level 4 Value-based criminal organisations
Management	Rules and regulations	Knowledge management	Goals and objectives	Organisational values
Structure	Networks of family members and temporary staff members	Network of competent and specialized associates	Hierarchical structure of power and influence	Hierarchical structure of mission, vision and ambition
Relationships	Family ties and random ties for temporary members	Members representing unique and valuable resources	Individual goals and rewards	Shared vision of a mutual goal aligning organisational and individual opinions
Division of labour	Multi-task members	Specialists	Managers and specialists	Specialists with shared knowledge base
Communication	Organisers are the core communicating orders	Communicators ensure feedback from knowledge workers	Management communicates goals and individual targets	Leadership shares values and global perspectives
Management	Dramatic management	Knowledge management	Strategic management	Charismatic leadership
Corruption	Randomly applied to succeed in a specific activity	No or little corruption	To achieve business goals for the criminal organisation, corruption might be one of the preferred strategies	Continuous corruption is applied in accordance with member values

based and strategy-based to a value-based criminal organisation. Von Lampe (2005) raises the question of whether the mafia is a stable organisation or a cultural phenomenon, state of mind and behavioural system that reflects certain aspects of Sicilian culture. Maybe the answer to this is that the mafia is both. The basic structural unit of the mafia Cosa Nostra is the cosca (family) under the leadership of a capo. Each family claims monopoly of power in a certain territory. At the provincial level, families are coordinated by a commissione or cupola.

The business of Cosa Nostra is focused on the protection and promotion of both legal and illegal economic, political and social interests of its members. In addition, the organisation is concerned with the regulation of internal conflicts. According to von Lampe (2005), these conflicts arise naturally from the main occupation of mafiosi, which is the provision of private protection in the absence of effective regulatory institutions. The guarantee of protection necessitates the absence of competition. This can best be secured when all providers are integrated into one centralized, hierarchical structure.

Cosa Nostra has developed according to the stage model for business criminal interaction from resource-based via agency-based to partner-based relationships with legal enterprises and government bodies. While the partnership exists between mafia organisations and legal organisations, partnership strength is determined by personal relationships between mafia bosses and industry executives as well as government officials and politicians.

The Russian mafia, like its Sicilian counterpart, is linked to the territorially based provision of protection services and to alliances between underworld and openworld. Corrupt government officials, shady business tycoons such as so-called oligarchs and members of criminal gangs are three types of actors often found in the Russian mafia (von Lampe, 2005).

Italian police arrested in 2007 a man believed to be the boss of the Sicilian mafia, Salvatore Lo Piccolo, but the long war between the Italian state and the mafia is far from over. With his son Sandro – who was also arrested – 65-year-old Lo Piccolo has been a major powerbroker in Sicily despite having been on the run for nearly 25 years. Nicknamed The Baron, he was believed by magistrates to have taken over from Bernardo Provenzano, who was the undisputed head of the Sicilian Cosa Nostra from 1995 until his arrest in 2006, according to Westcott (2007). Provenzano had run the Corleone mafia, which gained supremacy in the 1980s. It hailed from the town of the same name in central Sicily, immortalized as the birthplace of the Marlon Brando character in the film *The Godfather*. Sicily's regional governor, Salvatore Cuffaro, said he hoped the arrest of Lo Piccolo would be 'a mortal, definitive blow to Cosa Nostra'. But Leoluca Orlando, the former mayor of Palermo renowned for fighting the mafia, warned against making the mistake of thinking that the arrests would bring an end to the mafia in Sicily.

According to Westcott (2007), Lo Piccolo began his crime career as a bodyguard for a Sicilian mafia boss. He began his criminal career at the lowest level among friends who made money by being bodyguards. He is believed to have taken over after Provenzano's arrest in 2000. Magistrates believe he fought for the leadership with Matteo Messina Denaro. Lo

Piccolo had been on the run since 1983. 'This is an important arrest,' the MP told the BBC News website. 'Since the arrest of Bernardo Provenzano, the boss of the so-called Corleonesi Mafia, Salvatore Lo Piccolo was considered to be the new boss of the Corleonesi group.' But, he said, the fight against the mafia was far from over, as the imprisonment of Provenzano had also provided opportunities for other criminal groups to muscle in. He said investigators would need to focus on the so-called 'Americans' who he described as the new mafia bosses in Sicily.

There have been fears that members of Sicilian families who were forced to flee the island in the 1980s after losing the power struggle with the Corleone gang, were being brought back from the US to fill the void left by the arrests of Provenzano and many of his lieutenants. 'After the arrest of Provenzano, the Corleonesi Mafia lost its hegemony among the Sicilian Mafia,' said Mr Orlando. In August 2007, police arrested 14 people in an operation which uncovered close ties between local Cosa Nostra families and the US-based mafia. They included local bosses, businessmen, extortionists and municipal employees. 'Now we have to fight both the Mafias,' said Mr Orlando. 'And we need to cut the connections between the old and new Mafia and politicians. We will not be able to say we have won the battle against organised crime until then.' Professor James Walston, a writer on the Italian mafia from the American University in Rome, says the US connection harks back to the days when the gangs were running drugs through Sicily to the US. According to investigators, the trans-Atlantic alliance uncovered involved drug trafficking and money laundering. For many years, the Sicilian mafia's core criminal activity has concentrated largely on protection rackets and the construction business. Mr Orlando said the 'Americans' would no doubt view the arrest of Lo Piccolo as an opportunity to try to seize greater control (Westcott, 2007).

According to Westcott (2007), the arrest could clear the way for Matteo Messina Denaro, known as The Playboy boss, to take over from Lo Piccolo. Denaro, 47, whose power base is in the town of Trapani not far from Palermo, was considered a possible rival to Lo Piccolo after the arrest of Provenzano. He is still on the run. Lo Piccolo was arrested after almost quarter of a century on the run. According to reports, he and the other bosses were tracked to a country house outside Palermo where they were holding a summit. 'These guys would not have been picked up by chance,' says Professor Walston. 'Informers are most likely to have been involved and this could indicate some sort of division.' Asked whether the arrests could spell the decline of the mafia, he said: 'They will make life difficult for certain groups, it puts someone in a weaker position.' 'But,' he continued, 'the Mafia never dies.' As a value-based criminal organisation, the mafia is able to survive executive change because new leaders share the old values.

STAGES OF ORGANISED CRIME BY BUSINESS ORGANISATIONS

As organised crime receives increased attention, the corporate world of business enterprises is identified as an arena for organised crime. Based on organised crime literature, business organisation literature and stage model literature, this section conceptualizes a stage model for organised crime by corporate business organisations. The four stages are labelled legal, federal, hybrid and criminal business organisations respectively.

Similarly, the four stages for entrepreneurship are labelled legal, federal, hybrid and criminal entrepreneurship respectively. At one end, the entrepreneur makes sure that the organisation operates within the boundaries of the law. At the other end, the entrepreneur is himself or herself a regular criminal. The middle stages of federal and hybrid are the most interesting ones, as entrepreneurs at these stages are involved in both legal and illegal business activities. For example, a bank may have both legal businesses and criminal enterprises as customers. The bank manager, as was the case with Willem Endstra in the Netherlands, may be a criminal bank entrepreneur who enables money laundering for kidnapping entrepreneurs such as Willem Holleeder.

In the business management literature, stage models for organisational development are often applied. Various multistage models have been proposed for organisational evolution over time. We have mentioned Rao and Metts (2003), who presented a stage model for electronic commerce, while Dean and Gottschalk (2007) presented a stage model for knowledge management systems in police investigations, and King and Teo (1997) presented a stage model for strategy integration in enterprises. Already in this book, three stage models for criminal career, criminal organisation and alternative criminal organisation stages have been suggested.

As we look at organised crime by business organisations, we should remind ourselves that an organised crime is any crime committed by a person occupying, in an established division of labour, a position designed for commission of crime, providing that such division of labour also includes at least one position for a corrupter, one position for a corrupted and one position for an enforcer. Organised crime involves a continuing enterprise in a rational fashion, geared towards profit achieved through illegal activities (van Duyne et al., 2003, 2005; Wright, 2006).

While some legal organisations are involved in limited corruption locally, others are involved in a systematic blend of legal and illegal activities globally. This conceptualization is important, as classification of organisations in terms of illegal activities might help law enforcement gain new insights into organised crime.

Organised crime is crime committed by organisations whose existence has continuity over time and across crimes, and that use systematic corruption and other means to facilitate their criminal activities. These criminals have varying capacities to inflict economic, physical, psychological and societal harm. The greater their capacity to harm, the greater the danger they pose to society (van Duyne et al., 2003, 2005; Wright, 2006). It is an ongoing criminal conspiracy, with a structure greater than any single member, and the potential for corruption and/or violence to facilitate the criminal process.

Takeyh and Gvosdev (2002) phrased the question: How are international business organisations and global terrorist networks similar? Their answer is that both kinds of organisation need a home. However, they choose very different homes. While multinational corporations seek out states that offer political stability and a liberal business climate with low taxes and few regulations, failing or failed states draw terrorists, where the breakdown of authority gives them the ability to conduct their operations without risk of significant interference.

Failed states hold a number of attractions for criminal entrepreneurs behind terrorist organisations such as Al Qaeda and Al Wa'd. First, they provide the opportunity to acquire territory on a scale sufficient enough to accommodate entire training complexes, arms depots and communications facilities. Secondly, failed states have weak or nonexistent law enforcement, allowing terrorist groups to engage in smuggling and drug trafficking in order to raise funds for operations. Thirdly, failed states create pools of recruits and supporters for terrorist groups, who can use their resources and organisations to step into the vacuum left by the collapse of official state power and civil society. Finally, failed states retain the outward signs of sovereignty, preventing cross-border actions designed to eliminate terrorist organisations (Takeyh and Gvosdev, 2002).

Thorne (2005) argues that Al Qaeda is a virtual organisation. Criminal, virtual organisations are hard to locate, since they are characterized by working practices enabled by the Internet. Some virtual organisations exist solely within cyberspace, yet are able to interact with both physical and virtual places. Organised crime and many terrorist organisations are involved and may have substantial positions in a number of the world's largest industries – arms smuggling, people smuggling, prostitution, money laundering and illegal drugs – and they make extensive use of cyberspace and information technology.

When legal entrepreneurs of global businesses establish themselves in new locations, it is important to learn and adapt to local settings. Similarly, when criminal organisations do the same, they need to learn and adapt. As mentioned by Varese (2006), limited ability to collect

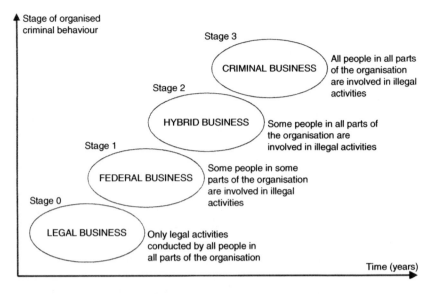

Figure 2.5   Stage model for organised crime by corporate business organisations

reliable information in unfamiliar regions is a major factor that hinders expansion.

Based on the reviewed literature on organised crime, business organisations and stages of growth models, we are now ready to present a potential stage model for organised crime by corporate business organisations, as illustrated in Figure 2.5.

- *Stage 0. A Legal business organisation* operates in all markets and in all departments according to the law. This is what is expected of legal enterprises. No staff member is involved in any kind of criminal activity on behalf of the organisation. We label this Stage 0, as we expect that most corporate enterprises all over the world are legal businesses and stay that way. We assume that well-known entrepreneurs such as Richard Branson of Virgin and Bill Gates of Microsoft have developed their business enterprises at this stage.
- *Stage 1. A Federal business organisation* is an enterprise where some people in some parts of the organisation get involved in illegal activities. The typical example is corruption. For example, oil companies are systematically bribing officials and their family members to get access to oil reserves in Iran. The Norwegian oil company Statoil was one of them. The chairman at Statoil is Helge Lund.

- *Stage 2. A Hybrid business organisation* is an enterprise where some people in all parts of the organisation are involved in illegal activities. The typical example is top management and corporate board manipulating corporate accounting to earn profits on high share prices. The US company Enron was one such company. The Norwegian entrepreneur Kjell Inge Røkke was involved in bribing officials to get fishing licences in Russia in the 1990s.
- *Stage 3. A Criminal business organisation* is an enterprise where all people in all parts of the organisation are involved in criminal activity. For example, when a local Hells Angels MC organisation runs a chain of legal tattoo shops, members are at the same time involved in drug smuggling, human trafficking and other criminal activities. The chairman and entrepreneur in HAMC Holland is Willem van Boxtel.

While few legal business organisations at Stage 0 develop into higher stages of 1, 2 and 3, some do. Effective law enforcement will have to look for symptoms in organisations leaving Stage 0 for criminal activities. However, one of the bottlenecks in international police cooperation is the targeting of the proceeds of crime. International agencies such as Interpol and Europol are sometimes involved in the interaction between the authorities and enforcement organisations of the countries concerned. Borgers and Moors (2007) studied bottlenecks in international cooperation for the Netherlands in targeting the proceeds of crime. While no bottlenecks were found in cooperation with countries such as Belgium and the United Kingdom, bottlenecks were found in relation to countries such as Spain and Turkey. In relation to Turkey, the Netherlands acts mainly as the requesting state and not the requested state (Borgers and Moors, 2007: 8):

> Regarding the cooperative relations with Turkey, Turkish respondents state that the framing of Dutch mutual assistance requests is inadequate. On the part of the Netherlands, there are different opinions on the depth of the investigation conducted at the request of the Netherlands. As far as the way in which people address one another is concerned, it is striking that the Turkish respondents sometimes consider the Dutch manner of operation as haughty and impatient. According to Dutch respondents, communication difficulties also occur if Dutch police officials directly contact the Turkish judges involved.

From the perspective of international cooperation, Borgers and Moors (2007) find that several bottlenecks are generic in nature. First, there is inadequate substantiation and framing of mutual assistance requests. Next, there are language barriers as well as cultural barriers. Furthermore, there is insufficient insight into the chain of cooperation, and successful cooperation in confiscation matters depends too much on personal contacts. Finally, international organisations play no or hardly any role, partly because of lack of international agreements in areas such as custody and management, asset sharing and processing times.

Tracking the proceeds of organised crime represents a knowledge challenge in policing. As an example, Chaikin (2000) argues that international lawyers have paid little attention to the problem of fraudulent enrichment and corruption by heads of state/government and top state officials. The Marcos case illustrates this clearly. When a greedy authoritarian leader or despot is in power, there are few, if any, opportunities for taking legal action to prevent or interdict stolen monies. However, if the dictator or authoritarian leader is deposed, the new government may seek the assistance of foreign governments and courts to investigate and ultimately to recover stolen assets which are located abroad.

The Marcos case represented a legal government organisation where proceeds of organised crime accumulated. Corrupt activities of Ferdinand Marcos commenced while he was a congressman and head of the import control board, which allowed him to gather large bribes in return for approving import licences. As legal congressman and criminal entrepreneur, Marcos soon became a millionaire largely based on his 10 per cent cut from government deals. When Marcos became president of the Philippines, he acquired an epic appetite for bribery, where several officials worked more or less full time in his value shop activities to acquire personal wealth (Chaikin, 2000).

The stage model for organised crime by corporate business organisations presented here is only conceptual in nature, as are all the other stage models in this chapter. Future research might develop benchmark variables for each stage, as was done for the alternative stage model for criminal organisations. Furthermore, future research might empirically evaluate this stage hypothesis by tracing the story of criminal organisations back to their roots.

In his classic article on organisational crime, Gross (1978) argued that different pressures on the organisation will influence the extent of criminal behaviour as illustrated by the stage model for organised crime by corporate business organisations. For example, a strong focus on ambitious goals for the organisation raises the probability that the attainment of the goals will subject the organisation to the risk of violating societal laws of organisational behaviour.

For many years, Siemens was a hybrid business at Stage 2. Corruption was part of the business practice in the German company. Siemens had 200 million euro as undeclared earnings, which were located in covert funds. The funds were used to pay bribes all over the world.

THE CASE OF DIAMONDS BY DE BEERS IN ANTWERP

This case is based on the article 'Diamonds and Organized Crime: The Case of Antwerp' by Dina Siegel (2008b).

There are many examples of intertwinement of illegitimate and legitimate activities. One example is the market for diamonds in the Belgian city of Antwerp (Siegel, 2008b: 87):

> Smuggling of diamonds is as old as the hills and it occurs in many places, often in periods of war and hunger and in countries with a troubled economy and instable government. But in times of peace smuggled diamonds are also a good investment and for some people, a guarantee of a better future. In contrast with drug trafficking or trading in rare species, trading in diamonds is legal. Naturally, smuggled diamonds are hidden from the view of customs and the police and when traders wish to evade taxes at the borders, smuggling can also be said to be taking place. But the smuggling which has attracted the most attention in recent years, is the smuggling of 'conflict diamonds'.
>
> The concept of 'conflict diamonds' or 'blood diamonds' refers to diamonds which have been obtained from areas which are under the control of rebel groups in Sierra Leone, Angola, Liberia and the Democratic Republic of Congo. This concerns a very small percentage of all mined rough diamonds, namely 4–5% of the total world production.

In 1998, the Belgian De Beers firm was accused of purchasing diamonds from the Angolan rebel organisation UNITA. Diamonds were traded against weapons. De Beers and the various companies within the De Beers family of companies engage in exploration for diamonds, diamond mining and diamond trading. Mining takes place in Botswana, Namibia, South Africa, Tanzania and Canada. For example, in Botswana mining is organised through the mining company Debswana, a 50–50 joint venture with the government of the Republic of Botswana. Trading of diamonds takes place through the Diamond Trading Company by wholly owned and joint venture operations in South Africa, Botswana, Namibia and the United Kingdom. The family of De Beers companies employs over 7000 people in Botswana, over 7100 in South Africa, 3800 in Namibia and 700 in Canada.

STAGES OF FINANCIAL CRIME BY BUSINESS ORGANISATIONS

Financial crime as part of organisational business activity has received increased attention in recent years (Abramova, 2007; Carpo, 2006; Chaikin,

2000; Europol, 2006; Gilinskiy, 2006; Lemieux, 2003). An organised financial crime is any crime committed by a person occupying, in an established
division of labour, a position in the organisation designed for commission
of such crime (van Duyne et al., 2003). Many researchers emphasize the
inherent business focus of much organised financial crime activities.

In the following, a stage model is developed for financial crime by corporate business organisations. While some legal organisations are involved
in limited corruption locally, others are involved in a systematic blend of
legal and illegal activities globally. Such categorization is important, as
classification of organisations in terms of illegal activities might help law
enforcement gain new insights into organised crime.

Money laundering (Abramova, 2007; Council of Europe, 2007; Elvins,
2003) and corruption (Chaikin, 2000; van Duyne et al., 2005; Finckenauer,
2005; Hagan, 2006; Kugler et al., 2005) are two typical examples of organised financial crime activities initiated by criminal entrepreneurship in legal
business enterprises.

Money laundering is an important activity for most criminal activity.
Money laundering has often been characterized as a three-stage process
that requires (1) moving the funds from direct association with the crime,
(2) disguising the trail to foil pursuit, and (3) making them available to
the criminal once again with their occupational and geographic origins
hidden from view. According to Joyce (2005), criminal money is frequently
removed from the country in which the crime occurred to be cycled
through the international payment system to obscure any audit trail. The
third stage of money laundering is done in different ways. For example,
a credit card might be issued by offshore banks, casino 'winning' can be
cashed out, capital gains on option and stock trading might occur, and real
estate sale might generate profit.

The proceeds of crime find their ways into different sectors of the
economy. A survey in Canada indicates that deposit institutions are the
single largest recipient, having being identified in 114 of the 149 proceeds
of crime cases (Schneider, 2004). While the insurance sector was implicated
in almost 65 per cent of all cases, in the vast majority the offender did not
explicitly seek out the insurance sector as a laundering device. Instead,
because motor vehicles, homes, companies and marine vessels were purchased with the proceeds of crime, it was often necessary to purchase insurance for these assets.

The Marcos case illustrates how legal business organisations use corruption to influence government decision making. Chaikin (2000) argues
that international lawyers have paid little attention to the problem of
fraudulent enrichment and corruption by heads of state/government and
top state officials. The Marcos case illustrates this clearly. When a greedy

authoritarian leader or despot is in power, there are few, if any, opportunities for taking legal action to prevent or interdict stolen money. However, foreign governments and multinational organisations may help recover stolen assets after a dictator has been removed. As an entrepreneurial head of state, Ferdinand Marcos in the Philippines was able to gain both personal power and personal wealth.

Corruption of police officers is made easier in many countries by the fact that they are modestly paid and, therefore, are subject to temptation. Combined with violence and threats of violence, corruption is an effective strategy for many criminal organisations. In their study, Kugler et al. (2005) found that when bribing costs are low, as a consequence of badly paid and dishonest law enforcers working in a weak governance environment, and the rents from criminal activity are sufficiently high, then increasing policing and sanctions can in fact generate higher crime rates. Further increases in expected punishment create incentives for organised crime to extend corruption rings that yields more rather than less crime.

Based on the reviewed literature on organised crime, business organisations and stages of growth models, we are now ready to present a potential stage model for organised financial crime by corporate business organisations, as illustrated in Figure 2.6.

- *Stage 1.* In *agency business*, an entrepreneurial employee acts as an agent for the legal business organisation when committing financial crime. To understand agency business, we apply agency theory, where a legal organisation is the principal while an employee is the agent. According to Eisenhardt (1985), agency theory is concerned with resolving two problems that can occur in agency relationships. The first is the agency problem that arises when the desires or goals of the principal and agent conflict, and it is difficult or expensive for the principal to verify what the agent is actually doing. The second is the problem of risk sharing that arises when the principal and agent have different risk preferences. The original impetus for the development of agency theory was large corporations' separation of control from ownership. The agency problem might arise when the two parties do not share productivity and other gains. For example, oil company employees are systematically bribing officials and their family members to get access to oil reserves in Iran. Employees working for the Norwegian oil company Statoil were among them. This first stage is also in line with the argument that collusion exists between some parts of business and criminal groups and the ever-present danger of terrorism. At this stage, we also find parasite organisational structures. Parasitism is a phenomenon in which

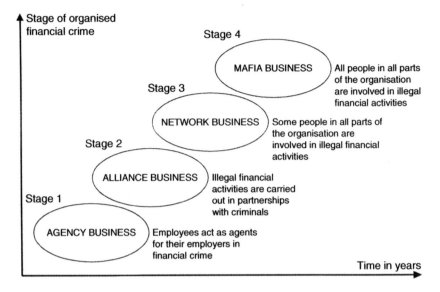

Figure 2.6   Stage model for financial crime by business organisations

two activities, which are unrelated, coexist over a prolonged period of time. Parasitism generally refers to the activities of organisms; usually the physically smaller of the two (the parasite) benefits and the other (the host) is harmed.

- *Stage 2*. In *alliance business*, the legal business is in alliance with criminals, where partnerships emerge. To understand alliance business, we apply partnership and alliance theory. Das and Teng (2002) studied how alliance conditions change over time, from formation via operation to outcome focus. An important stream of research in the alliance literature is about partner selection. It emphasizes the desirability of a match between the partners, mainly in terms of their resource profiles. The approach is consistent with the resource-based theory of the firm, which suggests that partners are defined by their resource profiles. Das and Teng (2002) found a lack of agreement concerning alliance performance in the research literature. This lack of agreement reflects an underlying conceptual puzzle: What does effective alliance performance mean? There are two distinct loci of alliance performance in the literature: the alliance itself and the partners forming the alliance. On the one hand, when alliances are viewed as separate entities, alliance performance is the success of these separate entities, in terms of, say, profitability or growth rate. On the other hand, because partners use alliances to achieve certain strategic objectives, alliance performance ought to be measured in terms of the aggregated results for the partner firms. Two or more entrepreneurs enter an alliance at this stage to achieve more profit from criminal activities than they would do separately. At this stage, we find parasite organisational structures as well. While parasite structures at Stage 1 are limited to certain people in certain parts of the organisation, here at Stage 2 parasite structures can be found in all parts of the organisation. One example at this stage is top management and corporate board manipulating corporate account- ing to earn profits on high share prices. The US business organisa- tion Enron did this, where top executives were the entrepreneurial parasites. This stage is in line with researchers who found organised crime in business, for example an increased involvement of criminal activities in the capital markets.

- *Stage 3*. In *network business*, persons and places in terms of nodes in the network are involved in both legal and illegal financial activities. According to network theory, the value of the network increases for all nodes when the network grows. This is called network externali- ties, where the number of nodes you can reach will increase expo- nentially with the number of nodes. Again, an entrepreneur will achieve more profit for his or her criminal enterprise by being part of the network than operating on his or her own. According to Beare (2000), empirical research has revealed that networks consist of a complex mix of criminals that range from the sophisticated special- ists to the opportunists – all operating within the same crime field. Lemieux (2003) argued that criminal organisations are both net- works and businesses. Criminal organisations, when viewed as net- works, have characteristics common to other social networks as well as specific characteristics associated with the fact that these organisa- tions are criminal businesses. Common characteristics include size of networks, density, couplings and ties. In criminal networks, the core is generally composed of entrepreneurial actors connected by strong ties, while the relationship between the core and the surrounding sub-networks is achieved through weak ties. These weak ties are ties through which information is transmitted in an upward direction and orders are transmitted in a downward direction (Lemieux, 2003). For example, the Verhagen Group in the Netherlands was trading cars in Europe and the United States. But more importantly for the business, the company was involved in trafficking hashish into cities such as Amsterdam, the Hague and Rotterdam. The core group con- sisted of five members, surrounded by a network of approximately 45 associates (United Nations, 2002). Similarly, Hells Angels is a legal motorcycle club, where the members are involved in criminal activity based on emerging networks. For example, when a local Hells Angels MC organisation runs a chain of legal tattoo shops, members are at the same time involved in drug smuggling, human trafficking and other criminal activities. This stage is in line with research that considers organised crime as various forms of business activity, which may or may not have attracted the label criminality. In particular, perceptions of legitimacy and effects of other normative factors will influence strongly whether activities, individuals and departments may be viewed as constituent parts of organised crime.

- *Stage 4*. In *mafia business*, there is a secret society, where the legal business is second to the illegal business. The mafia in Sicily is often regarded as the typical criminal business organisation. Similarly, the Camorra mafia in Naples is running the legal garbage collection system, which is dominated by illegal motivations and transactions. Von Lampe (2005) raises the question of whether the mafia is a stable organisation or a cultural phenomenon, state of mind and behavioural system that reflects certain aspects of Sicilian culture in the case of Cosa Nostra. Maybe the answer to this is that the mafia is both an organisational structure and an organisational culture, where the structure determines roles and responsibilities, while the culture determines norms and standards. The basic structural unit of the mafia Cosa Nostra is the cosca (family) under the leadership of a capo. Each family claims monopoly of power in a certain territory. At the provincial level, families are coordinated by a commissione or cupola.

Again, this stage model is only conceptual in nature. Future research might develop benchmark variables for each stage. Furthermore, future research will have to include empirical study of criminal organisations, tracing their evolution back to their roots.

Pinto et al. (2008) found that much that is labelled corporate crime and organisational crime is enacted by groups acting collectively, be it top management or a subset of organisational members. Organisational crime is defined as a type of white-collar crime that is enacted by collectivities or aggregates of discrete individuals in the context of complex relationships and expectations among boards of directors, executives and managers, and among parent corporations.

Pinto et al. (2008) developed the notion that corruption can manifest itself through two very distinct phenomena: an organisation of corrupt individuals in which a significant proportion of an organisation's members act in a corrupt manner primarily for their personal benefit; and a corrupt organisation in which a group collectively acts in a corrupt manner for the benefit of the organisation. The first phenomenon might be labelled the economics perspective, while the second is the sociology perspective. In both kinds of corruption, the organisation is the focal unit of analysis, as in our stages of growth model for for financial crime by corporate business organisations.

At Stage 4 of financial crime by business organisations, corruption becomes institutionalized within organisations. It becomes part and parcel of everyday organisational life. Leaders will sanction or authorize corrupt behaviours, explicitly or implicitly, by imposing reward structures that promote corrupt practices or by ignoring such practices when they occur. According to Misangyi et al. (2008), corrupt practices then become embedded within the scripts associated with depersonalized organisational roles, as well as within ongoing organisational processes. Corrupt practices become part of everyday routine and a habit for organisational members. As a consequence, corrupt activities then become less obvious as criminal activities, because routinization makes them normative and enacted automatically. They are made acceptable through socialization processes of repetition, reward systems for actors, rationalizing ideologies by leaders, expectations to follow norms, and presumptions that existing policy and practices are rational and indeed legitimate.

THE CASE OF SHIPOWNER ANDERS JAHRE

Norway has traditionally been a major shipping nation in the world. One of the great shipowners was Anders Jahre from the city of Sandefjord south of the capital Oslo. He founded the shipping company Anders Jahre Shipping in 1922, but he is better known for the whaling company Kosmos operating out of Sandefjord and catching whale in Antarctica. He contributed significantly to the development of the city of Sandefjord. Among other things, he financed the building of the new town hall.

Like so many other criminal entrepreneurs, Jahre did good deeds in his local community. Some support their local football club, some donate money to a new local hospital, others support education for children, and others again finance welfare programmes. Similarly, organisations such as Hamas have won elections in Palestine because they have helped schools and hospitals.

Anders Jahre was born in 1891 and died in 1982. He was a great philanthropist and was honoured with the Royal Norwegian Order of St Olav in 1950 as well as 1962. He became honorary doctor at the University of Oslo in 1961 – after having donated substantial amounts of money to research at that university.

Since his death, however, there has been much controversy surrounding alleged tax fraud and hidden funds in overseas accounts. In spite of several years of searching, the Norwegian government has not yet been able to retrieve the money in question. Norwegian authorities happened to stumble over information about Jahre's assets abroad for the first time in 1973. The finding occurred when Jahre had donated money for the new town hall and also favoured a bronze statue of himself outside the entrance to the hall.

Since then, Norwegian authorities have not got much out of banks such as Lazard Bank Limited and its chairman Lord Hugo Kindersley, who are in possession of both information and funds from Anders Jahre. A court case was initiated on Cayman Island, but without success.

One of Anders Jahre's partners in organised tax fraud was Thorleif Monsen. He was formally in charge of all money abroad and worked closely with the shipowner. He was based in Japan, where he was Norwegian consul and managing director of the shipbroker Aal & Co. Aal & Co. had its headquarters on Caymen Island.

Anders Jahre as a shipowner had prospered from the maritime cluster in Norway, without paying back in terms of taxes. He was a criminal entrepreneur whose reputation in society temporarily collapsed after his death. His reputation as a criminal is now overshadowed by his legal entrepreneurship as a shipowner. In 2008, Anders Jahre's Culture Prize was awarded again for the 18th time. Nobody questioned publicly whether the prize money should go to the government rather than the prizewinners. A furniture designer and a glass manufacturer received the prize of almost one hundred thousand US dollars each that year (Andreassen, 2008).

STAGES OF BUSINESS CRIMINAL INTERACTIONS

Since criminal entrepreneurs are in the business of making profit similar to legal enterprises and industries, they may benefit from interactions with business corporations. There have been a number of attempts to categorize the various ways in which criminals may interact with legitimate businesses. Beare (2007) found that criminal partnerships are often set up in a way that makes it almost impossible to identify, amid the multitude of transactions, those transactions that could be labelled as constituting various forms of criminality. Places to look for potential crime include improper payroll and labour billing, improper equipment billing, improper materials billing, safety and environmental issues, subcontractors, security and management of projects.

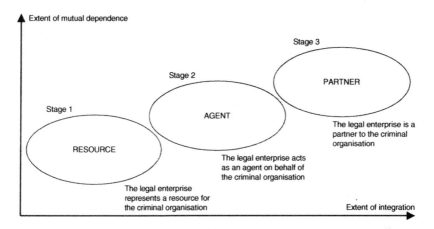

Figure 2.7   Stage model for relationships in crime

Figure 2.7 illustrates a stage of growth model for interactions and integration between legal enterprises and criminal organisations. The model consists of three stages:

- *Stage 1: Resource stage.* The legal enterprise represents a resource for the criminal organisation. A resource is characterized by being of important value, enabling criminals to do their business in more efficient and effective ways. For example, the drug trade in the city of Oslo in Norway is run by several criminal organisations. Some of these organisations use taxi companies in the city in their logistics operations. When drugs are to be transported or when weapons or people are to be transported, a taxi rather than a company car might be more useful in the operation. Another example is the production of counterfeit medicines; this has attracted organised crime, but it also requires the cooperation of people with some experience in pharmaceutical manufacturing and distribution. Counterfeit medicine is a product which is deliberately and fraudulently mislabelled with respect to identity and/or source (Reggi, 2007). The resource stage is critical in all entrepreneurship, as resources are enablers of activities aimed at exploring and exploiting opportunities. When an entrepreneur is unable or unwilling to mobilize his or her own resources, the alternative is to interact with another enterprise to gain access to resources required for successful crime.
- *Stage 2: Agent stage.* The legal enterprise acts as an agent on behalf of the criminal organisation. An agent is a representative of criminal activity. For example, a law firm might illegally claim money on

behalf of a criminal organisation. The law firm is the agent while the criminal enterprise is the principal. Agency theory is concerned with resolving two problems that might occur in agency relationships. First is the agency problem that arises when the desires or goals of the principal and agent are in conflict with each other, and it is complicated for the principal to verify what the agent is actually doing. Second is the problem of risk sharing, for example when the principal is risk seeking while the agent is risk averse.

- *Stage 3: Partner stage.* A partnership is a long-term alliance between two organisations, one legal and one illegal. When a legal business needs protection services from a mafia organisation in Russia, the legal business may in return carry out money laundering for the mafia organisation. There is an exchange of services on a permanent basis. A partnership may be found in relationships between two or more parties. Although the sharing of risk and rewards is the typical artefact of a partnership, often the emphasis is on intangibles, such as trust, comfort, understanding, flexibility, cooperation, shared values, goals, mutual problem solving, good interpersonal relations and regular communication. Partnership, often referred to as an alliance, has frequently been noted as a major feature of IT outsourcing and offshoring in legal industries. Partnership can reduce the risk of inadequate contractual provision, which may be comforting for clients about to outsource a complex and high-cost activity such as IT functions. Similarly, one legal organisation running manufacturing facilities for the production of heroin based on opium enters a partnership with a criminal organisation operating logistics functions from Afghanistan via the manufacturing plant in Kurdistan to wholesalers in Albania. While the production of heroin is legal, smuggling of heroin is not.

According to the European Union (Elvins, 2003), transnational criminal organisations are strengthening their international criminal contacts and targeting the social and business structure of European society, for example through money laundering, drug trafficking and economic crime. These groups appear to be able to respond easily and effectively both within the European arena and in other parts of the world, responding to illegal demand by acquiring and supplying commodities and services ranging from drugs and arms to stolen vehicles and money laundering. Their interactions with legal business enterprises are often vital to successful crime.

Elvins (2003) describes Europe's response to such transnational organised crime. The European Council meeting held in Tampere, Finland in

October 1999 was the first summit meeting specifically held to discuss crime. Later at the Amsterdam European Council, EU leaders decided to incorporate the Schengen system. In doing so measures that were highly secret and subject to no effective parliamentary scrutiny have been accepted without an assessment of the implications. The EU is now moving towards a European organised crime strategy (Levi, 2004).

3. Entrepreneurial leadership and management

Organising the business of crime requires a market-oriented approach, where market share is important. There are markets for heroin, cocaine and other drugs. There are markets for illegal weapons and stolen cars. There are markets for illegal gambling, prostitution, protection and money laundering. Whatever business a criminal organisation is in, the market share is important to establish, sustain and increase.

Typically contributions of an entrepreneur are to develop new markets and increase the market share on existing markets. Under the modern concept of criminal marketing, markets are people who are willing and able to satisfy their needs. An entrepreneur is creative and resourceful in satisfying invisible and visible demand. An entrepreneur can create customers or buyers. This makes an entrepreneur different from an ordinary businessman who mainly performs traditional functions of management.

ENTREPRENEURIAL JUDGMENT IN DECISION MAKING

Why does a criminal entrepreneur choose to organise a criminal business enterprise in order to exploit a market opportunity? Alvarez and Barney (2007) argue that entrepreneurial opportunities can be exploited in a variety of ways and seek to understand the conditions under which organising an enterprise is the most efficient way of exploiting a particular opportunity.

Opportunities to create new economic value exist because of demand for goods and services in illegal markets. Entering an illegal market as an entrepreneur is based on the assumption that there are competitive imperfections reflecting changes in technology, demand or other factors that individuals or groups in an economy attempt to exploit. For example, Ismael Zambada-Garcia is a Mexican drug lord. He is capo (captain) and head of the Sinaloa cartel in Mexico. He is 'El Mayo', Mexico's number one drug dealer. He climbed to the top by eliminating rivals and victory over Columbian cocaine producers. Zambada-Garcia got indirect help from the police because in 2002 police in Mazatlan shot and killed his most powerful rival, Ramon Arellano Felix. The Tijuana cartel operated by Felix was weakened while the Sinaloa cartel of Zambada-Garcia was strengthened (Small and Taylor, 2006). Competitive imperfections were created by the purposeful actions of Zambada-Garcia.

Whatever the source of competitive imperfections, their existence, per se, often only holds the potential for creating new economic value (Alvarez and Barney, 2007: 1058): 'The realization of this potential often requires additional economic activities, activities that sometimes require the organisation of a firm and sometimes can be organised through other governance mechanisms, such as arbitrage and alliances.' Alvarez and Barney (2007) argue that if a particular individual possesses all the resources – whether tangible or intangible – necessary to create economic wealth associated with a market opportunity, no additional economic organisation is required to exploit this opportunity. The individual is said to be engaging in arbitrage if he or she possesses all the resources necessary to exploit a market opportunity, and thus no additional coordination through economic organisation is required to create economic value.

If an individual does not possess all the resources required to exploit an opportunity, access to those resources will need to be obtained by the entrepreneur. This can be done in a variety of ways. For example, the entrepreneur can recruit the owners of these resources into a hierarchical structure to gain the access required to exploit an opportunity. Alternatively, the entrepreneur might form an alliance with the owners of these resources in a network structure to gain access.

Entrepreneurial leadership is characterized by judgment in decision making. Judgment is where individuals take decisions without access to any generally agreed rule that could be implemented using publicly available information known to be true. A drug dealer who buys before he or she knows the price at which the drug can be resold must make a judgment abut what the future price will be, for instance. Judgment refers primarily to business decision making when the range of possible future outcomes is generally unknown. Judgment is required when no obviously correct model or decision rule is available or when relevant data are unreliable or incomplete (Foss et al., 2007).

Entrepreneurial judgment is ultimately judgment about the control of resources. As an innovator, a leader, a creator, a discoverer and an equilibrator, the entrepreneur exercises judgment in terms of resource acquisition and allocation to prosper from criminal business opportunities. As founder and developer of the business enterprise, the entrepreneur must exercise judgmental decision making under conditions of uncertainty (Foss et al., 2007).

An important task in entrepreneurial leadership is to stimulate organisational citizen behaviour among criminals in the organisation. Organisational citizen behaviour supports the organisation and goes beyond an individual's job assignment and tasks. Examples include cooperation with others, volunteering for additional tasks, orienting new employees, offering to help others accomplish their work and voluntarily doing more than the job requires. Organisational citizen behaviour is performance that supports the social and psychological environment in which task performance takes place. This behaviour exceeds the minimum role requirements of the job, it is not easily enforceable, and performing it is usually at the discretion of the individual (Bergeron, 2007). Thus, individuals who spend time on these support activities are considered 'good citizens' in the criminal organisation.

ENTREPRENEURIAL MANAGEMENT

The emergence of criminal business enterprises is strongly associated with entrepreneurial innovation rather than an extension of managerial routine. It occurs at times of great volatility. Volatility reflects the fact that the economic, competitive and law enforcement environment is continually subjected to shocks (Casson and Godley, 2007). Shocks are extremely varied: they include disruptions because of police actions, fads and fashions in consumer tastes, and rivalry among competitors.

The dominant theoretical explanation of the creation of criminal business enterprises and managerial hierarchies remains transaction cost economics. According to transaction cost theory, internalization of resources is prompted under behavioural norms of bounded rationality and opportunism. Therefore, managing the crime business is no longer attributed only to great acts of entrepreneurial endeavour, but is also seen as the linear outcome of incremental cost- and risk-minimizing decisions by a far-seeing professional management pursuing optimal decisions. Vertical integration is here viewed as a managerial process focused on contractual change, rather than entrepreneurial innovation (Casson and Godley, 2007).

While the entrepreneur is the agent of development, the criminal business enterprise is the means of coordination and the agent of growth. As the agent of development, the entrepreneur creates change. Major changes include new goods and services, new methods of smuggling, new markets, new sources of supply and new ways of organising the business. As the means of coordination, the enterprise allows deployment of resources according to market opportunities. As the agent of growth, the enterprise is a structured arrangement of capabilities, which can produce economic development (Loasby, 2007).

Entrepreneurial management manifests itself in a regime in the organisation. A regime is the set of rules, both formal and informal, that regulate the operation of organised crime and its interaction with society. Regime change is sometimes needed to take advantage of new criminal business opportunities. One dimension of a regime is employment, where employment regime is dependent on the employees' major work motivation, the mode of coordinating and controlling employees, and the standard for selecting staff (Witt, 2007).

CHIEF EXECUTIVE OFFICERS

At the top of an organisation we often find a boss. In legal enterprises, the boss carries the title of chief executive officer (CEO), president, managing director or some similar title. The chief executive is the only executive at Level 1 in the hierarchy of an organisation. All other executives in the organisation are at lower levels. At Level 2, we find the most senior executives. Level 3 includes the next tier of executives (Zhang and Rajagopalan, 2004).

Being a CEO involves handling exceptional circumstances and developing a high level of tacit knowledge and expertise; these characteristics and experiences contribute to the accumulation of firm-specific human capital. The time a CEO spends in the position represents a significant investment in firm-specific human capital for both the individual and the firm. The firm is investing its resources to compensate the CEO, and the CEO is investing his or her productive time. Both make these investments with the expectation of future return, so age is a major factor determining the level of firm-specific human capital investment.

Criminal organisations seldom 'hire' a CEO like legal organisations do. Rather, a CEO is 'appointed' based on some criteria. Criteria might include family background, ownership in enterprise, position in the criminal underworld and successful beating of rivals.

If the CEO is also the founder of the organisation, then there are some similarities to legal organisations. Often, sons and daughters of founders take over their parents' top positions in shipping, manufacturing and trade.

It is not easy to identify the CEO in criminal organisations, but here are some examples:

- *Terry Adams* is head of the Adams family that is perhaps the most feared criminal organisation in England. The Adams family went into narcotics in the 1980s. There was a large demand for cocaine, cannabis and ecstasy at that time. The family built a network to

Colombian cocaine cartels. The family governs by means of violence. According to the police, the family is responsible for 30 murders (www.gangsterinc.tripod.com).

- *Jamal Ahmidan* was doing well in the narcotics trade. He was caught and put in jail, where he converted to Islam. While in prison, he planned terror attacks together with other inmates. On release, to finance the intended terrorism, he continued to head the narcotics trade. At the same time he planned the train station explosions in Madrid. With money from drug dealing he bought explosive material, that was used in the subway system in Madrid. Hence, Ahmidan was involved in both criminal business and terrorism (Shelley et al., 2005). The terror bombing in Madrid in 2004 hit commuter trains to Spain's capital on the morning of 11 March. 191 people were killed and 1460 injured. The attack was carried out by an Islamic group. The attack consisted of a coordinated series of 10 explosions onboard four commuter trains in the rush hour. A total of 13 bombs were placed but three did not explode.
- *Victor Bout* is claimed to be the world's largest weapons dealer. He was born in Tajikistan. He has Russian military training and speaks six languages fluently. He has supplied Afghan groups with weapons and ammunition. His headquarters are in the Arab Emirates, at first in Sharjah and later Ajman. In the summer of 2004 one of Bout's transport planes landed in Liberia, containing helicopters, armoured vehicles and firearms (www.gangsterinc.tripod).
- *Edoardo Contini* is chief executive of the Camorra mafia in Napoli in Italy. He is currently managing the mafia from his prison cell. Napoli is the hometown of the Camorra mafia, which is successful in narcotics and blackmail.
- *Lo Hsing Han* is the narcotics baron of Burma. He contributes to the finances of the military junta in Burma, which holds the Noble Peace Prize laureate Aung San Suu Kyi under house arrest. Lo Hsing Han mostly does business from Singapore, where he manages his narcotics empire. He started in the opium trade in the 1950s. He was arrested and sentenced to death in 1973 but was released from prison again in 1980. In 1992 he founded Asia World Company, which is the legal branch of his narcotics empire. He now controls the economy in Burma together with the 'spider man' Tay Za. In 2006, Han arranged the wedding of the daughter of the junta leader Tan Shwe. Tan Shwe is the military dictator in Burma by being the chief commander in the military junta (McKenna, 2005).
- *Ivo Karamanski* in Bulgaria was the 'godfather of the Bulgarian mafia'. Car theft was one of the many organised crimes he managed.

He was born in 1959 and died in 1998, when he and his bodyguard were gunned down in what police termed a drunken quarrel. He founded an insurance company as well as 20 other small firms. His personal signature and phrase was: 'The good boys go to heaven, the bad ones go wherever they like' (www.wikipedia.org).

- *Ahjed Wali Karzai* is the opium baron of Afghanistan. He is the younger brother of the country's president, Hamid Karzai. Sixty members of parliament in Kabul are assumed to be involved in opium production. Karzai's family is not only the wealthy owner of the Afghan Helmand restaurants in the US, but is also very influential in the Helmand and Kandahar provinces with 62 per cent of Afghanistan's opium production and more than half of the global production (Tunander, 2007).

- *Terry McGraw* is chief executive in a gang of bank robbers. When they robbed a nightclub, they were unable to switch off the alarm. Police came and arrested McGraw. The next day he was released because he had an agreement with the police to be an informant. His wife Margaret McGraw had calmed his friends that night by saying: 'The boys have been on to me already to say that it's okay, they have it in hand. Not to worry, he'll be home tomorrow. You have to just sit tight.' The boys to whom she referred were the Serious Crime Squad in the police force in Glasgow (www.gangstersinc.tripod.com).

- *Bernardo Provenzano* is the chief executive of Cosa Nostra on Sicily. His calling name is 'the tractor' because early in his mafia career he ploughed down people by shooting them down. He was jailed in 2006, but is probably still in charge of the organisation. Another calling name is 'the bookkeeper' because he in recent years has led the operations of his criminal empire in a discreet and careful way (Dickie, 2006).

- *Shinobu Tsukasa* is the sixth-generation boss (kumicho) in the criminal organisation Yamaguchi Gumi in Japan. The organisation consists of 750 clans with 17,500 members. The organisation is involved in almost all kinds of criminal business (www.gangstersinc.tripod.com).

- *Curtis Warren* is one of the greatest and richest drug dealers in the UK. He has a personal wealth of 185 million pounds. Warren is claimed to be an intelligent man, who neither drinks, smokes or uses narcotics. He has a photographic memory of telephone numbers and bank accounts. His organisation has good contacts with the Colombian Cali cartel, as well as Moroccan and Turkish criminal organisations. His organisation imports tons of cocaine and heroin

to the UK each year. Presently he is in prison and is expected to be released in 2014 (www.gangsterinc.tripod.com).
- *Ismael Zambada-Garcia* is capo (captain) and chief executive of the Sinaloa cartel in Mexico. He is 'El Mayo', Mexico's largest drug dealer. As in so many other situations when police get involved in rival criminal organisations, one criminal organisation may profit from police intervention, while others may lose. That was the case in Mazatlan, when police shot and killed Zambada-Garcia's strongest rival Ramon Arellano Felix in 2002. The Tijuana cartel of Felix was weakened, while the Sinaloa cartel of Zambada-Garcia was strengthened (Small and Taylor, 2006).

These examples illustrate the variety of backgrounds of chief executives in criminal business enterprises all over the world. These examples also illustrate the various ways chief executives have gained the power and position. This kind of executive career can be compared to the career of many executives in legal organisations.

When the top position in a legal business enterprise becomes vacant, the competition for the vacant CEO position starts. CEO succession is perhaps one of the most crucial events in the life of any firm because of the substantive and symbolic importance of the CEO position. CEO succession has been commonly viewed as an important mechanism for organisational learning and adaptation. A change in CEO can fundamentally alter the knowledge, skills and interaction processes at the top of a company, and these alterations can in turn significantly influence post-succession firm performance. Zhang and Rajagopalan (2004) studied CEO successions, and the following description of this topic is based on their research.

A distinction can be made between two types of CEO succession: inside and outside. Some have emphasized the role of outside successions in organisational learning and adaptation. However, Zhang and Rajagopalan (2004) argue that research evidence consistently indicates that outside new CEOs rarely succeed in their efforts to improve firm performance. It is plausible that although outside successions bring in new competencies and skills, they are disruptive to firms from a process standpoint, and thus the enhanced cognitive repertoire may not get translated into improved firm performance. Further, the simple distinction between inside and outside succession does not recognize crucial differences between relay and non-relay inside successions, which may have different implications for organisational learning and adaptation.

In relay succession, a firm identifies an heir apparent to its CEO well in advance of the actual succession event and uses the interval between designation and promotion to groom the heir for the top job. A relay CEO succession has two phases: during the first phase, the firm decides whether or not to designate an heir and during the second (the grooming phase), the firm decides whether or not to promote the heir to the CEO position. Both phases offer significant opportunities for organisational learning and adaptation. In the first phase, learning and adaptation occur primarily at the firm level. The firm assesses the availability and desirability of various candidates for the CEO position and evaluates their qualifications in light of key internal and external contingencies in order to decide whether to designate one of them as the heir apparent.

The second phase can be characterized as a two-way learning and adaptation process that occurs at both the individual level of the heir apparent and at the firm level. At the individual level, the heir now has the opportunity to carry out some of the tasks of the CEO position and to thereby acquire and enhance position-specific knowledge and develop broader leadership skills consistent with the position. Meanwhile, at the firm level, because one candidate has been designated the heir, the firm can now conduct a more focused assessment of this particular candidate's capabilities (cognitive and interpersonal) and continuously update its evaluation of whether the candidate's capabilities fit the CEO position. It can then use this evaluation to subsequently decide whether or not to promote the heir apparent. In this sense, the grooming phase is also a probation period for an heir apparent.

LEADERSHIP ROLES

In the following, differences between criminal and non-criminal organisations are studied in terms of leadership. Based on a set of managerial roles, this section is concerned with different emphases on entrepreneurial leadership roles in criminal versus non-criminal organisations.

This approach is important, as it is based on the fundamental issue of whether or not there are significant differences between legal and criminal organisations. One significant difference, of course, is the fact that criminal organisations are involved in organised crime. However, would these organisations stop their activities, if, say, trafficking became legal? Is the goal of criminal organisations to be criminal or is it to make above average profit? Again, this section is based on the assumption that the reason criminal organisations are involved in organised crime is that they have the possibility of higher profits or other benefits at relatively low risk. The enterprise paradigm of organised crime assumes that criminal entrepreneurs would become legal entrepreneurs if the profit-versus-risk ratio were better in legal business than in criminal business.

Criminal organisations need dynamic leadership in unstable and unpredictable environments. A manager's job consists of several parallel roles. At a certain point in time, the manager may perceive one role as more important than the others. Mintzberg (1994) found that it is a peculiarity of the management literature that its best-known writers all seem to emphasize one particular part of the manager's job to the exclusion of the others. Together they cover all the parts, but even that may not describe the whole task of managing.

Mintzberg's role typology is frequently used in studies of managerial work. When such role terminology is applied to a criminal organisation, some modification is required as a criminal will not necessarily be responsible for all aspects of each role. Furthermore, business management terminology does not always fit so well in a policing and law enforcement domain. Hence, some of the role labels have been changed to provide a more accurate fit with crime terminology.

These six crime manager roles, adapted from Karlsen et al. (2007), are briefly described below along with the specific role label noted in brackets:

- *Personnel leader* (motivating role). As a personnel leader, the entrepreneur is responsible for supervising, hiring, training, organising, coordinating and motivating a cadre of criminals to achieve the goals of the organisation. This role is mainly internal to the organised crime. The entrepreneur would not be generally responsible for hiring a particular individual in a business sense, but would have a say in which particular criminal might join his or her team for a particular crime. However, the main thrust of this role is that of motivating his/her troops and keeping such motivation up, especially in difficult and complicated situations.
- *Resource allocator* (resourcing role). The entrepreneur must decide how to allocate human, financial, technical and information resources to the different tasks of the crime. This role emphasizes planning, organising, coordinating and controlling tasks, and is mainly internal to the organised crime. Often, the entrepreneur has to be an advocate in this regard to get the necessary resources for his or her team to be able to complete the crime efficiently and effectively.
- *Spokesperson* (networking role). As a spokesperson, the entrepreneur extends organisational contacts to areas outside his or her own jurisdiction. This role emphasizes promoting acceptance of the unit and the unit's work within the criminal organisation of which it is part. For the entrepreneur it means contact with the rest of the

organisation. Frequently, he or she must move across traditional departmental boundaries and criminal cells to become involved in personnel, organisational, technical and financial matters. Hence, with regard to a crime manager, this key role is one of networking within the criminal organisation.

- *Solution manager* (problem-solving role). The entrepreneur identifies the criminal organisation's needs and develops solutions that change problematic situations. A major responsibility of the entrepreneur in this management role is to ensure that rapidly evolving criminal methods are understood, planned, implemented and strategically exploited in the organisation. Such a role is sometimes more akin to being a problem solver than a solution manager in a criminal setting. As a solution manager, the criminal entrepreneur identifies the needs and priorities of the criminal organisation. Based on identified needs and priorities, the crime manager implements criminal projects according to those needs.

- *Liaison* (liaising role). In this role, the entrepreneur communicates with the external environment, and this includes exchanging information with other criminal organisations, customers and vendors. This is an active, external role. This is a very similar role description for a criminal who has to liaise with a wide range of people throughout a crime who are external to the criminal organisation such as technical experts, property developers and financial experts. Bribing police and others is part of this role.

- *Monitor* (gate-keeping role). This role emphasizes scanning of the external environment to keep up with relevant changes, such as potential crime scenes, competitors and policing activities. The entrepreneur identifies new ideas from sources outside his or her organisation. To accomplish this task, the manager uses many resources, including vendor contacts, professional relationships and a network of personal contacts, including inmates in prisons. While the manager clearly monitors the progress or otherwise of an organised crime, the role description here is more like a gate-keeping role, in that it is not so much external politics or economics which the organised crime manager has to contend with, but rather making sure the police and other outside forces do not disrupt the progress of a crime. Hence, in that sense this is a gate-keeping role to protect the criminal team and undue external pressure.

These six crime manager roles for an entrepreneur are illustrated in Figure 3.1. As can be seen, the motivating and resource roles are internal to the criminal team for the manager. The networking and problem-solving

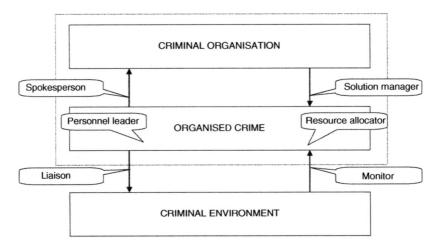

Figure 3.1   Leadership roles in organised crime

roles are directed towards the criminal organisation, and the liaising and gate-keeping roles are linked to the external environment.

Figure 3.1 illustrates the relationship between the criminal organisation and organised crime. While the criminal organisation is the basic social system, an organised crime is a temporary social system in terms of a criminal project.

We would expect that these roles are not equally important for a team manager creating criminal success. Furthermore, we would expect these roles to be different in criminal versus non-criminal organisations. Intrapreneurship in organised crime might be of critical importance (Drejer et al., 2004).

For example, in police investigations detectives in a pilot study in Norway found the role of solution manager to be most important (Karlsen et al., 2007). In a policing context, this means that the manager of an investigative unit, typically a senior investigating officer, finds the problem-solving role most important. Just as criminal investigations might be compared to organised crimes as temporary activities in a project, police organisations might be compared to criminal organisations as permanent base organisations for legal as opposed to criminal activities.

In a different empirical setting concerned with IT outsourcing projects, the project manager role of spokesperson was found to be most important. Previous studies have identified management role importance in other settings as well.

Because of the criminal nature of criminal organisation business, we will argue that the external roles are relatively more important for organised

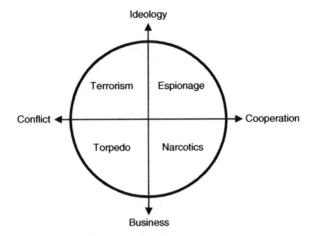

Figure 3.2 Entrepreneurial leadership depending on organised crime business

crime. For example, drug control systems (Chawla and Pietschmann, 2005) and trafficking control cooperation (Nicola, 2005) require criminal organisations to emphasize external management roles. Formulated as hypotheses, we suggest that: (1) the management role of liaison is more important in criminal organisations than in non-criminal organisations; and (2) the management role of monitor is more important in criminal organisations than in non-criminal organisations.

Successful entrepreneurs apply some kind of contingent approach to management. A contingent approach implies that the situation determines which management style is most appropriate. The situation in criminal entrepreneurship is characterized by the industry in which business is developed. Here we introduce two dimensions to classify criminal business: ideology versus business and cooperation versus conflict. An example of each combination is illustrated in Figure 3.2.

We argue that entrepreneurial leadership style will be different in terrorism, espionage, torpedo activity (the collection of debt by threats and violence) and narcotics. In terrorism, the entrepreneur will need funding as well as members willing to sacrifice their lives for the cause. In torpedo, the entrepreneur needs members who are willing to collect money as loyal agents of the entrepreneur. In espionage, the entrepreneur has to identify sources of information for which alien governments or competing corporations will pay. In narcotics, the entrepreneur will set up a physical logistics system where each individual has a limited and predefined role.

MANAGING CRIMINAL PROJECTS

Entrepreneurs in organised crime will typically set up a project each time a specific and significant criminal operation is to be carried out, such as kidnapping, bank robbery or extortion. While the criminal organisation is the basic unit in terms of a hierarchy, network or other structure, each organised crime of certain size and complexity might be set up as a project. The difference between organised crime and criminal organisation was visualized in Figure 3.1 illustrating leadership roles, where the two structures are linked in terms of the leadership roles of spokesperson and solution manager.

In order to speak about organised crime, according to the European Union, at least 6 out of a set of 11 characteristics need to be present, 4 of which must be those numbered 1, 3, 5 and 11 out of the list, as described by Elvins (2003) (see p. 5). As already mentioned, characteristic 8 suggests commercial or businesslike structures. Several other characteristics are similar to characteristics of traditional projects. For example, a project is normally a collaboration of more than two people (1), each with their own appointed tasks (2), and for a prolonged or indefinite period of time (3). While an organised crime seldom will be for an indefinite period of time, the criminal organisation might very well be. Compared with legal business projects, we suggest that criminal projects have a tighter control structure, thereby emphasizing the control side of the motivating role of personnel leader.

Therefore, an organised crime might be defined as a project. A project plan includes information on the general background of the case, goals, schedules, methods, division of labour, resources and risk analysis (Karlsen et al., 2007). It includes several horizontal properties, such as defining the exchange of information between participants, and a feedback section, the purpose of which is defined as trying to learn collectively by reflecting on the experience when the case is finished and tasks completed.

What is a project then? According to Frame (1995), a project has the following characteristics:

- *Goal orientation.* Projects are directed at achieving specific results – that is, they are goal oriented. It is these goals that drive the project, and all planning and implementation efforts are undertaken so as to achieve them.
- *Coordinated undertaking of interrelated activities.* Projects are inherently complex. They entail carrying out multiple activities that are related to each other in both obvious and subtle ways.
- *Limited duration.* Projects are undertaken in a finite period of time. They are temporary. They have defined beginnings and ends.

- *Uniqueness.* Projects are, to a degree, non-recurring, one-of-a-kind undertakings. However, the extent of uniqueness varies considerably from project to project.

Similarly, in order to speak of a project, the following criteria need to be met (Maylor, 2005):

- any non-repetitive activity;
- a low-volume, high-variety activity;
- a temporary endeavour undertaken to create a unique product or service;
- any activity with a start and a finish;
- a unique set of coordinated activities, with definite starting and finishing points, undertaken by an individual or organisation to meet specific performance objectives within defined schedule, cost and performance parameters.

We might add some criteria that need to be met to qualify as an entrepreneurial criminal project:

- an illegal business activity;
- an illegal business opportunity;
- limited access to information;
- ad-hoc decision making.

As illustrated in Figure 3.3, criminal projects have both general and specific characteristics. In the planning phase, significant attention is attributed to risk management, including competing criminal organisations as well as law enforcement personnel. Risk analysis may lead to bribery of law enforcement personnel as well as revision of crime plans.

In the implementation phase, a command structure rather than a cooperation structure is typically set up. In the closing phase of a criminal business project, the proceeds of crime have to be handled and the criminals involved have to be released from duty. Often, criminals involved in a criminal project will have as little information as possible based on the need-to-know principle.

Entrepreneurs investing in project organisation typically do so in order to become more flexible, adaptable and successful. There are specific properties of project organisation that contribute to instilling such capabilities for criminals. Project-based adaptation is characterized by goal-oriented and open-ended work process where emerging contingencies are handled. As a contrast, criminals may apply routines as a mode of adaptation, which

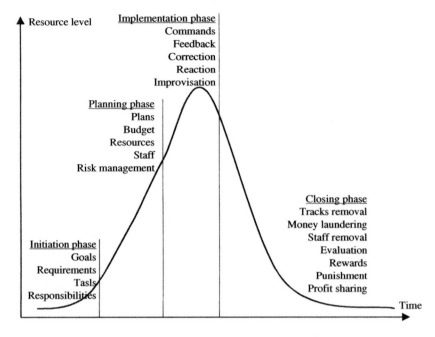

Figure 3.3   Criminal project life cycle phases

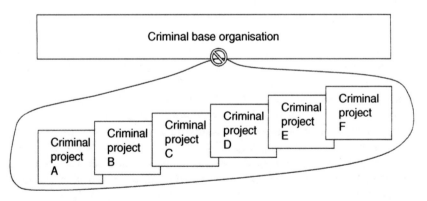

*Figure 3.4   The criminal organisation as base organisation, and organised
               crime as criminal projects*

rather relies on applying a pre-existing response pattern (Lindkvist, 2008).
While there is only one criminal base organisation, as illustrated in Figure
3.4, there are many criminal projects that may be implemented both simultaneously and sequentially.

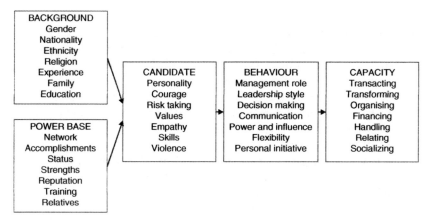

Figure 3.5   Selecting the project leader for organised crime

Therefore, the project organisation might represent a value creation logic that is far better than routine work in organised crime. Value creation in organised crime is handled in projects, where projects either create value or contribute to value creation.

According to Allum (2007), Sicilian mafia women are perceived as loyal and subordinate wives who do not interfere with their husbands' criminal projects and decisions. In contrast, Camorra women have always been much more involved and aware of their men's activities. They are not passive onlookers but are the active backbone of this criminal organisation and have become increasingly involved, sometimes out of necessity and sometimes because of a specific criminal intent. Generally, gender-dependent roles in criminal projects may define women in leadership roles such as monitor, liaison and spokesperson, while men are defined in leadership roles such as solution manager, personnel leader and resource allocator.

Selecting an appropriate project leader is an important task for the entrepreneur, as illustrated in Figure 3.5. Typically, the selection effort starts by establishing requirements for background and power base. In terms of background, some entrepreneurs may prefer a project leader with the same ethnic background, such as Albanian or Moroccan. In terms of power base, it is important that the project leader as a criminal has established a reputation for professionalism in organised crime. Based on background and power requirements, potential candidates can be identified. Their personality, courage, risk taking, values, empathy, skills and tendency towards violence are evaluated. The next phase in the selection process is behaviour, where some potential candidates have already been dropped based on results in the previous phase. Even fewer relevant candidates remain in the final phase of evaluating candidate capacity. At the end, only one person can be selected for the role of project leader.

A famous criminal project was the 9/11 terrorist attacks upon the United States. According to the 9/11 Commission (2004) report, terrorist entrepreneurs were in charge of the project. Khalid Sheikh Mohammed was the mastermind of the plot. He was the project manager of planes operations. He applied his entrepreneurial skills to hatching and planning an extraordinary array of terrorist schemes.

The 9/11 project goal was to kill Americans because America had declared war against God. It was inspired by Usama Bin Laden, who declared war against America (Commission, 2004: 47):

> We believe that the worst thieves in the world today and the worst terrorists are the Americans. Nothing could stop you except perhaps retaliation in kind. We do not have to differentiate between military and civilian. As far as we are concerned, they are all targets.

This was in 1998. Three years later, in 2001, 11 September, several thousand people were killed in lower Manhattan, on a field in Pennsylvania and along the banks of the Potomac. The United States suffered the single largest loss of life from an enemy on its soil.

There is a growing demand for project management skills as a consequence of the projectization of many legal as well as criminal organisations. Legal organisations adopt the project approach to handle special tasks more efficiently, while criminal organisations adopt this approach also to keep a distance between the criminal management and the organised crime, making it more difficult for law enforcement to identify executives and prove their involvement in the crime. For example, Hells Angels tends to have a matrix organisation, where the legal motorcycle club is along the vertical axis while the criminal activities of HAMC are along the horizontal axis. The criminal activities are not initiated and organised from the top. Instead, one core entrepreneurial member initiates a criminal project by identifying an opportunity and recruiting fellow members to the project. Top management is informed – but not necessarily involved.

Project management is being viewed as a flexible form of general management, which enables organisations to integrate, plan and control schedule-intensive and one-of-a-kind endeavours in order to improve performance and reach organisational goals.

The job of the project manager is demanding, complex and varied, requiring the ability to handle many loose ends in critical situations. Communication between team members and the entire network is vital to support a shared understanding of the project and its goals. Managing projects therefore requires a combination of skills including interpersonal ability, technical

Table 3.1 Comparison of general versus project management (adopted from Maylor, 2005)

General management	Project management
Responsible for managing the status quo	Responsible for overseeing change
Authority defined by management structure	Lines of authority 'fuzzy'
Consistent set of tasks	Ever-changing set of tasks
Responsibility limited to their own function	Responsibility for cross-functional activities
Works in 'permanent' organisational structures	Operates within structures which exist for the life of the project
Tasks described as 'maintenance'	Predominantly concerned with innovation
Main task is optimization	Main task is the resolution of conflict
Success determined by achievement	Success determined by achievement of stated end-goals
Limited set of variables	Contains intrinsic uncertainties

competencies, creativity, solution orientation and effectiveness, along with the capability to understand the situation and people and then dynamically integrate appropriate leadership behaviour. Differences between general management and project management are listed in Table 3.1.

Projects can be organised in different ways. Donk and Molloy (2008) classify projects into the following five categories:

- The *simple project* relies on the agency and vision of the project leader. It is typically an initiative of an entrepreneurial project leader. Here the enthusiasm, drive and charisma of one key person are needed to get things done.
- The *bureaucratic project* relies on stable and not too complex environments. Project management prescribes the work and work methods to be used in executing the project and order of execution, preparation of detailed instructions, and compilation of drawings and documents for the work to be done.
- The *divisionalized project* relies on managers who deal in the same way in different arenas. Such arenas may be markets, products and/ or clients.
- The *professional project* relies on professional experts working together. Each professional recognizes his or her own part and knows where the expertise ends. Project leadership will normally be

in the hands of a senior professional, who has proven expertise and knowledge in previous projects as a member of a team.

- The *adhocatic project* relies on an urgent task needing an urgent solution. Involved persons adjust their attention and make themselves available to solve problems that have occurred.

A criminal project seldom serves a single base or parent organisation only. Rather, criminal projects tend to live their own lives in complex environments with unclear overall governance schemes. Therefore, many criminal projects need a project strategy. According to Artto et al. (2008), *project strategy* is a direction in a project that contributes to the success of the project in its environment:

- *Project direction* might be goals, plans, guidelines, means, methods or governance systems including reward and penalty schemes. These elements include a capability to directly or indirectly affect the project's course. Project direction and its elements may change even on a frequent basis, which suggests that project and its strategy are dynamic.
- *Contribution* is the assumed effect of the direction. Since the direction matters and makes a difference, it will contribute an effect.
- *Success* refers to how well the project is able to accomplish its goals. Each project stakeholder may have different and conflicting criteria for evaluating projects' degrees of success. However, a project can be successful by meeting its self-established goals that may be against the interest of even major stakeholders.
- *Environment* refers to the world outside the project's boundaries with which the project as an open system must continuously interact.

Project strategy is related to survival of an organised crime. From a project's point of view, criteria for measuring survival and success and respective managerial actions may be quite different depending on the kind of crime to be carried out in the project. To implement the project strategy, there is a need for time planning, critical chain project management, cost and quality planning, plan analysis and risk management, project structure and team(s), as well as management and leadership.

THE CASE OF CURTIS 'COCKY' WARREN

This case was written up by David Amoruso and published on the Internet (Amoruso, 2007b).

Curtis 'Cocky' Warren is one of Britain's biggest and richest drug traffickers worth an estimated 185 million British pounds. Unlike most other drug traffickers or criminals, Warren is a highly intelligent force. Warren does not drink, smoke or use drugs. He has a photographic memory for telephone numbers and numbers of bank accounts. His organisation had contacts with the Colombian Cali cartel as well as Moroccan and Turkish criminal organisations. Curtis Warren was the main drug supplier in all of Britain, moving tons of cocaine, heroin and ecstacy.

Curtis Warren was born on 31 May 1963 in Liverpool, England. Warren grew up in the Granby district of Toxteth, a tough neighbourhood with a bad reputation. At age 11 Warren decided school was not for him and dropped out. He started doing petty crimes and was arrested several times. At age 12 he was arrested for stealing a car. When he reached his teens Warren became a bouncer at a Liverpool night club. In this position he got a close look at how the drug trade worked. A bouncer had the power to let the dealers (and the drugs) in or out; Warren realized this could be very good business. After some time Warren was promoted to head bouncer and had the task of bossing around the other bouncers. In this position he could fully exploit the dealers and have a good hold on the drug trade. He got his 'in' and began selling and controlling the drugs. As years passed by Warren got richer and richer and into bigger and bigger deals.

In the late 1980s he teamed up with another English drug trafficker named Brian Charrington from Middlesbrough, England. In September of 1991 they flew to Venezuela to set up a big cocaine shipment project. They had made a deal that the coke would be shipped in steel boxes sealed inside lead ingots. This way the shipment could not be x-rayed and opening it up would take a lot of effort. When the shipment hit England, it was held by customs out of suspicion. They cut open one ingot but found nothing and let the shipment through. Moments later they got a tip from the Dutch police that there was cocaine hidden inside the steel boxes inside the lead ingots, but by now the shipment and Warren were long gone. Luckily for law enforcement a second shipment was on its way, and this time they were waiting. When the shipment arrived the cocaine was found and Warren and Charrington and several others were arrested. It seemed Warren's criminal career was over and that he was going away to prison for a very long time.

Warren and his friend Charrington faced charges of importing shipments of cocaine with a combined worth of 500 million British pounds (around $600 million). All looked set but a surprise was about to happen; two detectives revealed that Charrington was a police informer. The customs agents knew nothing of this informer and it turned out that Charrington, with the help of his informer status, had shipped a lot of drugs to Britain. The case was dropped and in 1993 Curtis Warren was acquitted of all charges. Legend has it that after he was set free he went back to the customs agents, walked past them and said: 'I'm off to spend my 87 million pounds from the first shipment and you can't fucking touch me.'

Back on the streets of Liverpool things were getting dangerous; several organised crime figures were found in holes, burned and with several bullets in their head, others had been chopped up with machetes. And along with these problems came the thought that the English authorities would come after him with everything they had after their first effort ended in disgrace with the collapsed trial. With all this in mind Warren thought it was a smart idea to move to a nice safe country. And so it was that in 1995 Warren moved his headquarters to Holland. Whereas most drug traffickers would choose Amsterdam or Rotterdam as a good place to set up base, Warren decided that the quiet town of Sassenheim would be perfect. He moved into a very nice villa from where he conducted his business, made his deals and organised his criminal projects.

By this time Curtis 'Cocky' Warren was a very, very rich and powerful man. He owned houses, mansions and office blocks in Britain, casinos in Spain, discos in Turkey, a vineyard in Bulgaria and his villa in Sassenheim. The rest of his money was stashed away in Swiss bank accounts. Warren could have easily retired to some tropical island but for some reason he did not. For whatever reason he kept on going, setting up more and more drug deal projects and making more and more money. Perhaps it was the rush he got from the smuggling. In the quiet town of Sassenheim Warren felt safe and relatively hidden from the police. From his home he made phone calls to his friends in England. He did not know it but the police were listening in. Not that it mattered, Warren talked in code. He never referred to any of his friends by name, only by nicknames such as macker and tacker, the egg on legs, twit and twat, the werewolf and the vampire, badger and boo. But cops are what they are and one thing they are not is quitters, so they continued their surveillance hoping to catch Warren red-handed.

Warren's new shipment project was already set in place. This time the cocaine from Venezuela would be shipped to Bulgaria, where it would be cooked into liquid and held in suspension inside bottles of wine. From Bulgaria it would be shipped to Holland and then on to Liverpool to be sold. While Warren waited for his cocaine shipment from Venezuela he was already thinking where to stash his new heap of money, but this time people were watching. On 24 October 1996 the shipment from Bulgaria arrived in Holland and that night Dutch special police units raided Warren's home to arrest him. The unit, using stun grenades, totally surprised the sleepy Warren and put him under arrest without difficulty. Several members of his organisation were arrested that same night. At the homes they found three guns, ammunition, hand grenades, crates with gas canisters, 1500 kilos of heroin, 50 kilos of ecstacy and $600,000 in cash. The shipment was also caught, which combined with the stashes found before would be worth 125 million British pounds. All in all you could say 'Cocky' Warren's criminal business was severely hit, but then again he was arrested in Holland and right away things looked a little bit brighter.

At the trial Curtis Warren was charged with importing 800 kilos of cocaine into Holland and planning to ship it to the UK. On 19 July 1997 he was found guilty and sentenced to only 12 years in prison because of lax drug laws in the Netherlands. Immediately after his sentencing the authorities started the search for Warren's riches, estimated at 125 million British pounds by British authorities; so far they have only traced 20 million pounds. They traced it but they cannot touch it. Twenty million pounds found that they cannot touch and over 100 million pounds lost, hidden somewhere in bank accounts or buried somewhere in a backyard in England. The only person who knew where all that money was stashed was Warren and he never kept any records, never wrote it down and never kept numbers or accounts in a computer. He had it all in his mind, a photographic memory. And as the authorities continued their search the man who knew where the treasure was buried was serving his 12-year sentence in the maximum security prison Nieuw Vosseveld in Vught, Holland, and he was not planning on telling them anything regarding his golden stash.

After serving over two years of relatively quiet time Warren made some noise: he kicked in the head of a fellow inmate. It all happened on the afternoon of 15 September 1999 when Warren was walking around the prison yard. While Warren walked around quietly inmate Cemal Guclu started yelling abuse at Warren. Guclu was serving a 20-year sentence for murder and attempted murder. Yelling abuse at Warren Guclu walked towards him and tried to punch him in the face. Warren evaded the punch and pushed Guclu against the wall, after which Guclu fell to the ground. Guclu tried to punch Warren again but Warren was one step ahead and kicked him in the head four times. After this Guclu tried to get up once more before Warren again kicked him in his head, after which Guclu lay motionless in the prison yard, his head a bloody mess. Guclu was dead on the spot. In February 2001 Warren was back on trial; Warren said he 'acted in self-defence'. The Dutch judge did not feel the same way and found Warren guilty of manslaughter, adding: 'the defendant had used excessive violence'.

The judge sentenced Warren to four years in prison. Warren, now 37, was to get out in 2014 and would now serve 16 years instead of 12. And still it could have been worse for him. The Dutch authorities looking for

Warren's gold told him that he had to pay them 26 million guilders ($14 million) or face an added five years in prison. After some legal chat back and forth an agreement was struck: Warren would pay 15 million guilders ($8 million) and not face an added five-year term; the Dutch authorities agreed and took the money.

Curtis 'Cocky' Warren was still in prison serving his time and was expected to be out around 2014. Warren's stash of gold had still not been found and he remained the wealthiest British criminal, worth an estimated 125 million British pounds according to the authorities and 185 million British pounds according to insiders. It is all stashed away safely and the combination of the vault is safely locked away in Warren's head.

In February 2005 Warren was charged by Dutch authorities of running an international drug smuggling cartel from his Dutch prison cell. He was found guilty but successfully appealed and was released from prison in June 2007. He was escorted by Dutch police to a ferry terminal. He is currently back in Liverpool and made it clear he wants to 'get on with his life in a positive way'.

By late July 2007 it had become clear that Warren had not turned his life around. He was charged with conspiracy to import £300,000 of controlled drugs into Jersey (a British island near France). Probably Warren could not live without the 'high' of the smuggle, the crime and each criminal project.

THE CASE OF ECO-CRIME: THE TROPICAL TIMBER TRADE

This case is based on the article 'Eco-crime: The Tropical Timber Trade' by van Solinge (2008).

A cargo ship was boarded off the Dutch coast by Greenpeace activists who chained themselves to the ship. The activists climbed the mast and displayed a banner reading 'Europe, stop ancient forest destruction'. The Liberian timber targeted by the activists was a good example of what is labelled 'conflict timber'. Conflict timber refers to timber trade that is related to armed conflicts (van Solinge, 2008: 99):

> From the moment former rebel leader Charles Taylor was elected President of the West African country of Liberia in 1997, he used different sectors of the economy in order to buy weaponry. Firstly, he used the large revenues of ship registrations. Being a 'flag of convenience' tax haven, Liberia has the world's second largest registered commercial fleet (after Panama). About one third of all oil tankers, cruise ships and freight carriers are registered as Liberian. The ship registration represented 30% of Liberia's national budget.

A second important source of income for the corrupt president was dia-monds. A third important source was eco-crime (van Solinge, 2008: 100):

> Liberia was the only country in West Africa still having a significant portion of its original rainforest cover. Under Taylor's regime, large quantities of Liberian timber and especially the valuable hard wood were exploited and exported. It soon became clear that Liberia's timber industry was related to arms traffick-ing. The UN's Expert Panel Report on Sierra Leone made no doubt about it. 'The principals in Liberia's timber industry are involved in a variety of illicit activities, and large amounts of the proceeds are used to pay for extra-budgetary activities, including the acquisition of weapons'. One of the members of the 'Taylor's coterie', as the Report described it, was Simon Rosenblum, an Israeli based in Abidjan, Ivory Coast, carrying a Liberian diplomatic passport. 'He has logging and road construction interests in Liberia and his trucks have been used to carry weapons from Robertfield, Liberia, to the border with Sierra Leone'. The UN Report described how weapons were flown in by a BAC-111, owned by Leonid Minin, an Israeli businessman of Ukrainian origin and known arms trafficker.

4. Value configurations in criminal entrepreneurship

Based on the enterprise paradigm of organised crime, this chapter outlines how value configuration analysis might be applied to criminal organisations. Distinctions are made between value chains, value shops and value networks. In the value chain, an entrepreneur organises flows of goods. In the value shop, an entrepreneur organises knowledge work. In the value network, an entrepreneur organises connections between actors. Based on the contingent approach to management, entrepreneurs will initiate different criminal organisations depending on the value configuration of a value chain, value shop or value network.

For a long time, we thought the only possible value configuration for business organisations was the value chain developed by Porter (1985). Insights emerged, however, that many organisations have no inbound or outbound logistics of importance, they do not produce goods in a sequential way, and they do not make money only at the end of their value creation chain.

Similarly, organised crime does not necessarily involve logistics and production, as defined by the value chain concept. Some criminal enterprises provide services, while other activities are mainly problem solving for law firm clients, consulting customers and hospital patients. In such cases, neither the beginning nor end of value creation is characterized by physical goods changing attributes in a sequential chain.

Therefore, two alternative value configurations have been identified, labelled value shop and value network (Stabell and Fjeldstad, 1998). As we move into a knowledge economy, both legal and criminal organisations make their living from knowledge creation and knowledge application. The typical value configuration where we find such knowledge work is the value shop. The value shop is a value configuration creating value by applying knowledge to customer problems. Also, the number of value networks is growing as enterprises are in the business of connecting people and organisations. A value network is an organisation that creates value by connecting clients and customers that are, or want to be, dependent on each other.

To comprehend the value that organised crime provides to criminal organisations, we must first understand the way a particular organisation conducts its business and how primary organisational activities affect the performance within the organisation. Understanding how criminal firms differ is a central challenge for both theory and practice of law enforcement.

A value configuration describes how value is created in a firm for its stakeholders. A value configuration shows how the most important business processes function to create value. A value configuration represents the way a particular organisation conducts business. In this chapter, a set of three value configurations is explored for organised crime: value chain, value shop and value network.

Again, this chapter is based on the enterprise paradigm of organised crime, which is grounded in the theories of legal organisations (Liddick, 1999). Similarly, when applying the enterprise paradigm in their book, Lyman and Potter (2007) make a distinction between groups and businesses. They also stress hostile environment as well as unstable environment as two distinguishing characteristics making criminal organisations different from legal organisations.

This conceptual approach to classifying criminal organisations into value configurations is important to both criminology and policing in society, as it sheds new light and creates new insights into criminal entrepreneurship. This chapter is based on the assumption that most criminal organisations are involved in organised crime because they have the possibility of creating significant value in their value configurations at relatively low risk.

THE VALUE CHAIN

The best-known value configuration is the value chain. In the value chain, value is created through efficient production of goods based on a variety of resources. The organisation is perceived as a series or chain of activities. Primary activities in the value chain are (1) inbound logistics, (2) production, (3) outbound logistics, (4) marketing and sales, and (5) service (Porter, 1985).

A typical example of a value chain configuration is the cocaine business. More than 14 million people worldwide, 0.3 per cent of the global population aged 15 and above, are estimated to use cocaine. The main change in the cocaine value chains over the past decade has been, the end of cartelization. This followed the dismantling of the Medellin and the Cali cartels. The operations of cartels were increasingly taken over by a large number of decentralized production and distribution firms. Production of coca leaf shifted to Colombia. It used to take place mainly in Peru. Farming of coca leaf is now closer to the cocaine laboratories, thereby improving inbound

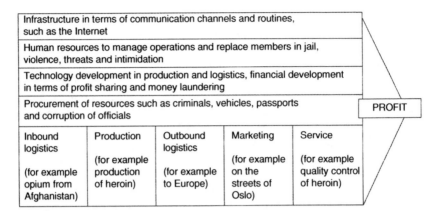

Figure 4.1   Primary and secondary activities in the criminal value chain

logistics for the value chains. The main outbound logistics of cocaine is from Colombia to the US and Europe (Chawla and Pietschmann, 2005).

In terms of the five primary activities of the value chain, (1) inbound logistics takes place when coca leaves are transported from farms to laboratories, where (2) production of cocaine takes place. Then (3) outbound logistics takes cocaine to markets, where distributors are doing (4) marketing and sales and also (5) service in terms of quality control, as illustrated in Figure 4.1.

Another typical example of value chains is the heroin business. While the bulk of heroin destined for European markets was manufactured in Turkey ten years ago, heroin production capacities within Afghanistan have increased significantly. The main trafficking route of opiates is from Afghanistan to Europe. As is the case for cocaine, one general trend in opiates has been a shift of manufacturing capacities closer to the areas of opium production (Chawla and Pietschmann, 2005).

The opiate trafficking chains are rather complex. Individual criminal groups generally transport opiates over shorter distances than for typical trafficking in cocaine. Opiate trafficking is often organised along ethnic lines. Typically, Pashtun traders sell the opium to operators of clandestine laboratories in Afghanistan. The opium or heroin is then sold to other Pashtun or Baluch traders who smuggle the goods across the border from Afghanistan to Pakistan or Iran, or to Afghan Tajiks who ship the heroin across the border to Tajikistan. Tajik groups from Tajikistan are then frequently involved in smuggling the heroin to major Russian towns. In another parallel route, Kurdish and Turkish groups transport the heroin across Turkey to Istanbul. Albanians then smuggle the heroin to wholesalers in Western Europe, where African criminal groups often take charge of retail distribution (Chawla and Pietschmann, 2005).

Other examples of criminal value chains include production of passports and pirate copies of computer software. Piracy was traditionally robbery at sea (Felsen and Kalaitzidis, 2005), but in our times piracy has moved into the virtual world of software and information on the Internet.

Secondary activities are also called enabling activities, since they are instrumental to achieve organisational goals and to make a profit (Wright, 2006).

The value chain as both a concept and a tool has been used for more than 20 years to understand and analyse industries. It has proved a very useful mechanism for portraying the chained linkage of activities that exist in the physical world within traditional industries, particularly manufacturing.

THE VALUE SHOP

A value shop creates value by solving problems. Eliminating trails for money from criminal activity through laundering is a typical example of problem solving. Knowledge is the most important resource in the value shop. A value shop is characterized by five primary activities: (1) problem finding and acquisition, (2) problem solving, (3) choice, (4) execution and (5) control and evaluation. In the case of money laundering, the problem is to make money clean. It can be done in different ways, such as real estate or financial transactions, and a choice has to be made in primary activity number 3. After implementation, the choice can be evaluated, as illustrated in Figure 4.2.

A value shop schedules activities and applies resources (mainly knowledge) in a fashion that is dimensioned and appropriate to solve a specific problem, while a value chain performs a fixed set of activities that enables it to produce a standard product in large numbers.

In the legal economy, typical problem-solving organisations, such as law firms and hospitals, are value shops. Not surprisingly, a law firm as value shop is also able to solve criminal problems such as money laundering. Generally, value shops are professional service firms, found in medicine, architecture, engineering, consulting and law.

The five activities in the value shop are interlocking, as illustrated in Figure 4.3, and while they follow a logical sequence, much like the management of any project, the difference from a knowledge management perspective is the way in which knowledge is used as a resource to create value in terms of results for the organisation. In the case of money laundering, different kinds of knowledge are needed to solve the problem.

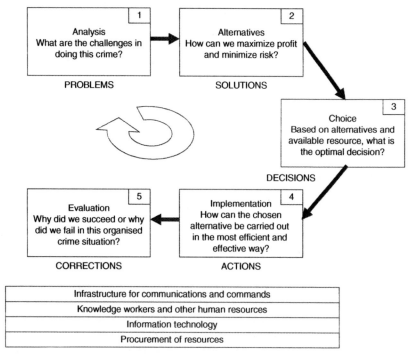

Figure 4.2   Primary and secondary activities in the criminal value shop

First, the funds have to be moved from direct association with the crime. Next, the trail to foil pursuit has to be disguised, and finally the money has to be made available to the criminals once again with its occupational and geographic origins hidden from view (Joyce, 2005). In this process of money laundering, alternative solutions are developed, and the implementation is evaluated.

The Marcos case represents a value shop where proceeds of organised crime accumulated. Ferdinand Marcos' corrupt activities commenced while he was a congressman and head of the import control board, which allowed him to gather large bribes in return for approving import licences. As congressman, Marcos soon became a millionaire, largely based on his 10 per cent cut from government deals. When Marcos became president of the Philippines, he acquired an epic appetite for bribery, where several officials worked more or less full time in his value shop activities to acquire personal wealth (Chaikin, 2000).

Deciding to bribe is the result of a problem-solving activity. Bribery activity can involve organisations in their home country or abroad and can involve the local or foreign governments with which organisations

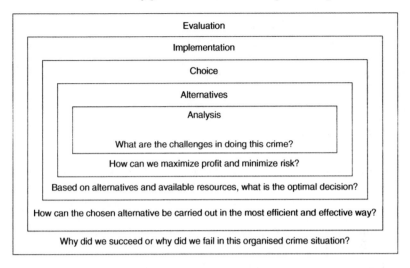

Figure 4.3   Interlocking primary activities in the criminal value shop

interact. Bribery activity differs on the basis of who is supplying as opposed to demanding the bribes, and whether public or private sector institutions are involved (Martin et al., 2007).

Bribery is corruption conducted to achieve favourable treatment. The criminal entreprenuer is dependent on favourable treatment to succeed in organised crime. The favourable treatment might be customs clearance, granting of a building permit or transaction acceptance. In the distinction applied by Pinto et al. (2008), an organisation of corrupt individuals is a behavioural phenomenon, while a corrupt organisation is a top-down phenomenon in which a group of organisation members undertake corrupt actions. Corrupt actions are carried out by the dominant coalition, organisational elites, or top management team; directly or through their subordinates to the benefit of the organisation.

Organisational corruption, which Lange (2008) defines as the pursuit of interests by organisational actors through the intentional misdirection of organisational resources or perversion of organisational routines, might ultimately impede the organisation's ability to accomplish its legitimate purpose and may threaten its very survival.

From an economic perspective, corruption is generally defined as the misuse of a position of authority for private or personal benefit based on external influences. The external influence supplies benefits to solve a problem. Typically, a problem is solved by providing benefits to persons in positions of authority. Corruption when applying the value shop con- figuration reflects rational, self-interested behaviour by the principal using its discretion to direct allocations to other social actors who offer rewards in return for favourable discretionary treatment. According to Misangyi et al. (2008), this approach assumes that corruption is a response to situations that present opportunities for gain and the discretionary power to appropriate that gain.

THE VALUE NETWORK

The third and final value configuration is the value network. A value network is a company that creates value by connecting clients and customers that are, or want to be, dependent on each other. These companies distribute information, money, products and services (Stabell and Fjeldstad, 1998). While activities in both value chains and value shops are carried out sequentially, activities in value networks occur in parallel. The number and combination of customers and access points in the network are important value drivers in the value network. More customers and more connections create higher value to customers.

The value network has only three primary activities, as illustrated in Figure 4.4. While network operations create communication, service provisions create services that are communicated, and marketing creates new contacts in the network.

The Russian–Italian mafia network extends the traditional Russian value networks, as exemplified by Solntsevo of Russia, when this criminal group decided to expand to Italy. The network structure is such that a few local actors in Italy are in touch with the Russians, while most of the Italian accomplices speak to each other and go through their point man, who is in touch with the Russian mafia (Varese, 2006).

While a value chain and a value shop each have five primary activities, a value network has only three. First, there is the infrastructure linking clients. In the legal economy, telephone companies and banks are examples: a phone company connects people who want to talk to each other while a bank connects people who want to borrow money from each other. This is done through the infrastructure of the value network. Next, the value network may have a small or extensive range of services. Finally, the value network is dependent on the persons and organisations that link through the network. More actors on the network will create more business.

The value creation logic in a value network is connecting clients to each other, so that they can do business. Typical examples are prostitution, the drug trade, slavery, theft of goods such as outboard motors and PCs, liquor smuggling, and cars stolen in Scandinavia sold in the Balkans.

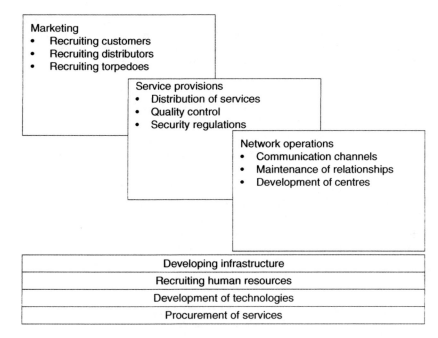

Figure 4.4   Primary and secondary activities in the criminal value network

In Taiwan, the Heavenly Alliance is a criminal organisation with the value configuration of a value network. It is involved in a number of businesses, such as the trafficking of mainland Chinese women to Taiwan for the purpose of prostitution. There are three ways for Chinese women to come to Taiwan: 'marriage', 'visit' and smuggling. Because rules for visiting relatives are very strict, it is difficult for the Chinese to obtain a visa to visit their relatives in Taiwan. Therefore, fake marriages are arranged for sex workers. The sex business is run in different ways, such as using a jockey (Finckenauer and Chin, 2006: 78):

> The 'jockey' (driver) is the bridge between a sex worker and a sex ring. Normally, one jockey will be assigned to one girl. . . . A driver will drive a sex worker around to the customers because most mainland Chinese women are not familiar with their new environment. Whenever a customer contacts a sex ring (normally the chicken head), the chicken head will select a sex ring after he or she listened to the special needs of the customer. An operator of the sex ring will then instruct a jockey to drive a sex worker to the customer's place. While the sex worker is with the customer, the driver will park his car around the vicinity to keep an eye on the people going in and out of the hotel and to keep track of the time. Ten minutes before the time is up, he will call the sex worker to hurry up. Of course, if the driver observes some law

enforcement personnel, he will also alert her and the customer. When the sex worker comes out of the hotel with the money collected from the customer, she will immediately hand it over to the driver to avoid being robbed by a subsequent customer. At the end of the day, the driver will turn over all the day's earnings to the sex ring.

The dream of mainland Chinese sex workers in Taiwan is to make a certain amount of money and then return home. Because they do not have legal status in Taiwan, they cannot settle down there, and the best they can do is return home unnoticed with some profit. However, due to police crackdowns, many of them are deported back to China.

If the Taiwanese police arrest a sex worker from China, the authorities will, according to the Kinmen Agreement between China and Taiwan, first check the detainee's background to make sure she is a Chinese citizen and then inform the Chinese authorities. While waiting for the Chinese government to take her back, she will be kept in a mainland Chinese processing centre, the so-called Jinru centre (Finckenauer and Chin, 2006).

COMPARISON OF VALUE CONFIGURATIONS

Value chain, value shop and value network are alternative value configurations that impact the business logic of organised crime. The value creation logic in a value chain is the transformation of input to output, such as opium to heroin. The value creation logic in a value shop is solving problems, such as eliminating the links to proceeds from crime through money laundering. Another example is cartels, which solve the problem of low prices by agreeing among members to raise prices. Murder is a third example of problem solving by a value shop, where the killing of a person is useful to the client. Further examples of value creation by value shops are torpedo activity, security services (such as Blackwater), insider stock trading, tax fraud and corruption.

When comparing the work form of value chains, value shops and value networks, we find important differences. While the value chain has a sequential production, the value shop has an integrated and cyclical problem-solving activity, and the value network monitors many simultaneous connections, as listed in Table 4.1.

Value configuration represents an organising framework in criminal entrepreneurship, by distinguishing between value chains, value shops and value networks. As has been documented in this chapter, the operations of these three configurations are very different, requiring law enforcement knowledge to be successfully understood.

Table 4.1   Comparison of value configurations

Characteristics	Value chain	Value shop	Value network
Value creation	Transformation of input to output	Solving clients' and customers' problems	Connecting clients and customers to each other
Work form	Sequential production	Integrated and cyclical problem solving	Monitored and simultaneous connections
Technology role	Making production more efficient	Adding value to the knowledge work	Infrastructure operations
Example	Production of drugs	Laundering of money	Trafficking of women

The issue of value network as a value configuration should not be confused with the issue of criminal network as a management structure. The United Nations (2002) found that the most frequent management structure in organised crime is a rigid hierarchy, followed by a developed hierarchy, a hierarchical conglomerate, a core criminal group and then an organised criminal network. An organised criminal network is defined by the activities of key individuals who engage in illicit activity together in often shifting alliances. They do not necessarily regard themselves as an organised criminal entity. Individuals are active in the network through the skills and capital that they may bring. For example, individuals in a criminal network may be active in narcotics supply, which is a value chain.

THE CASE OF ILLEGAL ALCOHOL IN NORWAY (VALUE CHAIN)

The illegal importation and distribution of alcohol has been organised crime in Norway for almost a century, since the Prohibition in the 1920s. According to Johansen (2007), the illegal entrepreneurs in this business have been forced to adapt to a number of changes over time. Demand and supply have fluctuated, wars have broken out, moral crusades against alcohol consumption have been launched, and new and aggressive police methods have been introduced and reduced.

Some criminal entrepreneurs have successfully managed to cope with these challenges and have survived as criminal professionals for decades. Many criminal smuggling teams have been successful for long periods, and they have learned from their mistakes. Some illegal enterprises are embedded in legal firms, which do not merely serve as a cover but have a legal existence of their own. This grey zone of overlapping legal and illegal business has been a familiar aspect of Norwegian criminal history since the Prohibition (Johansen, 2007).

Size is an important factor in organised crime. Large criminal enterprise in Norway is risky in such a small and transparent society, where rumours about sudden wealth travel fast. The more assistants an illegal entrepreneur keeps employed, the greater the chance of someone talking and telling.

Expressive lifestyle as a security risk is as old as the illegal markets in Norway. According to Johansen (2007), drinking and driving is also a very stupid thing for a Norwegian smuggler to do. A timid Norwegian loves to brag after some drinks. Smugglers with working class backgrounds from the East Side of Oslo, who socialize in West Side restaurants with gold chains, young women and fancy suits are easy targets. Even more so when they 'forget' about their wives, as the betrayed Norwegian wife is a classic informer.

For the successful illegal entrepreneur practical precautions are the first rule of thumb. A professional smuggler drives a certain trailer just once or twice before he switches to a new one. He does not own the trailer. It is normally rented. There is a new route across the border every time. Some teams have hideaways along the border as a place to rest, or isolated farms in Sweden or Denmark where they split up the cargo before crossing the border. Limiting smuggling loads to one thousand litres helps reduce the severity of sanctions, since smaller quantities are no longer seen as professional smuggling by the courts. Importers and drivers are very concerned about timing, adjusting the driving to hours, days and weeks when custom officers are known to be absent. Some customs stations even provide information about when their offices are open, as a service to legal importers who want to pay duty and need papers to show they have done so (Johansen, 2007).

Successful illegal entrepreneurs have established a kind of intelligence system. For example, they have a car in front of the trailer and another one behind that give warnings by cell phone in code if the police show up. Contacts within police and customs are seldom comparable to the level of corruption in Italy or Russia. Often, bribes are seen as a security risk because most officers are difficult and dangerous to bribe.

THE CASE OF THE RUSSIAN MAFIA (VALUE SHOP)

A qualitative transformation of Russian organised crime, particularly in organisational and behavioural patterns, was brought about by the changed economic and political situation in Russia since the 1990s. In particular, Abramova (2007) observes a pronounced shift from violent crime towards economic crime. Criminals try to establish and exercise control over legitimate businesses via corrupt politicians, local authorities and/or law enforcement officials. A tendency towards the consolidation of criminal groups within given territories is also discernible, while there are signs of increased interregional integration among different criminal organisations.

The core of Russian organised crime may be described as about 130 criminal communities (soobschestva), which comprise over 1,200 organised criminal groups (gruppirovski) of cumulative strength of approximately 11,000 men and women. The largest among the communities are 'Dalnevostochny Vorovskoi Obschak' and 'Uralmashski', while the more well known, especially in the West, are the 'Solntsevo', 'Chechen', 'Tambov' and 'Podolsk' communities. All of these criminal organisations, although they represent a blend of legal and illegal structures, were involved in both legal and criminal activity that originated from traditional violent crime (Abramova, 2007).

Abramova (2007) expects more transnational organised crime originating in Russia in the future. The leaders of Russian criminal organisations, having established and/or legalized their positions in the key industries at home, will try to expand their economic influence abroad. For this purpose, they are most likely to use the methods perfected in Russia – violence, fraud and corruption. They will not limit themselves to creating new affiliate criminal structures abroad, but will try to carve out a share of the existing criminal markets overseas. This will transfer hostilities between organised crime groups to other lands; in particular, Southern Europe, South East Asia and selected key countries in the West.

Among areas of economic criminal activity the following will be of special interest to Russian organised crime (Abramova, 2007): trafficking in arms, human beings, drugs, diamonds and rare metals; financial operations, especially illegal international transfers and money laundering as well as assistance in terrorist financing; and the introduction of fraudulent financial and other schemes.

The Russian mafia has quickly expanded its activities abroad. For example, in the Netherlands, the national police has registered a significant increase in the number of criminal suspects from the former Soviet republics. While there were 592 suspects in 1996, the number had risen to 2,068 suspects in 2002. Suspects and detainees from former Soviet republics are usually Russians and Lithuanians, followed by suspects born in the three Caucasus republics (Armenia, Azerbaijan and Georgia), Ukraine or Belarus. Estonia, Latvia and the five Central Asian republics are hardly represented in the police data (Weenink and Laan, 2007).

In the Netherlands, Weenink and Laan (2007) found Russian mafia activity in many markets:

- *Narcotic drugs*: Drug trafficking, including cocaine from Latin America, heroin production and synthetic drug production such as ecstacy. In most of these cases, Dutch citizens are also involved.
- *Human trafficking*: Ties to prostitution. Offender groups mostly consist of two to five persons, and women also show up in the files as offenders.
- *Human smuggling*: Persons from Eastern Europe to the Netherlands and the United Kingdom.
- *Illegal trafficking of firearms*: As firearms are not produced in the Netherlands, all weapons have to come from abroad. Several former Soviet republics are production centres.
- *Cigarette smuggling*: The Netherlands is mainly a transit country for cigarette smuggling to the United Kingdom, where excise duties are much higher than on the continent.
- *Illegal trade in plants and animals*: Russia plays an important global role as a transit port, source country and as a country of destination for endangered species as well. Limited quantities of endangered plants are smuggled from the Netherlands to the Czech Republic in particular and of endangered species from the Czech Republic and Russia to the Netherlands.

There is a growing illegal money flow from Russia to the Netherlands and other Western countries. The problems the money flow from Russia poses for the outside world are threefold. First, the illegal nature of the money flow affects the integrity of financial service industries. Second, unknown owners invest in strategic industries in the West. Third, it perhaps becomes more difficult to distinguish between funds that have their origin in criminal activities in Eastern Europe and the 'less dirty' money flows (Weenink and Laan, 2007).

THE CASE OF MARZOLA PAEDOPHILE SERVICES (VALUE NETWORK)

As a paedophile, Sergio Marzola discovered there was money to be made in the market. As an entrepreneur, he set up a secret Internet service for trading in images of children being raped by adults. The typical supplier of new images was a father raping his daughter. Marzola paid 250 euro for a daughter filmed in lingerie, 500 euro filmed naked and subsequently

750 euro filmed when raped (Independent, 2007). Marzola was selling the images through Internet bulletin boards whose existence was known only to paedophiles. They spent only minutes or even seconds on these boards before making contact and then disappearing into private chat rooms to conduct business. Marzola is an Italian but he moved to Ukraine, where he had bought a house and a studio in city of Karkov. Young Ukrainian girls were raped and filmed in Marzola's Studio.

Marzola was operating an Internet criminal organisation called 'Fun Club', where value was created by connecting supply and demand of paedophile images and films. Paedophile subscribers were found in Belgium, Denmark, Germany, Holland, Switzerland and many other countries. Many identifiable subscribers and contributors were fathers photographed or filmed with web cameras as they abused their daughters, aged between 2 and 14 years (www.droitfondamental.eu).

5. Entrepreneurial structure and culture

Organisational design is important in entrepreneurship. For example, when a criminal entrepreneur needs venture capital, the venture capitalist provides monetary and non-monetary resources to turn the entrepreneur's idea into a viable business. In order to maximize their returns from their investments, venture capitalists will pay considerable attention to the way the criminal enterprise is organised in terms of value configuration, organisational structure and organisational culture (Casson and Nisar, 2007).

CHARACTERISTICS OF ORGANISED CRIME GROUPS

The United Nations (2002) conducted a pilot survey of 40 selected organised criminal groups in 16 countries. The following characteristics of criminal organisations were identified:

- *Structure*. Rigid hierarchy was the most common structure, where there is a single boss and strong internal discipline.
- *Size*. The average size of the criminal organisations was 50–100 persons.
- *Activities*. Most of the criminal organisations had one primary activity, such as drug trafficking.
- *Transborder operations*. Most criminal organisations spread their activities across five or more countries.
- *Identity*. Half of the criminal organisations had members drawn from the same social background or ethnic background, while the other half had no such identity.
- *Violence*. Most criminal organisations saw the use of violence as essential to their activities.
- *Corruption*. Most criminal organisations considered the use of corruption to be essential to their primary activities.
- *Political influence*. Some criminal organisations had political influence at the local and regional level, while a few had influence at the national level in the country of intervention.

- *Penetration into the legitimate economy.* Most criminal organisations had extensive crossover between legitimate and illegitimate activities.
- *Cooperation with other organised crime groups.* Most criminal organisations had some kind of cooperation with other criminal organisations.

According to the United Nations (2002), globalization and growing economic interdependence have encouraged and promoted the transformation of crime beyond borders in all parts of the world. Improved communications and information technologies, increased blurring of national borders, greater mobility of people, goods and services across countries, and the emergence of a globalized economy have moved crime further away from its domestic base.

In a similar study, Europol (2006) employed the following indicators in its analysis of organised crime groups:

- *The international dimension.* The situation where a criminal group resorts to international operations, exploiting its presence in source, transit and destination countries, presents the most threatening feature.
- *Group structures.* Modern organised crime research is increasingly shifting its focus from criminal collectives, initially organisations and later criminal networks, to the individual organised criminal. Studies have revealed very flexible and fluid patterns of association between individual criminals. The existence of criminal organisations or networks should not be taken for granted; attention might instead be paid to the conditions under which patterns of criminal association and co-offending emerge and exist.
- *Use of legitimate business structures.* Organised crime does not operate exclusively within a criminal underworld, but makes regular and widespread use of legal businesses to support and facilitate its criminal activities.
- *Specialization.* Organised crime groups often have a need for someone with specialist skills or know-how, such as chemists, accountants, financial experts, IT specialists, those with access to particular goods and services such as firearms or false passports, or those willing to carry out specific tasks such as murder or debt enforcement.
- *Influence and corruption.* Corruption can be defined as the misuse of entrusted power for private gain. With regard to organised crime activities, this definition can be developed further to integrate facilitation payments made to receive preferential treatment for

something the individual receiving the bribe is required to do by law, or to obtain services the individual receiving the bribe is prohibited from providing.

- *Use of violence.* The use of violence is inherent in many types of crime, but organised crime groups can exert violence for several different reasons other than simply for the sake of committing a violent crime. Violence can be adopted as an offensive or defensive tactic, it can be planned or based on reaction, it can be brought to the extreme or limited to the necessary degree, and it can be publicly exposed or kept hidden.
- *Counter-measures.* A counter-measure is an action undertaken by an organised group to avoid detection and ultimately prosecution by law enforcement agencies.

According to Finckenauer (2005: 81–2), the attributes of the criminal organisations that make the crimes they commit organised crime include criminal sophistication, structure, self-identification and the authority of reputation, as well as their size and continuity:

> These criminal organisations exist largely to profit from providing illicit goods and services in public demand or providing legal goods and services in an illicit manner. But they may also penetrate the legitimate economy, or in the case of the mafia, assume quasi-governmental roles. However they choose to do it, and whatever they choose to do, their goal remains the same – to make money, as much as they can. Sometimes that can mean seeking political power in order to facilitate their greed, but the bottom line is the same. The members of a criminal organisation may comprise a crime family, a gang, a cartel, or a criminal network, but those labels are not important to the definition. These members may also share certain ethnic or racial identities; but that too is not essential to their being defined as a criminal organisation engaged in organised crime. What is essential to the definition of organised crime is the ability to use, and the reputation for use of violence or the threat of violence to facilitate criminal activities, and in certain instances to gain or maintain monopoly control of particular criminal markets. Also essential is that organised crime employs corruption of public officials to assure immunity for its operations; and/or protect its criminal enterprises from competition. It is these that are the defining characteristics of organised crime and that best answer the question of just what organised crime is.

Finckenauer (2005) makes a distinction between certain crimes that may be extremely complex and highly organised in their commission – but which are not committed by criminal organisations – and true organised crime. Criminal organisations can be envisioned as being arrayed across a spectrum based upon having a greater or lesser degree of the following characteristics (Finckenauer, 2005: 75):

- *Criminal sophistication* – What degree of planning is used in carrying out crimes? How long do individual criminal ventures last? How much skill and knowledge are required in carrying out these crimes?
- *Structure* – Is there a division of labour with clearly defined lines of authority and leadership roles? Does the structure maintain itself over time and over crimes?
- *Self-identification* – Do the participants in criminal activities see themselves as being members of a defined organisation? Is there, for example, an emphasis upon bonding, such as the use of colours, special clothing, language, tattoos, initiation rites, etc.?
- *Authority of reputation* – Does the organisation have the capacity to force others – whether criminals or non-criminals – to do what it dictates without having to resort to actual physical violence? In other words, is the organisation's reputation sufficient to instil fear and to intimidate others?

A criminal organisation building up a system of illegal operations is defined by the following characteristics (Gilinskiy, 2006: 279):

- A stable association of people, designed for long-term activity
- A complex hierarchical structure with functions assigned to specific units of the organisation
- The criminal nature of the activity and associated financial activities
- The deriving of maximum profits as the key goal of the activity
- The corruption of powerful organisations and individuals, especially law-enforcement bodies, as the main means of the criminal activity
- The aspiration to monopoly in a certain sphere of trade or on certain territories

According to Carpo (2006), an important multinational concept of organised crime is defined as follows:

> A criminal organisation means a structured association, established over a period of time, of two or more persons, acting in a concerted manner with a view to committing offences which are punishable by deprivation of liberty or a detention order of a maximum of at least four years or a more serious penalty, whether such offences are an end in themselves or a means of obtaining material benefits and, where appropriate, of improperly influencing the operation public authorities.

According to Carpo, the United Nations Convention on Transnational Organised Crime can be considered the most important attempt to date to arrive at a globally agreed upon concept of organised crime:

- *Organised criminal group* shall mean a structured group of three or more persons, existing for a period of time and acting in concert with the aim of committing one or more crimes or offences established in accordance with this Convention, in order to obtain, directly or indirectly, a financial or other material benefit.
- *Serious crime* shall mean conduct constituting an offence punishable by maximum deprivation of liberty of at least four years or a more serious penalty.
- *Structured group* shall mean a group that is not randomly formed for the immediate commission of an offence and that does not need to have formally defined roles for its members, continuity of its membership or a developed structure (Carpo (2006), p. 11).

Carpo (2006) states that organised crime groups are increasingly enlisting professionals such as lawyers, accountants, financial service experts and other specialists for their activities.

Ethnic Albanian organised crime groups are typically indigenous due to a persistent common mentality, clan-like relationships all over South Eastern Europe and beyond, mainly with Turkish organised crime groups, and often brokered by Egyptian middlemen and Asian and South American cartels. Some groups have both national and foreign members, mainly Italians (Carpo, 2006). Albania reported 13 organised crime groups involved in 74 recorded cases of trafficking of women for sexual exploitation and nine cases of trafficking of minors (Carpo, 2007).

Organised crime refers to continuing organised groups that monopolize illegal enterprises through violence and threats and enjoy immunity of operation through corruption (Hagan, 2006).

Organised crime can become ideological. Contrary to the claims that organised crime groups do not have political designs on their own, Schulte-Bockholt (2001) argues that such organisations may develop or acquire ideological preferences. The argument is made that criminal organisations acquire ideological preferences as they evolve into elite structures.

Criminal organisations are different from legal organisations, and many propositions concerning differences have been introduced. One proposition suggests that criminal organisations are more short-lived than legal organisations because illegal business enterprises are disadvantaged by the hostility of their task environment. In a study of criminal organisations in New York, Liddick (1999) did not find support for this proposition. Many criminal organisations exist for decades while many legal organisations go bankrupt after a short time. A comparison of legitimate business versus organised crime groups is listed in Table 5.1.

Another proposition suggests that illegal organisations will be smaller than legal organisations because the illegality of a product has consequences for the ways in which various participants (entrepreneurs, agents,

Table 5.1   *Comparison of legitimate business and organised crime groups*
(adapted from Wright, 2006: 60)

Dimension	Legitimate business	Organised crime groups
Enterprise	Activities cover the whole range of goods and services above the legal limit. May be involved in licit forms of power brokering or security/protection	Illicit; only covering a limited range of goods and services below the legal limit. These often involve illicit forms of power brokering or security/protection based on threats and violence
Transaction costs	Apply to all transaction costs, including incentives, cooperation and enforcement. There is a tendency to minimize such costs to support profits	Apply to all transactions, including incentives, cooperation and enforcement. In particular, they are relevant to the security and survival of the group
Organisation	Generally hierarchical; sometimes bureaucratic in structure but now less so. Exceptions to this in some specialist fields, where structures are less well defined. Transaction costs because of organisational structures may be somewhat higher than they are in organised crime groups	Hierarchical, non-bureaucratic, in loose confederation, often with partners. Organisational transaction costs may be lower than in legitimate business, although applying too many draconian sanctions may increase them
Boundaries	Legal and ethical boundaries. Businesses may impose strategic boundaries by choice. Multinational organisations have only limited jurisdictional boundaries	No jurisdictional, legal or ethical boundaries. Transaction costs comparatively low in this dimension
Goals and objectives	Generally accessible, although some business strategies are kept confidential for commercial reasons. Goals are often multiple to satisfy a range of constituencies within the firm	Clandestine to protect the group and its leaders. Except in 'expressive' gangs, goals generally are limited to those that maximize profitability. Transaction costs are minimized in this respect

Table 5.1   (continued)

Dimension	Legitimate business	Organised crime groups
Profitability	Optimizing 'satisfying' behaviour, depending on the type of business, the multiplicity of its goals and the character of its executive and stakeholders	Generally maximizing, although personal generosity is not unknown
Competition	Competitive edge preserved through technology, research, marketing and intellectual property rights. Not adverse to corruption to achieve their ends in some environments. Transaction costs more predictable than they are in a firm pursuing illicit enterprises	Competitive edge preserved by means of coercion, violence and use of capital resources for corruption on a regular basis. These may appear to reduce transaction costs but there may be a long-term price to pay
Rent-seeking behaviour	Some rent-seeking behaviour to achieve specific goals. It is rarely immanent in the functions and purposes of the business	Almost constant rent-seeking behaviour, which is often immanent in the functions and activities of the group

customers) seek to structure their relationships. The threat of police intervention, either to seize assets or to imprison participants, and the lack of court-enforceable contracts are likely to lead to the formation of small enterprises. Liddick (1999) found no support for this proposition. Many of the criminal organisations studied had several thousand employees.

A third proposition suggests that illegal enterprises can be expected to be local in scope, not to include branches in remote locations. Only 2 out of 33 illegal number operations studied by Liddick (1999) were observed to span state lines, thus supporting this proposition. As operation expands, the risk of drawing law enforcement agencies' attention might increase. Thus, a generally hostile environment seems to naturally limit the geographic scope of illegal organisations.

A fourth proposition suggests that pure conglomeration, diversification into unrelated product lines, seems not to occur in illegal markets. Illegal entrepreneurs are expected to diversify into related product markets such as marijuana importers also handling cocaine. Liddick (1999) did not find support for this proposition in his research, as the NYPD reports were filled with information about various legal and illegal business activities carried out by one criminal organisation. As proposed, most of the numbers entrepreneurs also offered other gambling services, including bookmaking, dice games and card games. Diversification, however, was not limited to provision of other gambling services. Every major numbers banker identified by the police also diversified into unrelated legal and illegal markets.

Using the theory of the firm enables analysts to compare aspects of legitimate business with those of organised criminal groups across a number of dimensions that generate transaction costs. These include their organisation, boundaries, goals and objectives, competition and rent seeking. Each of these involves transaction costs, which vary according to the extent to which an enterprise is licit or illicit. Table 5.1 adapted from Wright (2006) sets out a comparison of legitimate business and organised criminal groups across these dimensions.

ORGANISATIONAL STRUCTURE

It has long been argued that organisational structure is the result of organisational choices. This idea was developed by Mintzberg (1979) and applied by scholars such as Donk and Molloy (2008). According to this idea, the structure of organisations is the result of choices based on nine design parameters. Design parameters are used by organisations to divide and coordinate their work to establish desired patterns of behaviour.

The choices about each of the design parameters represent the building blocks of the organisational structure. The nine design parameters are as follows (Donk and Molloy, 2008; Mintzberg, 1979):

1. *Design of positions in terms of job specialization.* The number of tasks to be executed and the amount of control over that work. Jobs can be specialized in two dimensions. Job specialization in the horizontal dimension represents division of labour. At one extreme, the police officer is a jack-of-all-trades, forever jumping from one broad task to another. At the other extreme, he or she focuses his/her efforts on the same highly specialized task, repeated day-in and day-out, even minute-in and minute out. Job specialization in the vertical dimension represents separation of work from administration. At one extreme, the police officer merely does the work without any thought as to how or why. At the other extreme, he or she controls every aspect of the work in addition to doing it. In the first dimension we find narrowness

by horizontal job specialization (in that it deals with parallel activities) and breadth by horizontal job enlargement. In the second dimension we find depth by vertical job specialization and closeness by vertical job enlargement.

2. *Design of positions in terms of behavioural formalization.* Regulating the behaviour of individuals by formalization of job, workflow or rules. No matter what the means of formalization (job, workflow or rules), the effect on the person doing the job is the same: his or her behaviour is regulated. Power over how that work is to be done passes from the police officer to that person who designs the specification, often a manager in the police district or in the national police directorate. Organisations formalize behaviour to reduce its variability, ultimately to predict and control it. One prime motive for doing so is to coordinate activities. The fully formalized organisation, as far as possible, is the completely controllable, precise and predictable organisation. There should be no confusion in the organisation. Everyone knows exactly what to do. The alternative is a completely informal organisation, where neither jobs nor workflows or rules are specified.

3. *Design of positions in terms of training and indoctrination.* Training is the process by which job-related skills and knowledge are taught while indoctrination is the process by which organisational norms are acquired. Professionals are trained over long periods of time, before they ever assume their positions. Often, this training takes place outside the organisation, often in a police university college. The training itself usually requires a particular and extensive expertise, beyond the capacity of the organisation to provide. Indoctrination is the way an organisation formally socializes its members for its own benefit. Indoctrination is the process by which organisational norms are acquired.

4. *Design of superstructure in terms of unit grouping.* Establishing the formal lines of authority by combining people into units and departments. Grouping establishes a system of common supervision among positions and units. Grouping requires positions in the same group to share common tasks and resources. Grouping creates common measures of performance. When positions are to be allocated to groups, several criteria are applied, such as knowledge and skill, work process and function. Positions may be grouped according to specialized knowledge and skills that police officers bring to the job. Alternatively, positions may be grouped according to function. When grouped according to knowledge, the same kind of expert is organised in the same group. When grouped according to function, different kinds of personnel are organised in the same group to completely carry out all tasks in that function.

5. *Design of superstructure in terms of unit size.* The span of control (distinguishing between a narrow and a wide span). This design of superstructure concerns how large each unit or work group should be. This is a question of span of control. While a tall organisational structure will be the result of small groups, a flat structure will be the result of large groups. A linkage focusing on planning involves future thinking. A linkage focusing on control involves correcting actions as they occur.

6. *Design of lateral linkages in terms of planning and control systems.* The specification of the desired output and the assessment if the desired outputs or standards have been achieved. The purpose of a plan is to specify a desired output in the future. The purpose of performance control is to regulate the overall results of a given unit.

7. *Design of lateral linkages in terms of liaison devices.* Positions bypassing normal vertical channels to establish contacts between two units to coordinate the work of these units. Examples of liaison positions are task forces and standing committees. The standing committee is a more permanent interdepartmental grouping. It meets regularly to discuss issues of common interest. Another example of lateral linkage is the matrix structure. A weak liaison device would be a coordinator who attempts to make different parts of the organisation aware of other parts' needs. A strong liaison device would be a board with power to make decisions influencing several parts of the organisation.

8. *Design of decision-making systems in terms of vertical decentralization.* The power to make decisions down the chain of authority. When all power for decision making rests at a single point in an organisation with a single individual, the structure is completely centralized. When the power is dispersed among many individuals, the structure is decentralized. Centralization is the tightest means of coordinating decision making in an organisation. Vertical decentralization is concerned with the delegation of decision-power down the chain of authority.

9. *Design of decision-making systems in terms of horizontal decentralization.* Refers in general to the extent to which non-managers control decision processes. Decentralization implies transfer of power out of the line structure. Power is transformed into informal power, for example control over knowledge resources and information gathering and advice.

A comparison of these organisational structure parameters for criminal versus legal organisations is illustrated in Figure 5.1. We suggest that horizontal job specialization is applied to a greater extent in criminal organisations, while a deeper vertical job specialization is found in legal organisations.

In addition to these nine design parameters, the shape of the organisational

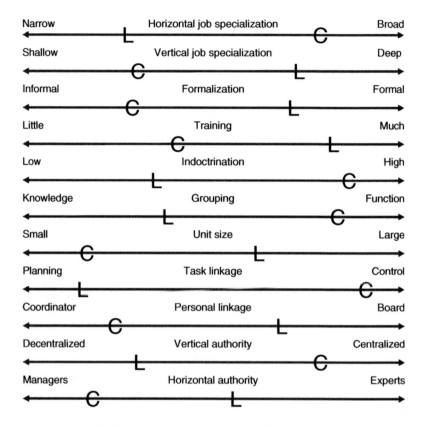

Figure 5.1   Organisational structure parameters for criminal versus legal organisations (C – criminal, L – legal)

structure is influenced by contingency factors. Examples of contingency factors are age and size of the organisation, regulation in the environment, stability in the environment, and power in terms of external control and internal control (Donk and Molloy, 2008).

A slightly different approach to organisational structure is organisational configuration. Organisational configuration is defined as a multidimensional constellation of conceptually distinct characteristics that commonly occur together. In this perspective, organisations are understood as clusters of interconnected structures and practices. It represents a systemic and holistic view of organisations, where patterns or profiles rather than design parameters are related to an outcome such as performance (Fiss, 2007). Ketchen et al. (1997) found that an organisation's performance is partially explained by its configuration.

When studying criminal organisations, organisational structures are often identified as either economic–bureaucratic in structure or independent-network in structure. Criminal networks have the merit of capturing the flexible and dynamic nature of interpersonal interaction. When studying Colombian cocaine firms, Zaitch (2002: 297) found a mixture of the two structures:

> By studying internal business and labour relations, I tried to capture both the economic and dynamic dimensions of cocaine enterprises. I found that Colombian cocaine firms are informal, small, mutating and decentralised. Some are individual enterprises; others adopt the form of temporary partnerships between two or three people. These coalitions are often formed solely for a single project, with some of the people involved also engaging in legal activities or in other coalitions. In many cases, a percentage system is used to divide profits, and payments in kind are not rare. A further conclusion of this study is that despite the importance of kinship ties and the frequent use of relatives, none of these enterprises are 'family businesses'. Brokers (people with contacts) play a central role in bringing about these coalitions and transactions.

Yet another, slightly different, approach to organisational structure is organisational architecture (Auteri and Wagner, 2007; Ethiraj and Levinthal, 2004; Moussavou, 2006). The issue of structuring organisational effort became popular in the 1990s with the promotion of the concept of organisational architecture. The architecture of an organisation provides the framework through which an organisation aims to realize its core qualities as specified in its ambitions. It provides the infrastructure into which business processes are deployed. It ensures that the organisation's core qualities are realized across the business processes deployed within the organisation.

According to most authors organisational architecture is a metaphor; like traditional architecture it shapes the organisational space where life will take place. It also represents a concept, which implies a connection between the organisational structure and other systems inside the organisation in order to create a unique synergistic system that will be more than just the sum of its parts.

Some systems are effective and efficient whereas others are not. Successful systems may be attributable to the skill exercised in designing the system or to the quality of management practised during operations, or both. Successful systems are characterized by their simplicity, flexibility, reliability, economy and acceptability:

- *Simplicity*. An effective organisational system need not be complex. On the contrary, simplicity in design is an extremely desirable quality. Consider the task of communicating information about the operation of a system and the allocation of its inputs. The task is not difficult when components are few and the relationships among them are straightforward. However, the problems of communication multiply with each successive stage of complexity.

- *Flexibility*. Conditions change and managers should be prepared to adjust operations accordingly. There are two ways to adjust to a changing operating environment: to design new systems or to modify operating systems. An existing system should not be modified to accommodate a change in objectives, but every system should be sufficiently flexible to integrate changes that may occur either in the environment or in the nature of the inputs.
- *Reliability*. System reliability is an important factor in organisations. Reliability is the consistency with which operations are maintained, and may vary from zero output (a complete breakdown or work stoppage) to a constant or predictable output. The typical system operates somewhere between these two extremes. The characteristics of reliability can be designed into the system by carefully selecting and arranging the operating components; the system is no more reliable than its weakest segment.
- *Economy*. An effective system is not necessarily an economical (efficient) system. It is often dysfunctional and expensive to develop much greater capacity for one segment of a system than for some other part. Building in redundancy or providing for every contingency usually neutralizes the operating efficiency of the system. When a system's objectives include achieving a particular task at the lowest possible cost, there must be some degree of trade-off between effectiveness and efficiency. When a system's objective is to perform a certain mission regardless of cost, there can be no trade-off.
- *Acceptability*. Any system, no matter how well designed, will not function properly unless it is accepted by the people who operate it. If the participants do not believe it will benefit them, are opposed to it, are pressured into using it or think it is not a good system, it will not work properly. If a system is not accepted, two things can happen: (1) the system will be modified gradually by the people who are using it, or (2) the system will be used ineffectively and ultimately fail. Unplanned alterations in an elaborate system can nullify advantages associated with using the system.

Organisational architecture parameters are compared in Figure 5.2 for criminal versus legal organisations. For example, we suggest that criminals

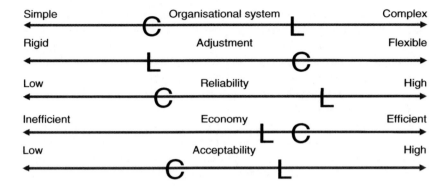

Figure 5.2   Organisational architecture parameters for criminal versus legal organisations (C – criminal, L – legal)

may be somewhat opposed to a system but they are pressured into using it, causing the extent of acceptability to be lower than in legal business enterprises.

Organisations are constructed, like any other kind of social system. An organisation is observable through the actions and interactions of its members, both between themselves and with people in the organisation's environment. To be observable, an organisation must have a domain for its activity and it must have a set of objectives and goals. The basic elements in organisation structuring include division of labour, structuring of work and coordination as first suggested by Mintzberg (1979).

Groth (1999) developed the idea of preconditions for organising and suggested six areas where we quickly run into limits restricting organisation building:

- *Capacity for work.* Both the need for organisations and their nature are strongly dependent on the nature and amount of work that has to be carried out.
- *Memory performance.* The brain has limitations in terms of storage capacity and retrieval capabilities.
- *Information processing.* The brain has limitations in terms of reasoning, problem solving and decision making.
- *Communication.* The amount of information a person can absorb is limited by communication bandwidth.
- *Interaction.* How fast a person can interact with other persons is limited.
- *Emotion.* Ambition, likes and dislikes, instincts and preferences represent limitations.

According to Groth (1999), it is difficult to ascertain which of these abilities or properties is most important, but they all represent limitations for organisational design. Since organisational design is about developing and implementing strategy (Bryan and Joyce, 2007), it is important to be aware of human limitations. Organisations can be designed to gain from strengths and compensate for weaknesses, and to avoid threats and to prosper from opportunities.

For example, hierarchy is efficient for setting aspirations, making decisions, assigning tasks, allocating resources, managing people who cannot direct themselves and holding people accountable. Even in internet times, hierarchy is needed to put boundaries around individuals and teams (Bryan and Joyce, 2007). All organisations are hierarchical, as compliance with authority is a universal feature of organisations. An authority structure is essential to decision making and its implementation (Andersen, 2002).

Furthermore, interdependencies among elements of organisational design might represent both barriers and enablers of strategy development and implementation. Since organisations are complex entities composed of tightly interdependent and mutually supportive elements, performance is determined by the degree of alignment among the major elements. The marginal costs and benefits associated with any design element depend on the configuration of others (Rivkin and Siggelkow, 2003).

OCCUPATIONAL CULTURE

The culture is created by an entrepreneur in a new criminal enterprise by setting priorities, determining rules and developing acceptable behaviour. Organisational culture is found to influence organisational performance. There is no consensus about its definition, but most authors will probably agree on the following characteristics of the organisational culture construct: it is (1) holistic, (2) historically determined, (3) related to anthropological concepts, (4) socially constructed, (5) soft and (6) difficult to change (Hofstede et al., 1990). Organisational culture represents an imperfectly shared system of interrelated understandings shaped by its members' shared history and expectations. It defines the 'shoulds' and 'oughts' of organisational life (Veiga et al., 2000).

To some extent, organisational culture contains what is taken for granted by members, invisible yet powerful constraints, and thus it connects cognition and action, environment and organisation, in an entangling and interwoven tapestry. They act as socially validated sources one for the other. An entrepreneurial culture is one that tends to foster positive social attitudes towards entrepreneurship (Williams, 2006).

Cooperation is often appreciated among close colleagues. At the same time, criminals may be competitive in criminal activities. They have a strong desire to achieve results, both individually and as a group. This attitude can stimulate individual competition, and competition among teams, organisations and networks. An important factor is the extent of workforce diversity (Yusuf, 2005), which might be needed in a criminal organisation.

Group orientation is often found in criminal work since a typical feature of organised crime is team cooperation or cooperation between two partners. This is a typical feature, developed as newcomers commit their first crime together. Partnerships of this kind tend to last for many years, long after they leave their guns in the closet. On the other hand, organised criminals are described as strong individuals with distinct leadership qualities. What is more, a criminal is often completely responsible for his or her personal actions, which leads to stronger emphasis on individualism.

Because of the group orientation of organised crime as well as the need for an organisation to avoid law enforcement, we suggest the following hypothesis that group orientation is stronger in criminal organisations than in non-criminal organisations.

Some criminal organisations only employ relatives. Here we find brothers, uncles and sons. Group orientation seems very strong in these organisations. A major narcotics business in Norway, for example, only employs relatives from Croatia. Employees live in Norway, Sweden, Austria, Croatia and the Netherlands. It is estimated that there are several hundred employees in this criminal organisation. Recently 30 employees were convicted, nine in Norway.

Top management of this multinational narcotics business is located in the Netherlands. Most of the goods are shipped from the Netherlands while weapons are supplied from the Balkans. When employees travel, they do so to visit relatives in different countries. In Norway, this criminal organisation has two cells, which operate independently of each other. This is similar to non-criminal organisations, which operate businesses with similar products under competing brands. A fast-food chain, for example, may operate two competing organisations, such as a pizza chain and a hamburger chain.

Both criminal and non-criminal organisations apply force or threat of force in their management. In non-criminal organisations, psychological force is often applied. Examples are threats and harassment, leading to uncertainty and other psychological problems for the employee. In criminal organisations, physical violence is in the management toolbox.

Perhaps the most significant difference between criminal and non-criminal organisations can be found in financial management. Since law enforcement agencies attempt to track the proceeds of organised crime, criminal organisations have to set up their financial management systems in a way that is non-traceable. Swiss and offshore banks may be used, where the obligation of secrecy in Swiss law and offshore law is found in various legislative provisions. Criminal organisations do not use their own names in illegal transactions; instead, they use nominees such as friends, cronies and layers of foundations and companies to conceal their activities (Chaikin, 2000).

Therefore, we suggest as another hypothesis that financial management is more critical to criminal organisations than to non-criminal organisations. Hence, knowledge of finance is important to organised crime leaders.

MANAGEMENT STRUCTURES

Criminal organisations have different characteristics but similarities to legal organisations exist. For example, competition is a key characteristic of business enterprises in capitalist parts of the world. Competition is found both in the legal and the illegal parts of an economy.

For example, tough competition characterized motorcycle organisations in Scandinavia a decade ago, where Bandidos, Hells Angels and Outlaws were the main competitors. Among other business areas, they were competing in the amphetamine market. This competition was labelled 'MC war', as a variety of competitive weapons were used by the parties, including bombs.

The similarities and differences between criminal and non-criminal organisations have been illustrated by management, projects, value configuration, network, culture and finance. More dimensions and characteristics may be included. For example, management structure is of interest. In a pilot survey of 40 selected organised crime groups in 16 countries, the United Nations (2002) found different management structures. The most frequent management structure was rigid hierarchy, followed by developed hierarchy and hierarchical conglomerate, defined as follows:

- *Rigid hierarchy*. Single boss. Organisation or division into several cells reporting to the centre. Strong internal systems of discipline. Example: Sizranskaya Groopirovska in Russia.
- *Developed hierarchy*. Hierarchical structure and line of command. However, regional structures, with their own leadership hierarchy, have a degree of autonomy over day-to-day functioning. Example: La Cosa Nostra in Italy.

- *Hierarchical conglomerate.* An association of organised crime groups with a single governing body. The latter can range from an organised umbrella-type body to more flexible and loose oversight arrangements. Example: Arellano-Felix Group in Mexico.
- *Core criminal groups.* Ranging from relatively loose to cohesive groups of core individuals who generally regard themselves as working for the same organisation. Horizontal rather than vertical structure. Example: Juvenal Group in Colombia.
- *Organised criminal network.* Defined by the activities of key individuals who engage in illicit activity together in often shifting alliances. They do not necessarily regard themselves as an organised criminal entity. Individuals are active in the network through the skills and capital that they may bring. Example: the Verhagen Group in the Netherlands.

The Verhagen Group, an example of an organised criminal network, was involved mainly in trafficking hashish into the main cities of Rotterdam, Amsterdam, Utrecht and the Hague. Key characteristics of this loosely organised group were the extensive use of transborder smuggling operations and the occasional use of violence and corruption (United Nations, 2002). Apart from drug smuggling, the group engaged in a diversity of other illegal activities.

The United Nations' (2002) attempt to develop a typology of criminal organisations is important, as typologies might provide greater detail to what is meant by the concept of organised crime. The identification of a series of typologies has important policy implications for law enforcement agencies. Different strategies of law enforcement must be used in confronting different types of organised crime groups.

Organisational structure and value configuration influence leadership roles. This is called the contingent approach to management. For example, the problem-solving configuration of value shops requires management of knowledge workers, while the production configuration of value chains requires management of production workers.

ENTREPRENEURIAL EDUCATION

The impact of entrepreneurial activity on both legal and illegal business enterprises has been well established. In the legal business sector, a wide range of institutional antecedents have traditionally been associated with both the choice of individuals to found ventures and various outcomes associated with venture founding. One institutional variable that has received significant attention is education based on the fundamental assumption that there is a positive relationship between education and the individual's choice to become an entrepreneur as well as the potential positive outcomes of such activity.

Similarly, it has been argued that criminal entrepreneurship is strengthened through education. Some business school students end up in organised crime after graduation. Some criminals attend business school courses. Some inmates in prisons become students at business schools.

However, the assumption that there is a positive relationship between education and entrepreneurship might be called into question. Dickson et al. (2008) report that the relationship between general education and venture formation is unproven although there appears to be a positive relationship between general education and entrepreneurial income. Regarding the linkage between education specific to entrepreneurship and entrepreneurial outcome, results are more significant, possibly because entrepreneurship students have already decided to move into venture formation.

Anderson and Jack (2008) examined how the context, approach and teaching techniques used for entrepreneurship education need to reflect the different roles that encompass enterprise. They identified role typologies and argue that teaching entrepreneurship needs to produce a combination of the creative talents of the artist and the skills and ability of the artisan, yet include the applied knowledge of the technician and the know-what of the professional. They argue that teaching of entrepreneurship requires a combination of theory and practice.

Similarly, the learning of criminal entrepreneurship requires a combination of theory and practice. Skilled entrepreneurs tend to apply different motivational factors from unskilled entrepreneurs. Unskilled traffickers, for example, tend to use threats and violence to accomplish criminal activities while skilled traffickers tend to use manipulation and bribes to accomplish tasks.

Entrepreneurial education in organised crime tends to be learning-by-doing education. Many criminal leaders believe that entrepreneurial behaviours are learned through experience and discovery. Their students can experience key aspects of the way of criminal life of the entrepreneur. Only experimental learning seems relevant to many, future criminal entrepreneurs.

As entrepreneurial learning requires a combination of theory and practice, prior entrepreneurial experience might reduce the number of mistakes and increase the number of successes in criminal entrepreneurship. Learning through previous experiences will strengthen entrepreneurial knowledge and contribute to the formation of organised crime. According to Huovinen and Tihula (2008), entrepreneurial experience has been examined as an individual characteristic influenced by the entrepreneur's personal history and work experience. Entrepreneurial experience consists of proficiency developed over time (stock of experience) and knowledge accumulated through events over time (stream of experience). Previous entrepreneurial experience might facilitate the recognition of new criminal opportunities.

Illegal entrepreneurial experience was studied by Aidis and Van Praag (2004) in terms of criminals who gathered experience during Soviet rule in Lithuania prior to starting up a private legal business. Their empirical results indicate that illegal entrepreneurship experience is not associated with overall business performance. The results render no support for a hypothesis that such experience would increase business performance in general. These results indicate that prior experience in the black or grey market under one economic system does not provide valuable human capital for entrepreneurs in a more open market-oriented setting. However, a closer look at their results indicates that illegally acquired experience is positively related to business motivation, where illegal experience can be seen as a signal for motivation to start a legal business after communism had disappeared in Lithuania.

THE CASE OF LONDON'S FIRST ORGANISED CRIME LORD

According to the BBC, Jonathan Wild was London's first organised crime lord. His story illustrates many of the points on criminal entrepreneurship we want to make in this book. First, illegal and legal activities were combined and benefitted each other in Wild's organisation. Next, political and other official contacts were useful in organised crime. Also, powerful mechanisms kept organisational members loyal to Wild. Here is his story according to the BBC (www.bbc.co.uk).

Jonathan Wild: London's First Organised Crime Lord

'Thief-takers' were the men and women who operated in England in the days before there was an established police force and a public prosecutor. Effectively created by the laws of the time – specifically the 1697 Act of Parliament, which offered rewards for the capture and successful prosecution of highwaymen – they captured those who had committed crimes, and either handed them over to the authorities or prosecuted them themselves. There have been women thief-takers, but the majority were men, and they worked for the cash rewards offered, as a very good living could be made this way. Highwaymen, coiners and burglars were worth £40 each (plus any equipment the criminal may have been using), with an additional £100 if robbery was committed within five miles of Charing Cross. This kind of sum would normally take three to four years to earn for the ordinary man. The reward also carried a free pardon for any offences the thief-taker may have committed. If the thief-taker died, any reward would be passed on to his descendants.

Although offering a reward was one of the few ways to encourage the catching of criminals and the breaking up of gangs without an organised police force, it paradoxically also encouraged corruption, blackmail and perjury. Rather than being an early form of 'Neighbourhood Watch', it caused criminals to turn on each other, creating suspicion and violence, and encouraged them to work both sides of the law. Thief-takers were very unpopular.

'Thief-taker General'

Jonathan Wild was the most famous thief-taker of his time. In the early 18th century he captured and brought to justice many London criminals. What was slow to come to the attention of the law was that he was at the same time involved in many criminal activities of his own.

Born in about 1682, he started his career in Wolverhampton as a buckle maker. He moved to London when he was in his mid-20s (leaving behind a wife and child), and soon found himself in a debtor's prison. Mingling with criminals for the two to four years he was incarcerated, Wild made sure that he not only learnt much from the others but also courted the acquaintance of those he felt would be useful in the future. In his last few months inside, he met Mary Milliner, a prostitute with plenty of under-world contacts. She became his mistress, and when they left prison they set up home in Covent Garden.

At first Wild returned to buckle making, but the temptation of easy money soon became too much to resist, and while Mary was busy enter-taining 'clients' in dark alleys, Wild would rob them. This led to them having enough money to take over a drinking house which was used by many other criminals – the King's Head. He began buying their stolen goods, and this was the start of his double life.

Wild set up an office in New Toner's Lane; he invited victims of crime to come to him with details of any stolen goods, and promised that he would recover them. His popularity as a receiver of stolen goods meant that he often either had the goods in his possession already or knew who had stolen them. One of his scams was to order the theft of specific goods so that he could return them to their grateful owners. He managed to please the thieves by paying for their goods and please the victims by reuniting them with their property (at a fee, of course). The thieves were also happy because it was a lot easier to steal small goods of sentimental value for which a good reward would be offered than to have to try to steal more valuable property that could be heavily protected.

London's First Criminal Underworld Boss

Wild began to expand his empire – he divided London into districts and set up gangs in each district, screening them from justice. He arranged for 'specialist' gangs, that robbed churches, or followed the various country fairs, gangs of conmen, gangs who ruled the prostitutes, gangs who collected protection money, to name but a few. He did not lead any gangs – he merely organised and advised them.

Anyone who didn't do his bidding, or crossed him, risked being reported to the authorities. They were framed with the assistance of witnesses who belonged to Wild. Once convicted, they could not testify against Wild himself in any subsequent court case. The same happened to those who operated outside of his empire. The rewards he gained from bringing criminals to justice helped him to become more powerful among the criminal underworld. Favours done for him were never forgotten and his loyalty to those who earned his respect never wavered. Treachery was likewise never forgotten and he was merciless in doling out revenge. He also turned in some of those depending on him to protect them from the law when he became tired of them, sometimes arresting them himself. He often joined the crowds at Tyburn when one of 'his' criminals was being executed, and he enjoyed passing on the tales of the men and women who were there due to his relentless pursuit of the criminal classes.

He avoided handling stolen goods himself, but had artists and craftsmen to alter and reset jewellery and objects of art. He owned warehouses to store large amounts of goods and he kept a sloop for carrying stolen items into Flanders and Holland; smuggling brandy, linen and lace to London on its return. He passed on information about wealthy travellers to highwaymen. His empire was so successful that no highwaymen were allowed to operate without his protection, and none were executed between 1723 and 1725. He moved out of the King's Head, took better premises in Old Bailey in 1719, and took a higher class mistress. His house was staffed by felons who had illegally returned from transportation. Knowing that they would be turned in if they displeased him made them very hard working.

Wild wasn't entirely unnoticed by the authorities although they hadn't been able to catch him getting up to anything. In 1717, the Solicitor-General

Sir William Thompson was instrumental in securing an Act of Parliament which made it a capital offence to take a reward under the pretence of helping the owner to recover stolen goods, without prosecuting the thief. This Act became known as 'Jonathan Wild's Act' because it had been designed specifically with him in mind.

Initially he was able to find ways around the new legislation. He had to close his office although work carried on in the coffee houses and on the streets, and sometimes adverts appeared in newspapers offering rewards with no questions asked. He brazenly drew attention when he petitioned the Lord Mayor for the Freedom of the City. He claimed that his efforts had resulted in more than 60 criminals being led to the gallows. He also claimed that he had spent five years apprehending and convicting felons who had returned from transportation before their time – all for no reward. He had certainly made the streets safer, as he cleared away many notorious gangs. Many of the wealthy London classes were impressed with him. He had consistently returned their stolen goods and accounts of criminals he had rounded up appeared in the papers every week. They saw him as their only defence against the crime wave of the time. His petition does not appear to have been rejected, but adjourned. We have no record of whether it was awarded but he was paid a handsome sum by way of gratuity.

In the spring of 1724 Wild had succeeded in apprehending a gang of around 100 street robbers in Southwark – most of them ended up in prison. It was clear evidence that not joining his empire meant certain prison for criminals.

Wild's Downfall

After ruling London for seven years, Wild's empire began to crumble in the winter of 1724/5. The captain of his sloop, Roger Johnson, stopped the value of some missing lace from the mate's pay. The mate informed against the captain and the sloop was exchequered. The captain returned to his old life as a thief and soon had a run-in with a man who kept a house of resort for thieves, Thomas Edwards. They turned each other in. Wild bailed his captain out, but as soon as the other man was released, he informed on Wild. Wild's warehouses were searched and the goods confiscated. Pretending that the goods belonged to his captain, Wild arrested Edwards, who was taken to the Marshalsea.

Wild was eventually convicted under the terms of the new Act for procuring the return of some stolen lace. For the sake of £40, he lost everything. He had sent a couple who had been drinking in his pub into a lace shop in Seven Dials and paid them for what they had stolen when they returned. While this was going on, Edwards had left the Marshalsea. He found Johnson, whom he immediately informed on. Johnson sent for Wild, who arrived and prompted a riot so that Johnson could escape. Wild then absconded as his part in the riot became known. On returning to his house three weeks later, he was arrested and taken to Newgate prison. In court he was accused of stealing the lace and then returning it to the shop owner for the reward.

As his past deeds were unravelled, the public turned against him and called for his blood. Nobody likes to be thought of as a fool. Despite defending himself vigorously, he was found guilty and sentenced to death.

In the early hours before his execution, he tried to commit suicide with an overdose of laudanum. It didn't work, and on the morning of 24 May 1725 he was taken to Tyburn, stupefied and delirious. On the journey, he was booed, pelted with a variety of missiles (including faeces and decomposing cat and dog corpses) and verbally abused. His execution attracted one of the largest ever crowds to Tyburn, and they rejoiced in his downfall and humiliation. Perhaps because of the confusion caused by the drugs, Wild did not give the customary last speech before he was hanged. His body was cut down quickly before the surgeons' men could seize it and was buried in St Pancras Churchyard. A few days later the coffin was dug up and found later in Kentish Town. His body had disappeared. An unidentified body was washed up on the banks of the Thames near Whitehall within days, and the extremely hairy chest led some to believe that it was Wild.

THE CASE OF THE VEHICLE THEFT MARKET IN BULGARIA

This case is based on the article 'The Vehicle Theft Market in Bulgaria' by Bezlov and Gounev (2008).

Bulgarian-run vehicle theft crime groups play a growing role in Europe. In Bulgaria ransom seeking, corruption, the communist legacy and the role of mafia racketeering that has changed economic and political life in the last two decades all contribute to a unique mix of underlying factors that shape the present-day stolen car market (Bezlov and Gounev, 2008: 72):

> The history of the vehicle theft market in Bulgaria to a large extent reflects the history of organized crime in the country. Until 1990, the purchase of private cars in Bulgaria was extremely restricted. The average wait time was 6–10 years. In addition, it required 10–15 years of savings from an average salary, while no financing schemes existed. Therefore, there were strong pull factors for a market for stolen cars. Nevertheless, the strong police control and the close to 100% recovery rate of stolen vehicles left only a handful of deviant youth to be

involved in joy-ride thefts. Between 1980 and 1985, the annual car thefts were only about 2,000; after 1985 the picture started to change.

In 1990, many car thieves were among the 4,000 prisoners that amnestied. Some of them headed to Western Europe to become involved in a range of criminal activities, including auto-theft, while others settled in the Czech Republic or Hungary, where they became intermediaries or itinerant groups that facilitated trafficking of stolen cars. These individuals' technical skills and connections with the Balkans and the Middle East provided the key competitive advantage that allowed them to compete with local and former Soviet Union crime groups. By 1992, a large group of car thiefs, including the late Ivo Karamanski, later to be known as the godfather of Bulgarian mafia, were repatriated to Bulgaria by Hungarian and Czech authorities. This accelerated even further the growth rate of stolen cars, while at the same time these individuals had developed the connections to import stolen vehicles from Western Europe.

6. Entrepreneurial growth in illegal business

Opening up new markets and developing new products are part of a strategy to sustain and develop a business. Ruggiero (2000) tells the story of how organised criminals opened up the new criminal market for heroin in the United Kingdom. Until 1968, heroin was bought legally with a medical prescription, which partly ended up feeding a grey market. Then new legislation limited medical doctors' power to prescribe, which stimulated criminal entrepreneurs to develop a black market. A turning point for drug distribution occurred a decade later, as locally centred and poorly structured supply was replaced by organised professionals' well-structured supply chains. The explosion of heroin consumption probably stimulated this turning point in the early 1980s.

Developing new products is always important. When everyone in the rich part of the world had a telephone in each home and each office, the demand for telephones dropped. What did producers such as Ericsson, Nokia and Sony do? They developed the mobile phone. In the beginning, you could only talk with the mobile phone, like you did with the stationary phone. Soon, you were able to use your cellular phone for e-mail, pictures and music. This is a typical example of new product development in legal business. Similarly, criminal business enterprises need to develop new products to sustain their crime business over time.

According to Davidsson (2008: 15), entrepreneur and entrepreneurship are often implicitly understood as someone successful and something successful in terms of growth and prosperity:

> Many scholars include in their understanding of the concept 'entrepreneurship' the criterion that the outcome is somehow successful or influential. Others hold that entrepreneurs act under genuine uncertainty and that therefore one should base the definition on the behavior itself and not the outcome, which is more or less contingent on luck.

Davidsson (2008) therefore argues that this is a strong indication that one needs to separate entrepreneurship as a societal phenomenon – its role in societal organisations and/or the economic system – from entrepreneurship as a scholarly domain. In this chapter we apply the outcome criterion of growth in illegal business.

ENTREPRENEURIAL STRATEGY

Entrepreneurial strategy is based on entrepreneurial vision. Entrepreneurial vision is a tacit perception of business opportunities for the criminal business organisation. To successfully reorganise resources into the envisioned business opportunities, 'resource owners must be coordinated on the entrepreneur's conception of the business and be motivated to perform properly' (Witt, 2007: 1125). An essential part of the entrepreneurial role of restructuring resources (knowledge, weapons, money, cars, etc.) is the provision of a clear image of why and how the business needs to change to sustain the crime business over time.

Strategy is both a plan for the future and pattern from the past; it is the match an organisation makes between its internal resources and skills (sometimes collectively called competencies) and the opportunities and risks created by its external environment. Strategy is the long-term direction of an organisation. Strategy is the course of action for achieving an organisation's purpose. Strategy is the direction and scope of an organisation over the long term, which achieves advantage for the organisation through its configuration of resources within a changing environment and to fulfil stakeholders' expectations.

Given an entrepreneurial strategy, strategic management is important in a criminal business enterprise. Strategic management includes understanding the strategic position of an organisation, strategic choices for the future and turning strategy into action. Understanding the strategic position is concerned with the impact on strategy of the external environment, internal resources and competencies, and the expectations and influence of stakeholders. Strategic choices involve understanding the underlying bases for future strategy at both higher and lower unit levels and the options for developing strategy in terms of both the directions in which strategy might move and the methods of development. Translating strategy into action is concerned with ensuring that strategies are working in practice. A strategy is not just a good idea, a statement or a plan. It is only meaningful when it is actually being carried out.

In entrepreneurial criminal businesses, strategic management must stimulate entrepreneurship in the whole organisation. Entrepreneurial employees can provide a wide range of entrepreneurial services to their organisation, including generating and evaluating innovative ideas related to potential crimes (e.g. money laundering, trafficking, fraud, corruption).

An entrepreneurial strategy pays attention to entrepreneurship that focuses on individuals, their knowledge, resources and skills, and the processes of discovery and creativity, which constitute the heart of entrepreneurship (Kor et al., 2007).

As part of an entrepreneurial strategy, symbiotic entrepreneurship might be considered by criminal management. The success of entrepreneurs is a function of their ability to be globally competitive, even if they refrain from competing globally. Small-scale entrepreneurs can develop relationships with other criminals and their organisations, thereby creating multi-polar networks. Criminal entrepreneurs are shedding their desire for independence, as they discover interdependence and relationships. The result is symbiotic entrepreneurship, which is defined by Dana et al. (2008) as an enterprising effort by multiple parties, each of which benefits from the joint effort, such that added value is created. Symbiotic entrepreneurship is leading to multi-polarity in the world of business. We are thus moving beyond the focus of the criminal enterprise towards a focus on relationships with multi-polar networks.

According to Grotenhuis and Kamminga (2008), criminal enterprises can choose from a broad range of strategic partnerships to sustain and expand crime business over time. Depending on the strategic goals, criminal enterprises can decide on the most suitable type of partnership. When the aim is to gain access to new markets or distribution channels, a full-scale merger would not be necessary but a strategic alliance could be sufficient. However, if sustaining the crime business requires improvements in economies of scale as well as control mechanisms not present within the current organisation, a merger or acquisition could be a better option. Another option is to enter into a joint venture, where both partners together start a third new enterprise.

The choice of strategic partnership is also a choice of depth of commitment and level of investment between organisations. Although the motives for mergers and acquisitions, joint ventures and alliances seem to be rather similar, that is to sustain and expand crime business, the choice of a specific type of partnership can make a significant difference in terms of potential benefits and risks. Often, a combination of motives is underlying partnerships. For mergers and acquisitions, motives can range from fast penetration of new and foreign markets to acquisition of knowledge and expertise. For strategic alliances, motives are often short-term profit and growth without losing autonomy for either partner. For cooperative ventures, motives include risk sharing and knowledge sharing (Grotenhuis and Kamminga, 2008).

EXPANDING CRIME BUSINESS

Despite mature markets, aging assets, imprisoned staff members, aging procedures and increased competition, attractive growth opportunities still exist. Similar to legal enterprises, criminal enterprises may have five ways to develop their business (Perkowski, 2007):

1. *Establish a joint venture or strategic alliance in a high-growth geographic market.* It used to be that the large size of many markets meant that local organised crime did not need to look beyond the border for new markets. It made sense to focus on serving and expanding domestic markets. But today, globalization, increased offshore manufacturing and the breakdown of trade barriers call for joint ventures (Luo, 2002). For example, the Russian mafia has entered into joint ventures with Colombian cocaine cartels to expand their criminal activity into more markets.

   A joint venture is an entity formed between two or more parties to undertake economic activity together. The parties agree to create a new entity by both contributing assets, and they then share in the revenues, expenses and control of the enterprise. The venture can be for one specific criminal project only, or a continuing business relationship. This is in contrast to a strategic alliance, which involves no assets by the participants and is a much less rigid arrangement.

   A joint venture exists between the Heavenly Alliance in Taiwan and trafficking organisations in mainland China. While a trafficking organisation supplies women, Heavenly Alliance arranges 'marriages' and 'visits'. Women are smuggled from mainland China to Taiwan (Finckenauer and Chin, 2006). As the prostitution market is growing in Shanghai and other cities in China, Heavenly Alliance may be interested in a new kind of joint venture, where its business concept of a jockey is implemented.

   By joining forces with developing foreign businesses, local criminal businesses gain access to high-growth markets in a developing country, and they may better serve existing and new customers who are expanding there. For example, in terms of joint venture projects, criminal organisations dealing in drugs, gambling and prostitution may find it attractive to make money during Olympic Games in foreign locations, such as in Beijing 2008.

2. *Collaborate to satisfy an unmet customer need.* Rather than focusing on supply of certain illegal goods and services, attention should shift to distinctive solutions for customers. To break away from the pack and offer a more distinctive solution to customers, producers need to

learn how to collaborate with suppliers, customers and/or competitors to find new and better solutions. This is difficult to do effectively and needs a strong commitment by all parties in order to work. Fortunately, if successful this difficulty represents a barrier to entry and therefore ensures less competition and higher margins.

This growth strategy is common in a number of legal as well as illegal businesses. For example, if the criminal organisation is in the business of stealing and smuggling stolen cars, it may increase its revenues if it at the same time is able to handle money laundering for customers buying the cars.

3. *Diversify or expand product offerings to the best customer segment.* Based on a demand curve, the criminal business enterprise knows that the best customers are willing to pay more than the market price for its products. If the enterprise were to offer complementary goods and services, then the highest prices would be achieved in the best customer segment. It is necessary first to have a clear understanding of who the most profitable customers are and identify what additional goods and services they need.

4. *Eliminate the bottom 10 per cent of the business.* To develop a criminal business, it is necessary to ensure that it only competes in markets where it has a strong competitive advantage. Where an advantage does not exist, it is necessary either to invest to attain it or to withdraw from the market completely. While withdrawal means lower volumes in the short term, it often ultimately leads to a stronger, more sustainable enterprise and one that is better positioned to grow in core markets.

5. *Leverage underused intangible assets in the business.* Internal capabilities, competencies and knowledge that have evolved to support the current business are often overlooked as possible sources of competitive advantage. Even worse, they are sometimes viewed as expendable when the focus is on cost cutting and streamlining the organisation. These intangible assets are typically information based and include customer relationships, access to supply networks and corrupt politicians. The critical challenge is often to identify how best to leverage these assets.

Similarly, DiModica (2007) suggests methods to expand a business. The first step is to identify the market gap, which is to discover and uncover sales opportunities where market demand is greater than supply. The next step is to pick a growth model, where the alternatives are labelled market duplication, market variation, market symbiotic attachment, market consolidation, market innovation and new market launch.

Growth as a goal has to be both short term and long term to achieve both prosperity and viability. Business growth has to be accompanied and supported by growth-oriented leaders, otherwise it may go wrong. US managers in Hyundai Motors and Kia Motors never seemed to please their Korean superiors, and the North American management staff was in constant turnover. Then, the chairman of Hyundai Motors, Chung Mong-koo, and his son, Kia Motors president Chung Eui-sun, came under investigation for their roles in scandals involving political slush funds and the misuse of company money.

Matthews (2005) identified four factors essential for growth:

1. *Talent*. An entrepreneur takes the risk to create something from nothing. Such talent must be developed by educating people about the basics of enterprise and fostering their entrepreneurial instincts. Some people are more predisposed and willing to take risks than others. Not everyone has the skills or knowledge to develop a business enterprise.
2. *Idea*. To meet a target customer's needs and wants the criminal enterprise must have a 'better idea' than competitors and law enforcement. The idea is broken down into resources and organising, as well as products and markets.
3. *People*. Good criminals may be hard to find. They will often tend to favour opportunistic behaviour, where their own goals are more important than goals of the criminal business enterprise. Thus, it is important to recruit knowledgeable people who stay loyal in critical situations. Management needs to lead people, build an organisation for growth and develop an approach to align criminals' efforts around execution of a growth strategy.
4. *Capital*. While entrepreneurs may have the personal resources to start a company, very few have enough to expand a company. This is especially the case in criminal business enterprises where the entrepreneurs enjoy a luxurious standard of living, without securing funds through money laundering for future investments. Most need to learn how to manage their balance sheet, do debt financing, trust strategic alliances and joint ventures, and understand finance.

The mafia in Japan – the Yakuza – went for business growth through market expansion into Korea. For the Yakuza, Korea's greatest attraction lies in smuggling drugs out of the country. Korea is the centre of drug traffic, and the drug is methamphetamine, known on the streets of America as speed, crank and meth, and on the streets of Japan as shabu and white diamonds. According to Kaplan and Dubro (1986), it had quite possibly become the world's most massive unpublicized drug route, a dope connection of little interest in the West because so far it had affected only East Asia. But that changed slowly as crime syndicates from both China and Korea also expanded their activities across the Pacific to the USA.

The expansion of Yakuza business from Japan to Korea might be understood in a network perspective of international entrepreneurship. Social networks exist among criminal persons. These people have contacts which extend far beyond the borders of the criminal organisations in which they are working. Networks by definition are constantly evolving and changing. Hinttu et al. (2004) argue that the critical elements in an enterprise's strategic success are the ability of the organisations in the network to influence these changes over time and thus create and maintain the most advantageous membership. The composition of the network and the degree to which actors in the network are rich in information, skills, referrals and other resources an organisation needs abroad are significantly important for the organisation's success.

MANAGING RESOURCES FOR CRIME

Entrepreneurship can be perceived as a resource-based process, where entrepreneurial innovation is the carrying out of new combinations of existing resources. It is such a process of recombination that leads to the innovation on which an organisation can build its competitive advantage. To manage resources successfully, there is a need to understand how resources promote corporate entrepreneurship and how different kinds of resources contribute to the enterprise's competitive advantage (Vita et al., 2008).

Again, we apply the resource-based theory of the enterprise that has established itself as an important perspective in strategic management. According to the resource-based theory of the enterprise, performance differences across enterprises can be attributed to the variance in the enterprises' strategic resources and capabilities. Resources that are valuable, unique and difficult to imitate can provide the basis for enterprises' competitive advantages.

The central tenet in resource-based theory is that unique organisational resources, both tangible and intangible in nature, are the real source of competitive advantage. With resource-based theory, organisations are viewed as a collection of resources that are heterogeneously distributed within and across industries. Accordingly, what makes the performance of an organisation distinctive is the unique blend of the resources it possesses. An enterprise's resources include not only its physical assets such as plant and location but also its competencies. The ability to leverage distinctive internal and external competencies relative to environmental situations ultimately affects the performance of the business.

The resource-based theory of the enterprise holds that, in order to generate sustainable competitive advantage, a resource must provide economic value and must be scarce, difficult to imitate, non-substitutable and not readily obtainable in factor markets. This theory rests on two key points. First, that resources are the determinants of enterprise performance and second, that resources must be rare, valuable, difficult to imitate and non-substitutable by other rare resources. When the latter occurs, a competitive advantage has been created. Resources can simultaneously be characterized as valuable, rare, non-substitutable and inimitable. To the extent that an organisation's physical assets, infrastructure and workforce satisfy these criteria, they qualify as resources. An enterprise's performance depends fundamentally on its ability to have a distinctive, sustainable competitive advantage, which derives from the possession of enterprise-specific resources.

A criminal entrepreneur needs to mobilize and successfully apply resources in organised crime. Since the resource environment is characterized by scarcity rather than abundance, it is sometimes argued that a conducive environment is crucial in developing entrepreneurship. Results of a study by Tang (2008) suggest a strong relationship between environmental munificence and an essential individual characteristic of entrepreneurs: alertness, especially when the entrepreneurs have high levels of self-efficacy in performing the roles and tasks of new venture creation activities.

The resource-based theory is a useful perspective in strategic management. Research on the competitive implications of such enterprise resources as knowledge, learning, culture, teamwork and human capital was given a significant boost by resource-based theory – a theory that indicated it was these kinds of resources that were most likely to be sources of sustainable competitive advantage for enterprises.

A fundamental idea in resource-based theory is that an enterprise must continually enhance its resources and capabilities to take advantage of changing conditions. Optimal growth involves a balance between the exploitation of existing resource positions and the development of new resource positions. Thus, an enterprise would be expected to develop new resources after its existing resource base has been fully utilized. Building new resource positions is important if the enterprise is to achieve sustained growth. When unused productive resources are coupled with changing managerial knowledge, unique opportunities for growth are created.

The term resource is derived from the Latin word 'resurgere', which has the meaning 'to rise' and implies an aid or expedient for reaching an end.

A resource implies a potential means to achieve an end, or as something that can be used to create value. The first strategy textbooks outlining a holistic perspective focused on how resources needed to be allocated or deployed to earn rents. The interest in the term was for a long time linked to the efficiency of resource allocation, but this focus has later been expanded to issues such as resource accumulation, resource stocks and resource flows.

Enterprises develop specific resources and then renew these to respond to shifts in the business environment. Enterprises develop dynamic capabilities to adapt to changing environments. According to Pettus (2001), the term dynamic refers to the capacity to renew resource positions to achieve congruence with changing environmental conditions. A capability refers to the key role of strategic management in appropriately adapting, integrating and reconfiguring internal and external organisational skills, resources and functional capabilities to match the requirements of a changing environment. If enterprises are to develop dynamic capabilities, learning is crucial. Change is costly; therefore, the ability of enterprises to make necessary adjustments depends upon their ability to scan the environment to evaluate markets and competitors and to quickly accomplish reconfiguration and transformation ahead of the competition. However, history matters. Thus, opportunities for growth will involve dynamic capabilities closely related to existing capabilities. As such, opportunities will be most effective when they are close to previous resource use.

Knowledge has long been recognized as a valuable resource for organisational growth and sustained competitive advantage, especially for organisations competing in uncertain environments. According to the knowledge-based theory of the enterprise, knowledge is the main resource for an enterprise's competitive advantage. Knowledge is the primary driver of an enterprise's value. Performance differences across enterprises can be attributed to the variance in the enterprises' strategic knowledge. Strategic knowledge is characterized by being valuable, unique, rare, non-imitable, non-substitutable, non-transferable, combinable and exploitable. Unlike other inert organisational resources, the application of existing knowledge has the potential to generate new knowledge.

An entrepreneur might be driven by a compulsive need to find new ways of allocating resources. He or she might be searching for profit-making opportunities and engineer incremental changes in products and processes. While strongly innovative entrepreneurs tend to champion radical changes in resource allocation by making new product markets and pioneering new processes, weakly innovative entrepreneurs tend to seek small changes in resource allocation to explore profit-making opportunities between already established activities (Markovski and Hall, 2007).

The criminal entrepreneur's task is to discover and exploit opportunities, defined most simply as situations in which there is a profit to be made in criminal activity. Opportunity discovery is about valuable goods and services for which there is a market. Hence, identification of valuable goods and services is linked to the identification of valuable markets that they serve. Opportunity discovery relates to the generation of value, where the entrepreneur determines or influences the set of resource choices required to create value.

The entrepreneurial theory of the criminal enterprise suggests that the criminal enterprise represents a realization of entrepreneurial vision. Setting up an enterprise organisation means hiring staff whose services are not completely specified in advance by the employment or network arrangement. This incompleteness is compensated by entrepreneurial vision. An essential contribution from entrepreneurial vision to enterprise organising of resources is the provision of a cognitive input in the form of a business conception. A business conception consists of subjective, sometimes highly idiosyncratic imaginings in the mind of an entrepreneur of what business is to be created, and how to do it. Like a business frame, Witt (2007: 1127) argues that 'a business conception is the basis for the entrepreneur's interpretation of incoming information with respect to its relevance and meaning for the imagined business venture'.

Opportunism is self-interest seeking with guile, and includes overt behaviours such as lying, cheating and stealing, as well as subtle behaviours such as dishonouring an implicit contract, shirking, and failing to fulfil promises and obligations. It is the equivalent of bad faith, the implication being that the party who is opportunistic is not trustworthy. In a criminal network, opportunism may involve misrepresentations, unresponsiveness, unreasonable demands and lying. The notion of opportunism is what differentiates transaction cost theory from alternative conceptualizations of the organisation, such as agency theory, relational exchange theory and resource view. The transaction cost economics presumption is that economic actors attempt to forecast the potential for opportunism as a function of unfolding circumstances, then take preventive actions in transactions where opportunism is likely to be high. Opportunism is an explanatory mechanism, not readily observable and typically empirically untested. However, it is important because it has potential for enormous impact on economic performance.

Opportunism is likely to increase if there are only a small number of owners of strategic resources for organised crime, as only a few are able and willing to contract. Transaction costs appear to be difficult to avoid and may be unavoidably greater in some settings than in others. For example, it can be argued that in transnational and global crime contract creation and monitoring are more difficult because of the complexity and because there are costs associated with varying ethnic backgrounds and distances which are hard to allocate to specific functions.

It is often argued that criminal organisations have a network structure. For example, similar to other forms of organised criminality, including weapons trafficking, immigrant smuggling and prostitution, drug trafficking in Colombia occurs in fluid social systems where flexible exchange networks expand and retract according to market opportunities and regulatory constraints. This durable, elastic structure did not emerge overnight but developed over many years as entrepreneurs built their enterprises through personal contacts, repeated exchanges and resources they accumulated gradually, while drawing on social traditions, such as contraband smuggling, that extend far back to Colombia's colonial past (Kenney, 2007).

IMPROVING BUSINESS PROCESSES

A business process is a collection of interrelated tasks which solve a particular work assignment. A business process is a structured, measured set of activities designed to produce a specific output for a particular function or client. It implies a strong emphasis on how work is done within an organisation. A process is a specific ordering of work activities across time and space, where activities occur both in sequence and in parallel. A business process has a beginning and an end, and clearly defined inputs and outputs. It uses one or more resources and creates a result of value for the receiver in the organisation or the client outside the organisation. Activities in the business process are primarily important to the extent that they contribute to complete the process, that is, that the business process delivers expected results in the form of governance and services.

This definition represents certain characteristics of a process. These characteristics focus on the business logic of the process (how work is done), such as having clearly defined boundaries, input and output, as well as activities ordered in time and space. Business processes are concerned with how work is organised, coordinated, staffed and focused on producing outputs. Business processes are workflows in the form of materials and information. Hence, business processes are collections of activities. Furthermore, business processes are the very special way the organisation has chosen to coordinate work and knowledge, and the way management chooses to coordinate all production of services. Business processes normally cross departmental borders. They may involve several levels in a hierarchy as well as nodes in a network.

People smuggling and money laundering may represent two business processes in a criminal business enterprise. People smuggling divides into at least three phases: recruitment, transfer and entrance into the destination country. Human trafficking involves a further stage: exploitation, which may take place in a variety of markets operating in the destination countries. Recruitment usually takes place in the home countries of the would-be migrants or trafficked victims. According to Nicola (2005), among trafficking victims women may be offered work as au pairs, dancers, models, housemaids, waitresses or airhostesses. In the case of sexual exploitation, women already working as prostitutes are also contacted.

In an organisation, many business processes take place at the same time. These processes are often dependent on each other, as they produce services through process interactions. The organisation also interacts with its environment. The environment includes everything and everyone influencing the organisation.

Today, executives are interested in identifying and improving business processes. This interest has emerged as executives realize that organisational success is dependent on the ability to deliver services at low cost, with high quality and professional performance. This interest has also emerged as more and more business processes have important interactions with the environment.

Efforts at business process interdependence have typically emphasized the view that the organisation should develop its own vision for internal integration after assessing the benefits of integrating current business processes. If an organisation deems the current processes to be effective, then it is important to articulate the specific objectives of internal integration: for instance, some organisations may seek to create cross-functional, horizontal business processes that are parallel to the traditional organisation. Alternatively, the logic for internal integration may reflect a transition towards fundamentally redesigning the business processes over a period of time.

Efforts at business processes interdependence should then emphasize the need to ensure that inter-organisational needs guide internal integration efforts. Simply fine tuning existing outmoded processes through current organisational and technological capabilities does not create the required organisational capabilities.

Four critical questions for exploiting benefits of business process redesign are: (1) What is the rationale for the current organisational design? (What are the strengths and limitations?); (2) What significant changes in business processes are occurring in the criminal underworld? (What are the likely impacts?); (3) What are the costs of continuing with the status quo? (When should we redesign the business process? What should be our pace of redesign?) and (4) What changes are occurring in local, national and global law enforcement impacting criminal business enterprises? (How should we redesign our business processes to compensate and strengthen our business?)

Professional enterprise management will initiate business process redesign after ascertaining the significant changes in its key allies' business processes – especially those of leading organisations – so that it can formulate appropriate responses beforehand.

Benefits from business process redesign are limited in scope if the processes are not extended outside the focal organisational boundary to identify options for redesigning relationships with the other organisations that participate in ultimately delivering criminal value. For example, in the case of people smuggling the business process of smuggling is mainly focused on crossing borders with minimal costs. Improvements in this business process may include change of port, airport or street, as well as change in staff and other resources. Relationships with recruiting organisations may change as a consequence of smuggling change, to ensure an optimal, redesigned business process.

HOW SUCCESSFUL LEADERS THINK

'We look for lessons in the actions of great leaders. We should instead be examining what goes on in their heads – particularly the way they creatively build on the tensions among conflicting ideas' says Martin (2007) in his article 'How Successful Leaders Think'. He argues that brilliant leaders excel at integrative thinking. They can hold two opposing ideas in their minds at once. Then, rather than settling for choice A or B, they forge an innovative 'third way' that contains elements of both while at the same time improving on each of them.

Martin (2007) identified four stages of decision making in the minds of successful leaders (See Figure 6.1):

- *Step 1: Identifying key factors*. Successful leaders do not only consider obviously relevant factors while weighting options, they also seek less obvious but potentially more relevant considerations.
- *Step 2: Analysing causality*. Successful leaders do not only consider one-way, linear relationships between factors, they also seek less obvious multidirectional relationships.
- *Step 3: Envisioning decision architecture*. Successful leaders do not only break a problem into pieces and work on them separately, they

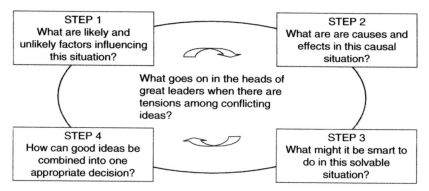

Figure 6.1   Decision making in the minds of successful leaders (adopted from Martin, 2007)

also seek to understand a problem as a whole – examining how its various aspects affect one another.

- *Step 4: Achieving resolution.* Successful leaders do not only make either–or choices, they often refuse to accept conventional options.

Successful leaders are what Martin (2007) calls 'integrative thinkers' who generate options and new solutions. They create a sense of limitless possibility.

Terrence 'Terry' Adams is the head of Britain's most enterprising, and feared, organised crime gang, according to Amoruso (2007a). He has an imaginative mind capable of sophisticated, complex and dishonest financial manipulation. When moving into new territories and new businesses, his integrative thinking helped build up links with other groups and cocaine cartels.

Curtis 'Cocky' Warren was one of Britain's biggest and richest drug traffickers. Unlike most other drug traffickers, Warren is a highly intelligent force, according to Amoruso (2007b).

Tam 'The Licensee' McGraw is head of a criminal organisation in Glasgow. His integrative thinking enabled him to balance and integrate law enforcement officials and competitors into his organised crime. When one of the criminals in McGraw's organisation phoned Margaret McGraw (his wife) late at night with the news that her husband had been arrested, her reply left the caller stunned. 'It's okay', she said, 'the boys have been on to me already to say that it's okay, they have it in hand, not to worry, he'll be home tomorrow, you have to just sit tight.' The boys that Margaret McGraw had been referring to were the Serious Crime Squad police unit who investigated crimes of the type committed by organised crime gangs and bank robbers. Tam McGraw was a police informer (Amoruso, 2007c).

WOMEN ENTREPRENEURS IN ORGANISED CRIME

Often, women are considered victims of organised crime. A typical example is trafficking in women, where women are exploited in prostitution by criminal organisations. However, there are examples of women playing a quite different role in organised crime.

For example, Frossard (2007) tells the story of Alete, who was the daughter of Jose Baptista da Costa in Brazil. He was killed in 1981. This crime remains unsolved – like most other homicides involving the cupola – despite the fact that suspicion fell on a former policeman and aspiring competitor. Arlete took over her father's business to protect the territory. She was dissatisfied, claiming that she should receive half the monthly proceeds from her territory. She decided to use violence to resolve the question. She contacted three policemen – all of them later killed in crimes that have also remained unsolved – known for violent dealings in the criminal underworld. Arlete and her three bodyguards also invaded competitors' territories.

Another example of daughter takeover in Brazil is Suely Correia de Mello. Her father was murdered in Rio de Janeiro over a territory dispute for the 'jogo dos bichos'.

Women in the Neapolitan criminal underworld of the Camorra mafia take on active, formal roles as directors of legal companies, which represent the front end of the organisation. They also take on leadership positions internally, making strategic decisions regarding the clan's activities, taking matters into their own hands, and even killing. For example, in May 2002 in Lauro, a town in the province of Avellino, a shoot-out between women from the Graziano clan and women from the Cavas clan left three women dead and six injured. According to Allum (2007), this suggests that Camorra women are now definitely taking centre stage as major players.

As directors of front-end companies, Camorra women received public contracts, as was the case of Maria Orlando, mother of Lorenzo Nuvoletta of the Nuvoletta clan, and Antonietta Di Costanzo, wife of Antonio Orlando, the uncle of Lorenzo Nuvoletta (Allum, 2007).

Anna Mazza in Napoli became involved in Camorra activities when rival gangs murdered her husband, Gennaro Moccia, capo and boss of Afragola. She became known as 'the Black Widow'. She supported her sons in avenging their father's murder and became the leader of the gang, directing its activities and influencing its ideology. She became a capo in her own right – one of the most dangerous and most bloody. She led the group while her sons were in prison. When her eldest, Angelo, became a leader of the Alfieri confederation her leadership role became less important, although she still managed local criminal activities, as well as relationships with politicians, while her sons were involved in regional Camorra warfare. Today, it appears to Allum (2007) that she still runs the clan, directs its activities and visits her sons in prison.

Successful women entrepreneurs in organised crime are hard to find. It is somewhat easier to find successful women entrepreneurs in legal businesses. For example, Reavley and Lituchy (2008) conducted a six-country analysis of self-reported determinants of success. They studied female entrepreneurs in Canada, Ireland, the Czech Republic, Poland and Japan. The women became entrepreneurs because they felt rejected – a phenomenon sometimes labelled the 'push factor'. While some women defined success in terms of profits, many used non-financial factors such as number of client, number of employees, years in business or because 'my peers say so'. The most important factor identified in the study was networking. Business education and training were second.

The contribution of female entrepreneurs is seldom acknowledged in either legal or criminal business. For example, in a study of female immigrant entrepreneurs, Low (2008) found that female immigrant entrepreneurs made a significant contribution to the Australian economy. The study examined the economic contributions of a group of Asian-born women entrepreneurs in Sydney. The empirical study showed that they made significant economic contributions to the creation of new businesses and jobs in addition to other non-quantifiable economic benefits to Australia.

In the United States, Georgia Durante saw the local mafia as her ticket out of boredom and poverty. In Rochester, New York, Durante started running errands for local mafioso Sammy Gingello. These errands involved taking packages into New York City, and she claims that she once delivered a letter directly to the powerful New York boss Carlo Gambino. She was also instructed to keep an eye on local comings and goings and to keep Gingello informed – a traditional female role in organised crime according to Longrigg (2007): when men's movements are restricted or attract more attention, it is often easier for women to pick up information.

Georgia Durante's principal role was as a driver: she started driving for mafia associates who collected extortion money from premises including building sites. Sometimes these shakedowns involved violence, and she became an expert at getting away fast from the scene of the crime. According to Longrigg (2007), Durante's mafia career was in some way similar to a man's: she was attracted to local mafia figures by their money and the strange fascination that violence exerts; she saw a way out of a dreary existence by associating with them. As they got to know her, they began to give her more demanding tasks. She always accepted these commissions, feeling they gave her status and enjoying the trust that was invested in her. It gave her a sort of fascination to be trusted at this level. She felt connected to fear but the thought never crossed her mind that she might be in any kind of danger. She was too engrossed in the intrigue.

The research by Allum (2007), Frossard (2007) and Longrigg (2007) can be found in a book entitled *Women and the Mafia – Female Roles in Organised Crime Structures*. There are many more research chapters in the book, all trying to shed new light on the role of women in organised crime. For example, the emancipation of women in society at large might have an impact on female roles within such organisations. The very interesting, while still incomplete, analyses in the book demonstrate a wealth of ideas even if they cannot yet lead to definite conclusions. One of the many interesting insights in the book is the underestimation of female criminality, the main reason being judges' consideration that women's roles in criminal episodes are as victims or at the most accomplices.

In a study of legal entrepreneurs, Seet et al. (2008) were interested in differences between female and male entrepreneurs in Singapore in terms of personality traits. Personality traits studied included sociable, decisive, authoritative, goal oriented, self-confident, anxious, risk taker, intuitive, internal locus of control, optimist, and leader. Their results showed that a majority of the female entrepreneurs regarded themselves as more anxious as compared with their male counterparts. Females rated themselves lower in the aspects of self-confidence and optimism. The study findings also showed that Singaporean male entrepreneurs have significantly higher internal locus of control than their female counterparts.

INTEROPERABILITY IN ORGANISED CRIME

To secure growth and to avoid law enforcement, criminal entrepreneurs need to initiate interoperability among criminals, criminal groups and criminal organisations on a local, national and transnational basis. Improved interoperability will cause lower transaction costs when criminals plan and complete organised crime. Improved interoperability between criminal parties as well as between illegal and legal organisations is of critical importance to make organised crime more successful.

Interoperability refers to a property of diverse systems and organisations that enables them to work together. Interoperability is the ability of criminal organisations to share information and integrate information and business processes by use of common standards. Successful service innovation and multi-channel service delivery depend on strategies, policies and architectures that allow data, systems, business processes and delivery channels to operate, so that services can be properly integrated. If channels and back office processes are integrated, different channels can complement each other, improving the quality of both services and the delivery to both criminals and customers. The ideal is to create an environment in which data, systems and processes are fully integrated and channels become interoperable instead of merely coexisting.

When systems and organisations are able to inter-operate then information and services are provided and accepted between them. In a narrow sense, the term interoperability is often used to describe technical systems. In a broad sense, social, political and organisational factors influencing systems and systems performance are also taken into account.

In the business world, where electronic commerce and electronic business rely on interoperability, enterprise interoperability might be defined as follows (Doumeingts et al., 2007: 1):

> Interoperability in the context of enterprises and enterprise applications can be defined as the ability of a system or a product to work seamlessly with other systems or products without requiring special effort from the customer or user. The possibility to interact and exchange information internally and with external organisations is a key issue in the enterprise sector. It is fundamental in order to produce goods and services quickly, at lower cost, while maintaining higher levels of quality and customisation. Interoperability is considered to be achieved if interaction can, at least, take place at the three levels: data, applications and business enterprise through the architecture of the enterprise model and taking into account the semantics issues. It is not only a problem of software and information technologies. It implies support of communication and transactions between different organisations that must be based on shared process models and business references.

An approach to identify benefits of interoperability is in terms of transaction cost reduction. In his seminal paper, Coase (1937) suggested transaction costs as the primary determinant of the boundaries of the organisation. Ideally, contracts between buyers and sellers provide adaptation strategies for all possible contingencies. However, this requires either certainty regarding the future economic environment or unbounded rational reasoning (knowing all possible future states). Transaction costs arise because complete contracting is often impossible, and incomplete contracts give rise to subsequent renegotiations when the balance of power between the transacting parties shifts (Williamson, 1979). Transaction costs include the costs associated with writing contracts as well as the costs of opportunistic hold-up at a later date. Although internal organisations or hierarchies are posited to offer lower costs of coordination and control and to avert subsequent opportunistic behaviour, related problems can occur in decentralized organisations. A major concern is the loss of high-powered incentives when the pay-for-performance link is attenuated by internal production (Anderson et al., 2000).

Interoperability represents a dynamic capability for transacting organisations. Teece et al. (1997) define dynamic capabilities as the organisation's ability to integrate, build and reconfigure internal and external competencies to address rapidly changing environments. Dynamic capabilities thus reflect an organisation's ability to achieve new and innovative forms of competitive advantage given path dependencies and market positions.

Dynamic capabilities are identifiable, specific processes. Some dynamic capabilities integrate resources. For example, product development routines by which managers combine their varied skills and functional backgrounds to create revenue-producing products and services are such dynamic capability (Eisenhardt and Martin, 2000).

Interoperability strategy is concerned with agreeing to common goals and ground rules for achieving mutual benefits. The decision to make information resources more widely available has implications for the organisations concerned (where this may be seen as a loss of control or ownership), their staff (who may not possess the skills required to support more complex systems and a newly dispersed user community), and the end users (Mason and Lefrere, 2003).

THE CASE OF THOMAS 'THE LICENSEE' MCGRAW

This case was written by David Amoruso and published on the Internet (Amoruso, 2007c).

Thomas 'The Licensee' McGraw was born in 1953 in the east end of Glasgow. He was a product of the ghetto-like housing schemes of Glasgow's inner city. He took to thieving at an early age like a duck to water. Most kids around him did likewise; how else could a 12 year old get the luxuries in life like cigarettes or a night at the cinema? Shop lifting, housebreaking, anything to earn a few pounds and escape the torturous-like boredom that was par for the course in the huge sprawling housing estates which sprang up around the city in the early 1960s. Later, through having spent time in approved schools, McGraw became known among the criminal community and was recruited as part of a gang of armed robbers known as the Bar-l team from the Barlanark housing estate.

With this gang McGraw was involved in raids on post offices all over Scotland. The raids were so successful that the police ran a national campaign to try to catch the perpetrators. After every raid/job the proceeds were hidden and collected at a later date, which meant if they were ever stopped on the way back from the raid by the cops none of the proceeds of the job would be found on them.

The gang were very security conscious and took a lot of pride in planning criminal projects with almost military precision. In spite of all their precautions all team members were arrested and charged at one time or another. In one particular night-time raid on a large social club on the outskirts of Glasgow things went disastrously wrong. A pre-check on the club's security system failed to register an important aspect of the system. Once the outer alarm systems had been dismantled and the pulsar neutralized for entry to the internal system, the entire area surrounding the club would light up, with heavy-duty spotlights illuminating the entire area up like a Christmas tree. This was an add-on to that particular alarm system the normally efficient crew were not aware of. The job took place as planned, when the lights lit up as a result of the pulsar being disarmed. Instead of abandoning the job the crew decided to take hurried measures to countermand the lighting system long enough to get in and out with the goods.

The spotlights on the ground were turned over face down on the grass; the ones on the roof were turned over to face downward on the asphalt and tarmac that covered the roof. With the place in darkness the team continued with the job at hand, relieving the club of all takings, all alcohol and all cigarettes. While the team were busy loading up the vans with the goods a crackling and popping sound could be heard coming from the roof. 'Fuck's sake . . . . Fire!' The high-powered spotlights had set fire to the asphalt on the roof and the whole roof was ablaze, lighting the area up once again brighter than before. Everyone ran, and the blue lights of the cop cars could be seen in the distance. Despite several guys shouting at McGraw to leave it and run, he stayed and kept loading the van.

Greed kept him there trying to get a few more crates of booze on board before the cops got near. The cops arrived, and McGraw got in the van and smashed straight through a cop car, ramming it against an iron fence; he accelerated up to around 80 mph and smashed through another cop car that had blocked his way to the street; he lost control and over-turned the van while trying to negotiate a sharp bend. He half crawled, half ran from the scene but was captured by the pursuing cops, who threw him into the back of a cop car and drove off.

This incident throws some light on the reason that McGraw is now suspected by many of Glasgow's underworld fraternity as being a police informer, giving information on fellow crooks in exchange for a green light to operate his own illegal activities unhindered by police enquiries. McGraw had enough money (even back then) to buy that club he was raiding with his buddies. He could have been charged with the following: conspiracy and organised crime, theft of the van, driving while banned, breaking and entering, and attempted murder (the cops in the cars he smashed into during his getaway).

When one of the guys on the team phoned Margaret McGraw (McGraw's wife) later that night with the news that her husband had been arrested, her reply left the caller stunned. 'It's okay,' she said. 'The boys have been on to me already to say that it's okay, they have it in hand. Not to worry, he'll be home tomorrow. You have to just sit tight.' 'The boys' referred to were police officers investigating crimes of the type committed by organised crime gangs, bank robbers, and so on. Maybe he just had a few cops on a payroll? That was allowed, no harm there.

For whatever reason he was set free the next morning just as his wife had said he would. That made it the sixth time McGraw had walked free from conspiracy and organised crime charges without the case ever making it to court. And remember he had been caught in the act this time.

In 1978 McGraw got into more trouble when he was arrested for the attempted murder of a policeman – but just like he walked on the social club fiasco he walked free again. On this occasion it had at least made the court-room but it was merely an inconvenience for 'The Licensee' – he was found not guilty and acquitted.

In the early 1980s McGraw started expanding his empire, getting into drugs and buying up pubs and other property. McGraw was now openly bragging to his associates about his connections on the force and of the cops on his payroll. That is how McGraw came by the nick-name 'The Licensee' – it seemed to be the case that he had been granted a licence to operate freely by the cops. It had been these cop connections that had got McGraw involved in the lucrative heroin trade. Confiscated drugs were channelled through to McGraw, who sold them on. McGraw, at that time being unfamiliar with the intricacies of the heroin business, sold almost 100 per cent pure heroin directly to the junkies on the streets, who as a result of over-dosing were dropping dead like flies.

In 1998 he was arrested and charged with drug smuggling. But again his 'luck' held; he was acquitted while others were jailed. Then there was the book written by Paul Ferris. Ferris wrote the book *The Ferris Conspiracy* partly as a way of getting his own back on the City of Glasgow's police department who Ferris claimed had waged a war of harassment against him for years and had fitted him up and attempted to fit him up on numerous occasions. He tells how in his opinion the police force was full of cops getting envelopes filled with cash from a chosen few to turn a blind eye. Ferris had no problem with that in itself but he also states how McGraw took this a stage further with his friends on the force to enable him to go about his business unobstructed but at the expense of other criminals' liberty.

Paul Ferris at one time did some 'work' with McGraw but they had fallen out when Ferris figured McGraw had tried to fit him up on a few occasions. Ferris took some enjoyment in 'outing' McGraw for his deeds in his book. This 'deeply pissed him [McGraw] off'. In the book Ferris says: 'I don't fear for my personal safety. I can live with the likes of the Licensee and his cronies because I tell them to their faces what they are. Not only should McGraw fear me, he should fear my book and the onslaught that will follow. He chose to deal with the police and break the criminal code and now I'm punishing him very publicly for doing so.' A new war had begun.

In 2002 it reached a boiling point. In April of that year Tam McGraw was stabbed several times, less than a mile from his home in the city's east end. He was wearing a bullet-proof vest and was left relatively unscathed. He received 20 blows but suffered only injuries to his arms and wrists which were minor defensive injuries; slightly more serious than these and the wounds to his buttocks were the wounds to his pride. 'The Licensee', known as the most protected gangster in the city due to his hired body-guards, some of whom had been brought in from Ireland and were a product of 'The Troubles', he also had the surveillance of the Serious Crime Squad to ward off the attentions of most would be assassins.

After the attack sources said that Ferris and McGraw had held a meeting in which Ferris discussed McGraw paying him two million pounds ster-ling in compensation which Ferris felt he was due for his loss of business while serving prison time on a weapons charge. McGraw had grasped the opportunity of Ferris's incarceration to make some moves into Ferris's operations. Ferris now wanted what he saw as being rightfully his. Things got out of hand, resulting in the stabbing of McGraw later on. Whatever deal was or was not made between the two rivals it is certain that the 'dis-cussions' have not ended.

McGraw's personal fortune has been estimated at 10 million pounds. He has properties in Scotland and Ireland and a home in Tenerife. In Glasgow he owns a number of legitimate businesses from security companies to taxi firms through which drugs money is laundered. There are some in Glasgow's underworld who think it is time Tam McGraw retired to his Spanish villa; some think he must have by now used all his good 'luck'. Recently his right hand man Billy McPhee was stabbed to death by an as yet unknown assailant. A few months prior to that another close McGraw associate was murdered, stabbed to death outside a bar in the city.

On 30 July 2007 McGraw had a heart attack in his Mount Vernon home. Paramedics tried to resuscitate him and he was taken to Glasgow Royal Infirmary but was found to be dead on arrival. McGraw was labelled the richest gangster in Scotland, and one of the richest in Britain. He was labelled a 'grass' (informer) by his fellow criminals and was believed to shy away from the streets during his last years. Perhaps the stress of an imminent attack by one of his enemies caused his heart attack. Glasgow Godfather Arthur Thompson died the same way – he too was an informer.

THE CASE OF NEW PLAYERS IN AN OLD GAME

This case is based on the article 'New Players in an Old Game: The Sex Market in Italy' by Becucci (2008).

The sex trade in Italy has changed as Italian criminal groups have been replaced by foreign entrepreneurs. The foreign groups appear to adopt different organizational models in recruiting immigrant women destined for the sex trade. Therefore, street prostitution in Italy and other European countries has undergone profound transformations over the past few years (Becucci, 2008: 57):

> The progressive disappearance of Italian prostitutes has been witnessed since the end of the 1980s. Increasing dangers in street work, and the absence of any generational replacement for local women, have made room for a new female population arriving from various other countries. Italian women have continued to ply their trade in apartments, considered safer locations, frequently relying on regular customers they had become familiar with during their previous street activity.

The Albanian model introduced into the Italian sex trade is based on an exclusive relationship between the prostitute and her protector. Certain rules govern the management of women being exploited. The protector (exploiter) has brought one or more women to Italy and has exclusive rights over them. The pimp's agreement is required in the case of decisions that could put a woman's life at risk. The pimp typically comes from the same city or village in Albania as the girl and they often share blood ties: brother, cousin, and sometimes uncle or nephew.

The Nigerian model is more comprehensive as a Nigerian organisation controls recruitment as well as the subsequent introduction into the Italian sex market. Major figures supervising recruitment in the country of origin are the so-called madam, a sort of priestess, and the sponsor. The first has the job of using magic rituals from juju (a local variation of traditional voodoo) to bind girls to the agreements stipulated by the organization. The second – the sponsor – advances travel costs. When arriving in Italy, girls are placed under the control of other madams. They are different from the previous Madam, since they usually do not perform magic rituals.

7. Strategic planning for criminal entrepreneurship

Developing a strategy for criminal entrepreneurship is taken to mean thinking strategically and planning for the effective long-term application and optimal impact of resources to support organized crime in criminal business.

Strategy can simply be defined as principles, a broad-based formula, to be applied in order to achieve a purpose. These principles are general guidelines covering the daily work to reach business goals. Strategy is the pattern of resource development and application decisions made throughout the organization. These encapsulate both desired goals and beliefs about what are acceptable and, most critically, unacceptable means for achieving them.

Part of an entrepreneurial strategy is typically what Davidsson (2008) labels 'new offer' by introducing a new product or service. Also included in an entrepreneurial strategy is organizational change, which will be applied in this chapter in terms of new information and communication technology. Such organizational entrepreneurship is typically labelled *intrapreneurship*.

Strategy is both a plan for the future and pattern from the past; it is the match an organisation makes between its internal resources and skills (sometimes collectively called competencies) and the opportunities and risks created by its external environment. Strategy is the long-term direction of an organization. Strategy is the course of action for achieving an organization's purpose. Strategy is the direction and scope of an organization over the long term, which achieves advantage for the organization through its configuration of resources within a changing environment and to fulfil stakeholders' expectations (Johnson and Scholes, 2002).

Based on the resulting strategy for resource mobilization and application in criminal business, strategic management is important in criminal entrepreneurship. Strategic management includes understanding the strategic position of an organization, strategic choices for the future, and turning strategy into action. Understanding the strategic position is concerned with the impact on strategy of the external environment, internal resources and competencies, and the expectations and influence of stakeholders. Strategic choices involve understanding the underlying bases for future strategy at both higher and lower unit levels and the options for developing strategy in terms of both the directions in which strategy might move and the methods of development. Translating strategy into action is concerned with ensuring that strategies are working in practice. A strategy is not just a good idea, a statement, or a plan. It is only meaningful when it is actually being carried out (Johnson and Scholes, 2002).

Resource-based strategy is concerned with development and application of resources. While the business strategy is the broadest pattern of resource decisions, more specific decisions are related to information systems (IS) and information technology (IT). IS must be seen both in a business and an IT context. IS is in the middle because IS supports the business while using IT. As part of a resource-based strategy, both IS and IT represent capabilities and resources that have been developed. As an example of strategic planning for criminal entrepreneurship, strategic planning of IS/IT is described in this chapter.

STRATEGY LEVELS AND ELEMENTS

Business strategy is concerned with achieving the mission, vision and objectives of an organization, while IS strategy is concerned with use of IS/IT applications, and IT strategy is concerned with the technical infrastructure, as illustrated in Figure 7.1. An organization typically has several intra-organizational as well as inter-organizational IS/IT applications. The connection between them is also of great interest, as interdependencies should prevent applications from being separate islands. Furthermore, the arrows in Figure 7.1 are of importance. Arrows from business strategy to

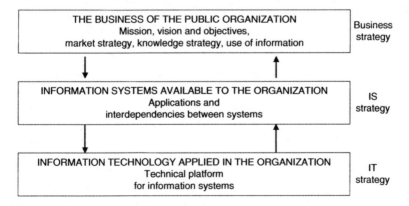

Figure 7.1   Relationships between strategies at three levels

IS strategy and from IS to IT strategy represent the alignment perspective; they illustrate *what* before *how*. What do we want to achieve? How might we achieve it?

Arrows from IT to IS strategy and from IS to business strategy represent the extension from *what* to *how* to *what*. This is the impact perspective, representing the potential impacts of modern information technology on future business options.

Necessary elements of a *business strategy* include mission, vision, objectives, market strategy, knowledge strategy and our general approach to the use of information, information systems and information technology.

Mission describes the reason for firm existence. For example, the reason for law firm existence is clients' needs for legal advice. The mission addresses the organization's basic question of 'What business are we in?' This single, essential, sentence should include no quantification, but must unambiguously state the purpose of the organization and should, just as carefully, define what the organization does not do. According to Ward and Peppard (2002: 189), the mission is an unambiguous statement of what the organization does and its long-term, overall purpose:

> Its primary role is to set a direction for everyone to follow. It may be short, succinct and inspirational, or contain broad philosophical statements that tie an organization to certain activities and to economic, social, ethical or political ends. Values are also frequently stated alongside the mission. Three widely-differing examples of missions are:
> - To be the world's mobile communications leader, enriching the lives of individuals and business customers in the networked society (large global telecommunication company)
> - To eradicate all communicable diseases worldwide (World Health Organization)
> - The company engages in the retail marketing on a national basis of petroleum products and the equitable distribution of the fruits of continuously increasing productivity of management, capital and labour amongst stockholders, employees and the public (a large public company).

Vision describes what the firm wants to achieve. For example, the law firm wants to become the leading law firm in Norway. The vision represents the view that senior managers have for the future of the organization; so it is what they want it to become. This view gives a way to judge the appropriateness of all potential activities that the organization might engage in. According to Ward and Peppard (2002), the vision gives a picture, frequently covering many aspects that everyone can identify with, of what the business will be in the future and how it will operate. It exists to bring objectives to life and to give the whole organization a destination that it can visualize, so that every stakeholder has a shared picture of the future aim.

Objectives describe where the business is heading. For example, the law firm can choose to merge with another law firm to become the leading law firm in Norway. Objectives are the set of major achievements that will accomplish the vision. These are usually small in number but embody the most important aspects of the vision, such as financial returns, customer service, manufacturing excellence, staff morale, and social and environmental obligations.

Market strategy describes market segments and products. For example, the law firm can focus on corporate clients in the area of tax law. Public schools can focus on students and their learning material.

The most important part of business strategy part is concerned with knowledge strategy. According to Zack (1999: 135), a *knowledge strategy* describes the overall approach an organization intends to take to align its knowledge resources and capabilities to the intellectual requirements of its strategy:

> It can be described along two dimensions reflecting its degree of aggressiveness. The first addresses the degree to which an organization needs to increase its knowledge in a particular area vs. the opportunity it may have to leverage existing but underutilized knowledge resources – that is, the extent to which the firm is primarily a creator vs. user of knowledge. The second dimension addresses whether the primary sources of knowledge are internal or external. Together these characteristics help a firm to describe and evaluate its current and desired knowledge strategy.

That part of business strategy concerned with use of information and IT is sometimes called an information management strategy. The general approach to the use of information, information systems needs and information technology investments is described in this part. For example, the ambition level for IT in knowledge management is described, and the general approach to selection of ambition level and combination of ambition levels I–IV are discussed.

Necessary elements of an *IS strategy* include future IS/IT applications, future competence of human resources (IS/IT professionals), future IS/IT organizational structure and control of the IS/IT function. An important application area is Knowledge Management Systems. The future applications are planned according to priorities, how they are to be developed or acquired (make or buy), how they meet user requirements and how security is achieved. The future competence is planned by types of resources needed, motivation and skills needed (managers, users, IS/IT professionals), salaries and other benefits. The future IS/IT organization defines tasks, roles, management and possibly outsourcing.

Necessary elements of an *IT strategy* include selection of IT hardware,

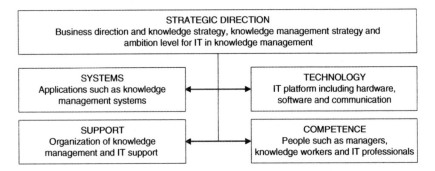

Figure 7.2   IS/IT strategy elements and interdependencies

basic software and networks, as well as how these components should interact as a technological platform and how required security level is maintained. The IT platform consists of hardware, systems software, networks and communications, standards and support from selected vendors.

An *IS/IT strategy* is a combined strategy including business context, the IS in a narrow sense and the technological platform. Necessary elements of an IS/IT strategy include business direction and strategy (mission, vision, objectives, knowledge strategy), applications (knowledge management systems), people (future competence of human resources), organization (future organization and control of IT function) and IT platform (future technical infrastructure). Hence, IS/IT is quite a broad term. The term is broad to take care of all connections and interdependencies in a strategy, as changes in one element will have an effect on all other elements, as illustrated in Figure 7.2.

Why is strategic IS/IT planning undertaken within business organizations? Hann and Weber (1996) see IS/IT planning as a set of activities directed towards achieving the following objectives:

- Recognizing organizational opportunities and problems where IS/IT might be applied successfully.
- Identifying the resources needed to allow IS/IT to be applied successfully to these opportunities and problems.
- Developing strategies and procedures to allow IS/IT to be applied successfully to these opportunities and problems.
- Establishing a basis for monitoring and bonding IT managers so their actions are more likely to be congruent with the goals of their superiors.
- Resolving how the gains and losses from unforeseen circumstances will be distributed among senior management and the IT manager.

- Determining the level of decision rights to be delegated to the IT manager.

THE Y MODEL FOR IS/IT STRATEGY WORK

In the following, we present a model for development of an IS/IT strategy for knowledge management. However, we do not limit strategy work to knowledge management. Rather, we describe the complete IS/IT strategy work of which knowledge management is a natural part. This is done to keep a complete strategy work process. A limited strategy only for knowledge management can cause sub-optimal solutions for the organization.

Empirical studies of information systems/information technology planning practices in organizations indicate that wide variations exist. Hann and Weber (1996) found that organizations differ in terms of how much IS/IT planning they do, the planning methodologies they use, the personnel involved in planning, the strength of the linkage between IS/IT plans and corporate plans, the focus of IS/IT plans (e.g. strategic systems versus resource needs), and the way in which IS/IT plans are implemented.

It has been argued that the Internet renders strategic planning obsolete. In reality, it is more important than ever for companies to carry out strategic planning (Porter, 2001: 63):

> Many have argued that the Internet renders strategy obsolete. In reality, the opposite is true. Because the Internet tends to weaken industry profitability without providing proprietary operational advantages, it is more important than ever for companies to distinguish themselves through strategy. The winners will be those that view the Internet as a complement to, not a cannibal of, traditional ways of competing.

In the following, the Y model for strategy work is discussed and applied. The model provides a coherent step-by-step procedure for development of an IS/IT strategy.

In all kinds of strategy work, there are three steps. The first step is concerned with analysis. The second step is concerned with choice (selection and decision), while the final step is concerned with implementation.

We now introduce a model for strategy work. This is illustrated in Figure 7.3. The model consists of seven stages covering analysis, choice and implementation. The stages are as follows:

1. *Describe current situation.* The current IS/IT situation in the business can be described using several methods. The benefits method identifies benefits from use of IS/IT in the business. Distinctions are made

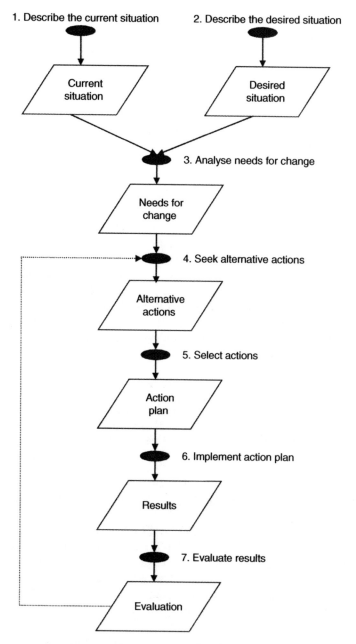

Figure 7.3   The Y model for IS/IT strategy work

between rationalization benefits, control benefits, organizational benefits and market benefits. Other methods include the three-era model, management activities and stages of growth.

2. *Describe desired situation.* The desired business situation can be described using several methods described in the first chapter. Value configurations, competitive strategy, management strategy, business process redesign, knowledge management, the Internet and electronic business, and information technology benefits.

3. *Analyse and prioritize needs for change.* After descriptions of the current situation and the desired situation, needs for change can be identified. The gap between desired and current situation is called needs for change. Analysis is to provide details of needs, what change is needed and how changes can take place. *What*-analysis will create an understanding of vision and goals, knowledge strategy, market strategy, and corporate problems and opportunities. *How*-analysis will create an understanding of technology trends and applications. These analyses should result in proposals for new IS/IT in the organization.

4. *Seek alternative actions.* When needs for change have been identified and proposals for filling gaps have been developed, alternative actions for improving the current situation can be developed. New IS/IT can be developed, acquired and implemented in alternative ways. For example, an information system can be developed in-house by company staff, it can be purchased as a standard application from a vendor, or it can be leased from an application systems provider (ASP).

5. *Select actions and make an action plan.* When needs for change and alternative actions have been identified, several choices have to be made and documented in an action plan. Important issues here include development process, user involvement, time frame and financial budget for IS/IT projects.

6. *Implement plan and describe results.* This is the stage of action. Technical equipment such as servers, PCs, printers and cables is installed. Operating systems are installed. Application packages, software programs, programming tools, end user tools and database systems are installed. Development projects are organized. Management and user training takes place. Results should be documented over time.

7. *Evaluate results.* Implementation results are compared with needs for change. It is determined to what extent gaps between desired and current situation have been closed. This is the beginning of the IS/IT strategy revision process, where a new process through the Y model takes place. Typically, a new IS/IT strategy process should take place every other year in business organizations.

While Stages 1 to 3 cover *analysis*, 4 and 5 cover *choice*, and 6 and 7 cover *implementation*. In some strategy models, Stage 2 is listed as the first stage. It is here recommended to carry out Stage 1 before Stage 2. It is easier to describe the ideal situation when you know the current situation. If you start out with Stage 2, it often feels difficult and abstract to describe what you would like to achieve. Having done Stage 1 first makes the work more relevant.

Stage 3 is a so-called gap analysis, looking at the difference between the desired and actual situation. This stage also includes prioritizing. Stage 4 is a creative session as it calls for ideas and proposals for alternative actions. Stages 5 and 6 are typical planning stages. The final stage, 7, is important because we can learn from performing an evaluation.

Stages 1 to 3 cover strategy analysis in the Y model. While Stage 1 is concerned with describing the current IS/IT situation, Stage 2 is concerned with describing the current and desired business situation, and Stage 3 is concerned with analysing needs for change based on the gap identified when comparing current and desired situations.

DESCRIBING THE CURRENT IS/IT SITUATION

The Y model starts with a description of the current situation. We focus on the IS/IT situation, as this will be the subject of change later in the model. First of all we have to understand the ways in which the company is using IS/IT. Many approaches can help us gain an understanding of the present IS/IT situation. Some methods are listed in the following:

1. *Benefits of IS/IT.* IS/IT is applied in business organizations to achieve benefits. We can study current IS/IT in the organization to understand what benefits have been achieved so far. Here we can determine what main benefit categories are currently the case. We will make distinctions between rationalization benefits, control benefits, organizational benefits and market benefits.
2. *Stages of IS/IT growth.* IS/IT in business organizations changes over time. New hardware and software, new areas of applications and new IS/IT support functions emerge. Most business organizations develop through stages over time. Here we can determine at what stage the business organization is for the time being. We will make distinctions between a total of nine stages. These nine stages are classified into three eras: data processing, information systems and information networks.
3. *IS/IT in management activities.* Management activities can be studied in a hierarchical perspective of operational, tactical and strategic

management. Current IS/IT in the organizations can be assigned to these levels to determine the extent of support at each level.

4. *IS/IT in business processes.* In a company, many business processes take place at the same time. Some of the processes may rely heavily on IS/IT while others are mainly manual at the current point in time.

5. *IS/IT support for value configuration.* We make distinctions between value chain, value shop and value network. In each of these value configurations, IS/IT can support activities. The current IS/IT situation is described by identifying activities in the value configuration depending on the extent of technology support.

6. *Strategic integration.* Business strategy and IT strategy have for a long time suffered from lack of coordination and integration in many organizations. Here we measure the current IS/IT situation by use of ten integration mechanisms to determine integration stage in an organization.

7. *IS/IT in e-business.* For most firms, becoming an e-business is an evolutionary journey. We introduce six stages to describe the evolving e-business: external communications, internal communications, e-commerce, e-business, e-enterprise and transformation.

8. *IS/IT-enabled business transformation.* IT-enabled transformation can include business direction change but more often we find examples at lower levels, such as business design change and business process change.

9. *IS/IT support for knowledge management.* The stages of growth model for knowledge management technology can be applied, where the current IS/IT situation is described by the stage at which the firm currently is performing.

Description of the current situation assumes that we have been able to define borders for our study. Borders exist for both breadth and depth. Breadth is a question of whether the whole company or only one division should be studied. Depth is a question of whether all aspects, such as technology, marketing, management and finance, should be included in the study. We recommend both extensive breadth and thorough depth to ensure that a wide range of alternative solutions and alternative actions can be identified in later stages of the Y model. In the case of breadth, this may imply that both suppliers and customers are included because there may be electronic market places used by our suppliers and customers. In the case of depth, this may imply that analysis of top management is included because management competence in the area of IS/IT can influence both management attitudes and ambitions concerning future applications of IS/IT.

Description of the current IS/IT situation should focus on issues of importance in technology and knowledge management. Less emphasis should be put on technology itself, such as drawings of company networks and servers. Technology management is focused on the management of information technology, while knowledge management is focused on knowledge strategy and knowledge management systems.

DESCRIBING THE CURRENT AND DESIRED BUSINESS SITUATION

We have used some of the nine methods to describe the current situation of IS/IT. Now we have to consider whether the current IS/IT applications are what the company needs or if chances might be needed. We use the Y model as our guiding approach. We compare the present business situation (with its support from IS/IT) with the desired business situation. If the current IS/IT applications are not able to serve the needs of the future desired business, then there is need for change in IS/IT applications and the way we do business. At this point we are moving into Stage 2 of the Y model.

There are many techniques for business analysis. Some are general while others are more specific. General analysis techniques include SWOT analysis and the X model. Specific analysis techniques include business direction (mission, vision, objectives), market strategy, value system, competitive forces and product life cycle. Some of these analytical tools are listed in the following:

1. *SWOT analysis.* SWOT analysis is an analytical tool for assessing the present and future situation focusing on strengths (S), weaknesses (W), opportunities (O) and threats (T). The whole company may be the object of analysis, but also a department in a company or a project in a company may be the study object. How can knowledge management exploit our strengths, compensate our weaknesses, use opportunities and avoid threats? How can knowledge management technology help make it happen?
2. *The X model.* The X model is a tool for description and analysis of both the current and a desired situation. It is a method for assessing the situation within a company, a project or a department. The situation consists of a time period in which work is done. At the beginning of the time period there are both factual and personal inputs, and at the end of the period there are both factual and personal outputs. How can knowledge management improve factual and personal outputs? How can knowledge management technology help make it happen?

3. *Business direction.* Important business concepts are mission, vision and objectives. How can knowledge management make the firm achieve its vision? How can knowledge management make the firm reach its objectives? How can knowledge management technology help make it happen?

4. *Market strategy.* The market strategy shows our position and ambition in the marketplace. We can either have the same product as our competitors, or we can have a different product. If we have the same product as everyone else, it has to be sold at the same price as all the others (as in a vegetable market or through the Internet). It is not possible for an Internet bookstore to sell at a higher price than others, when there is perfect information and information searching is associated with no costs. This is called the law of indifference. In order to survive, the company must have a cost advantage that will give higher profits and result in higher earnings for the owners. How can knowledge management cause a cost advantage? How can knowledge management technology help make it happen? If we are selling a product that our customers perceive to be different from our competitors' product, then we have differentiation. A service may in its basic form be the same for all companies, like airline travel, in the sense that all airlines are supposed to bring you safely to your destination. The product is differentiated by supplementary services. How can knowledge management make our customers perceive our products and services to be different from our competitors'? How can knowledge management technology help make it happen?

5. *Competitive forces.* The basis of this method is that a company exists within an industry and to succeed it must effectively deal with the competitive forces that exist within the particular industry. For example, the forces in an emerging industry such as mobile communications are considerably different from those of established industries such as financial services. The company interacts with its customers, suppliers and competitors. In addition, there are potential new entrants into the particular competitive marketplace and potential substitute products and services. To survive and succeed in this environment, it is important to understand these interactions and the implications in terms of what opportunities or competitive advantage can occur. How can knowledge management reduce the threat of new entrants, reduce the bargaining power of suppliers, reduce the bargaining power of buyers, reduce the threat of substitute products and services, and reduce the rivalry among existing competitors? How can knowledge management technology help make it happen?

6. *Product portfolio analysis.* There are a number of approaches that aim to relate the competitive position of an organization to the maturity of

its product. The models assume there is a basic S-shaped curve description to the growth phenomenon of products. Four stages in the life cycle of any product can be identified as introduction, growth, maturity and decline. When we look at the life cycle of all products in the firm, we can apply product portfolio analysis. This method shows the relationship between a product's current or future revenue potential and the appropriate management stance. The two-by-two matrix names the products in order to chart symptoms into a diagnosis so that effective management behaviour can be adopted. The matrix classifies products according to the present market share and the future growth of that market. A successful product that lasts from emergent to mature market goes around the matrix. This strategy is simply to milk the cows, divest the dogs, invest in the stars and examine the wild cats. How can knowledge management get more milk for a longer period of time from the cows? How can knowledge management eliminate the dogs? How can knowledge management explore and exploit the stars? How can knowledge management help develop uncertain potentials (wild cats) into profitable service (stars)? How can knowledge management technology help make it happen?

7. *Environmental analysis.* Environmental analysis is concerned with the external corporate environment. An analysis of the environment is important because it increases the quality of the strategic decision making by considering a range of the relevant features. The organization identifies threats and opportunities facing it, and those factors that might assist in achieving objectives and those that might act as a barrier. The strategy of the organization should be directed at exploiting the environmental opportunities and blocking environmental threats in a way that is consistent with internal capabilities. This is a matter of environmental fit that allows the organization to maximize its competitive position. An external analysis can investigate politics, the economy, the society and the technology. This is sometimes called PEST analysis. If we include the study of legal and environmental matters, we call it PESTLE. The analytical work that has to be done in the company when doing environmental analysis is concerned with questions such as: What are the implications of the trends (changes in the environment)? What can the company do in order to meet the opportunities and threats that follow? How can knowledge management meet the opportunities and threats that follow? How can knowledge management technology help make it happen? For example, how can knowledge management technology help in global competition (politics)? How can knowledge management technology help in alliances and partnerships (economy)? How can knowledge management help serve an increasing number of older people (society)?

8. *External knowledge analysis.* Distinctions can be made between core knowledge, advanced knowledge and innovative knowledge. While core knowledge is required to stay in business, advanced knowledge makes the firm competitively visible and innovative knowledge allows the firm to lead its entire industry. The knowledge map can be applied to identify firm position. The map in terms of the strategic knowledge framework illustrates firm knowledge levels compared with competitors' knowledge levels.

9. *Internal knowledge analysis.* While the knowledge map represents an external analysis of the firm's current knowledge situation, the knowledge gap represents an internal analysis of the firm's current knowledge situation. The knowledge gap is dependent on business strategy. What the company does is different from what the company will do, creating a strategy gap. What the company knows is different from what the company has to know, creating a knowledge gap. Two important links emerge: the strategy–knowledge link and the knowledge–strategy link.

STRATEGIC ALIGNMENT

IT is recognized as a critical business discipline because it is central to all business activities of modern enterprises in the creation of organizational and customer value. To create business value from IT, business needs to understand the role IT plays, not only in supporting the running of the business in such back-office functions as human resources, finance and inventory control, but more importantly the special and competitively differentiated ways that IT plays in delivering products and services to the cooperating agencies and citizens. The integral role that IT has enmeshed into all business functions today means that IT has become a central nervous system of a business. In particular, information *is* the bloodstream of business, which flows through all business functions (processes) supported by the IT nervous system. Business value is created by each business function or process through dynamic consumption (processing) of input information and creation of new output information, which in turn will be 'consumed' by another business function (process) as defined by the value configuration of the business.

The fundamental principle of all the critical success factors of IT strategy is therefore IT and business acting as one. This requires each IT task to be aligned with and 'justified' by the business function it is designed to contribute, for and based on which its business value is measured.

IT and business acting as one is easier said than done, however. In reality not many enterprises have yet fully mastered the practice of the fundamental principle of IT and business acting as one. This is because of the bad old tradition of IT in the past (and even today for some enterprises) working (either being treated or wanting to be treated) as the 'back-office techie guys' who seemed to do as they were told (or requested) by the business without having any concern for the end customers or indeed the business purpose of the tasks being requested. In the past, IT saw itself as the technical guys who would do whatever technical task was requested of them by the business. There was no need to understand the business, let alone the business strategy or points of differentiation. The 'us-versus-them' working relationship or company culture permeated most enterprises in the past, and indeed even today.

While this scenario may be an extreme example for today's enterprises, it is nonetheless still a common issue for most enterprises today that some degree of misalignment still exists between business and IT. The varying degrees of organizational misalignment and functional disconnect between business and IT have been the key inhibitor of value creation by IT in all enterprises, past and present. Despite rigorous and diligent attempts by researchers and practitioners alike, in the past 20 years, various surveys have shown that business–IT alignment remains a strategically critical priority for business and IT leaders to manage and achieve.

In a classical study of alignment, King and Teo (1997) investigated the degree of alignment and integration between business strategy and IT strategy in enterprises, as illustrated in Table 7.1.

King and Teo (1997) found that companies go through four stages of strategic integration, with increasing degree of integration as the company becomes excellent (mature) in exploiting and managing IT for business differentiation. The first stage is separate planning with administrative integration. The second is one-way linked planning with sequential integration, while the third is two-way linked planning with reciprocal integration. The fourth stage is fully integrated business and IT planning – the most mature level of business and IT acting as one.

There are many factors affecting the ability of business and IT to act as one. The combination of these factors defines the level at which business functions and IT functions do act as one in strategy formulation, planning and execution. King and Teo (1997) identify ten factors affecting business–IT partnership in business–IT strategic management. They call these factors benchmark variables. The four stages of integration can be described in terms of benchmark variables, as shown in Table. Benchmark variables indicate the theoretical characteristics at each stage of integration. For example, organizations at Stage 1 can theoretically be expected to conform to values of benchmark variables listed under Stage 1. However, this does not mean that it is not possible for organizations

Table 7.1   Stages of integration between business strategy and IT strategy (adapted from King and Teo, 1997)

Benchmark variables	Stage 1 Administrative integration	Stage 2 Sequential integration	Stage 3 Reciprocal integration	Stage 4 Full integration
Purpose of integration	Administrative and nonstrategic	Support business strategy	Support and influence business strategy	Joint development of business and IT strategies
Role of the IT function	Technically oriented and nonstrategic	Resource to support business strategy	Resource to support and influence business strategy	Critical to long-term survival of organization
Primary role of the IT executive	Functional administrator responsible for back-room support	IT expert who formulates IT strategy to implement business strategy	IT expert who provides valuable inputs during strategy formulation and implementation	Formal and integral member of top management who is involved in many business matters
Performance criteria for the IT function	Operational efficiency and cost minimization	Contribution to business strategy implementation	Quality of IT inputs into business strategy formulation and implementation	Long-term impact on organization
Triggers for developing IT applications	Need to automate administrative work processes	Business goals considered first	Business goals and IT capabilities considered jointly	IT applications are critical to success of business strategy
Top management participation in IT planning	Seldom	Infrequent	Frequent	Almost always
User participation in IT planning	Seldom	Infrequent	Frequent	Almost always
IT executive participation in business planning	Seldom	Infrequent	Frequent	Almost always
Assessment of new technologies	Seldom	Infrequent	Frequent	Almost always

Table 7.1   (continued)

Benchmark variables	Stage 1 Administrative integration	Stage 2 Sequential integration	Stage 3 Reciprocal integration	Stage 4 Full integration
Status of IT executive (number of levels below the CEO)	Four or more	Three	Two	One

at Stage 1 to have values of benchmark variables applicable to other stages.

Each of the ten benchmark variables can be explained in more detail as follows (King and Teo, 1997):

1. *Purpose of integration.* At Stage 1, integration focuses primarily on the support of administrative work processes. IT is still a commodity service and not critical for business strategy. This gradually changes as the IT function begins to support business strategy (Stage 2) or influence business strategy (Stage 3). At Stage 4, there is joint strategy development for both business and IT strategies – at which business and IT truly act as one, with strategic influences going both directions.
2. *Role of the IT function.* The general transition from being technically oriented to business oriented is a trend for most IT functions. At Stage 1, the IT function is viewed as being primarily technically oriented. Gradually, this role changes when the IT function is used as a resource to support the implementation (Stage 2) and formulation (Stage 3) of business strategies. At Stage 4, the IT function is viewed as critical to the long-term success of the organization. To be able to act as one with the business, IT acts and thinks like a business with strong business skills. Similarly business becomes very IT savvy.
3. *Primary role of the IT executive.* There seems to be a general decrease in the size of the central IT function. This may have resulted in a shift in the responsibilities of the IT function from systems design to systems integration, and from the role of a developer to that of an advisor. Due to increasing decentralization, the IT function may assume a staff role similar to a federal government in coordinating dispersed IT resources. The skill requirements of the senior executive have also changed over the years, with increasing emphasis on both knowledge about changing technology and knowledge about the business. In addition,

significant political and communication skills are required. The role of the IT executive gradually changes from being a functional administrator responsible for providing backroom support (Stage 1), to being an IT expert who formulates IT strategy to implement business objectives (Stage 2). As the organization begins to apply IT for strategic purposes, the role of the IT executive becomes more important. He or she begins to play a major role in facilitating and influencing the development and implementation of IT applications to achieve business objectives (Stage 3). Finally, in Stage 4, the IT executive becomes a formal and integral member of the top management team, and provides significant inputs in both IT- and non-IT-related matters.

4. *Performance criteria for the IT function.* As the IT function matures in terms of alignment to business needs and influence on business solutions, performance criteria for the IT function change from a structured focus on operational efficiency to a more unstructured concern for the impact of IT on strategic direction. The early performance criteria (Stage 1) for the IT function are primarily concerned with operational efficiency, technical quality and cost minimization. When the IT function begins to play a more strategic role by adapting to and influencing business processes, the emphasis gradually shifts to effective strategy implementation (Stage 2), and then to the quality of IT inputs into business strategy formulation and implementation (Stage 3). Ultimately, the performance criterion for the IT function is its long-term impact on the organizational performance (Stage 4) where IT is becoming a business transformer to create a sustainable strategic advantage.

5. *Triggers for developing IT applications.* Initially, triggers for development of new IT applications are opportunities for achieving greater efficiencies through process automation. As IT applications begin to be increasingly used to support business direction, business goals become trigger mechanisms in deciding appropriate IT applications to be developed (Stage 2). At Stage 3, joint considerations of business goals as well as IT capabilities become important as the organization attempts to develop systems for sustainable competitive advantage. Finally, in Stage 4, IT applications are developed because they are critical to the success of the organization's strategy and the creation of business value for sustained superior performance.

6. *Top management participation in IT planning.* Traditionally, as in Stage 1, top management did not pay great attention to the IT function because it was considered to be an overhead function that generated only cost. Top management's concern was only what IT caused in terms of technology expenditures, not what kind of benefits were

achieved from applying information and communication technologies and systems. At Stage 2, greater top management participation in IT planning begins when IT strategies come to be used to support business strategies rather than just specifying technical solutions. The realization that strategic IT planning can also influence business strategy motivates top management to participate more actively in this kind of strategy work by applying a business language rather than a technical language (Stage 3). For example, e-business influences the way government works in terms of e-government. Finally, in Stage 4, when the IT function becomes critical for the survival or sustainable superior performance of the organization, top management and senior IT executives jointly formulate business and IT plans – business and IT truly acting as one.

7. *User participation in IT planning.* Before the availability of end-user computing, user management was generally not significantly involved – they were mainly complaining when something went wrong (Stage 1). However, as end-user systems and tools begin to dominate individual work, and the IT function begins to influence functional units in terms of its effects on everyday work as well as business strategies, participation of users becomes more important and natural in order to fully exploit the potential of information technology. User participation gradually increases through the stages, until Stage 4, where users participate and contribute extensively in IT planning.

8. *IT executive participation in business planning.* The other side of business management alignment in IT planning is having IT executives participate in business planning. The traditional role of the IT function in providing administrative support does not assume the senior IT executive to participate in business planning (Stage 1). The senior IT executive reacts to business plans and does not have any influence on their formulation. Often, the IT executive simply does not understand the business plan and is unable to translate business strategy into IT solutions. At Stage 2, senior IT executive participation is initiated. As the IT function in the eyes of business executives becomes more important in achievement of business objectives, it becomes necessary and smart to include more frequent participation of the senior IT executive in business planning because the traditional participants are relatively unfamiliar with the potential of information technology (Stage 3). With greater participation, the senior IT executive learns the business, becomes more informed about business objectives and is better able to provide higher-quality inputs into the planning process. At Stage 4, the senior IT executive becomes an integral member of the top management team and participates extensively in both business

planning and IT planning based on alignment expertise acquired at earlier stages.

9. *Assessment of new technologies.* During IT planning, new technologies, which can impact on IT operations as well as business operations, are usually assessed. The level of expertise and sophistication involved in assessing new technologies is the basis for this ninth benchmark variable. In the early stages of IT planning (Stages 1 and 2), assessment of functionality as well as impact of new technologies, if any, is usually done rather informally and infrequently. At Stage 3, the need for formal, knowledge-based and frequent procedures for assessing new technologies becomes apparent as the IT function begins to play a more important role in business planning. At Stage 4, assessment of the impact of new technologies becomes an integral part of business planning and IT planning when the CIO (chief information officer) and the CEO have established a mutual communication platform. The business and IT executives are constantly seeking out potential disruptive technologies with which to transform the business.

10. *Status of IT executive.* The responsibilities of the IT function have changed over the years due to technological and conceptual changes that made information technology more important to organizations. IT line responsibilities are being rapidly distributed in many organizations as the IT function begins to take on more staff responsibilities. With these changing responsibilities of the IT function, the status of the senior IT executive is likely to become higher. The position of the senior IT executive – in terms of the number of levels below the CEO – can serve as an indication of the importance of the IT function to the organization's strategy.

So what must business and IT do to act as one – resonating harmonically even in the event of a changing business environment? In addition to the mutual understanding of business and IT roles and capabilities in customer value creation described above, two more ingredients are required: behavioural and organizational.

The behavioural component of staff personnel deals with the establishment of strong relationship and trust between business and IT. This component requires IT to work proactively to engage the business. It requires strong leadership and communication skills, as well as business skills. IT is a means to a business end. IT executives must therefore have a deep understanding of their company business and master the art of business communication. All IT activities and service performance levels must be explained in terms of business context. For instance, instead of saying IT has improved the order management process by implementing a business process management platform using the state of the art service-oriented architecture, we say that the order management process has been redesigned with in-built flexibility for ease of adaptation for future business change and has reduced the order-to-cash time from x days to y hours. This business context communication will improve the business understanding of the IT role, and indeed IT value to business.

CRIME STRATEGY

According to Felson (2006), the intellectual study of organized crime suffers from at least four major distractions: (1) mixing overall analysis with the requirements of prosecution; (2) understating the diversity of criminal cooperation; (3) underestimating how crime cooperation inter-acts with legitimate activities and (4) overestimating the degree of planning and sophistication needed for offender symbiosis to occur. Hence, the current chapter may suffer from such distraction, as many criminal projects are opportunity-based activities with a low degree of planning and sophistication.

Crime generally requires a degree of concealment. According to Felson (2006), this process is largely physical. Concealment is concerned with the privacy of a transaction, a setting and a location. A few small pills are easily hidden while victimized individuals may be hard to transport in public.

An example of crime strategy is the robbing of cash-in-transit vans. Cash-in-transit vans are an attractive target for robbers because they are lucrative. Yet they are risky as well, since guards have to be confronted directly and there are higher levels of security than are found in most other targets (Gill, 2001).

When comparing entrepreneurial robbers of cash-in-transit vans with entrepreneurs in the legitimate world, Gill (2001) finds many similar behaviours and characteristics. Both are operational in attitude, and they sharpen their skills and awareness via experience when doing the job. Both seem to be rational actors that need to conduct an intuitive cost–benefit analysis, where they are weighing up the benefits and disadvantages of each venture because the costs of getting it wrong can be high. While the legitimate entrepreneur may lose his or her reputation and go bankrupt, the robber may lose freedom for a long time and may well be injured or even killed. They both live a life where there often is a lot to lose, and this in itself sharpens expertise.

According to Gill (2001) such characteristics lead to the conclusion that both types of entrepreneur have to plan their ventures in terms of strategy, and they need to carefully consider the risks and manage them to best advantage. Both need to be good risk takers, having the characteristics of courage and sound judgment.

One kind of crime strategy is to develop business in the underground economy by doing underground work. Underground workers are defined by Williams (2006: 5) as those engaged in the production and sales of goods and services that are unregistered by, or hidden from, the state for tax, social security and/or labour law purposes but which are legal in all other respects:

> Importantly, therefore, for those who might assume that drug dealers, those selling stolen goods and so forth are being discussed, this definition explicitly denotes that the only criminality about underground work is the fact that the production and sale of the goods and services are not registered for tax, social security and/or labour law purposes.

The underground economy covers only work where the means are illegitimate, not the ends (goods and services) themselves, according to the definition applied by Williams (2006). In Norway, the underground economy as a percentage of the total economy is estimated at 5 per cent while in the UK it is estimated at 6 per cent and Greece 29 per cent (Williams, 2006).

Williams (2006) presents portraits of underground enterprises, where examples of tasks typically conducted by underground workers include house maintenance, home improvements, routine housework, making and repairing goods, car maintenance, gardening and caring. This suggests that the vast majority of underground work takes place in the domestic service and construction sectors.

THE CASE OF SAM GOODMAN

This case is based on the book *Confessions Of A Dying Thief: Understanding Criminal Careers and Illegal Enterprise* by Steffensmeier and Ulmer (2005), presented at www.books.google.com.

Sam Goodman was a long-time thief, fence and quasi-legitimate businessman. He had a criminal career that spanned 50 years, beginning in his mid-teens and ending with his death when he was in his mid-60s.

The book *Confessions of a Dying Thief* is an in-depth ethnographic study of Sam and his world based on continuous contact with him for many years, on multiple interviews with his network of associates in crime and business, and on a series of interviews before he died. The book combines Sam's narrative accounts with commentary by the authors to provide a more nuanced portrayal of criminal careers, illegal enterprise and the broad landscape comprising organized crime.

To more fully understand pathways into and out of crime as well as the social organization of illegal enterprise, the authors of the book propose an integrative learning–opportunity–commitment framework that combines differential association/social learning theory and an extended conceptualization of criminal opportunity with a three-fold theory of commitment to crime. This framework offers a way of understanding mechanisms that underlie criminal offending and criminal careers. It also recognizes the complexity and scope of the criminal landscape and its embeddedness in the fabric of the larger society, including its criminal justice system. Sam's illness and death are a sobering backdrop throughout the whole book. The book is a journey into the dynamics of criminal careers and the social organization of criminal enterprise, as experienced by a veteran thief and fence and his network of key associates.

THE CASE OF STRATEGIC ADAPTION BY THE BEDOUIN

This case is based on the article 'Hashish Smuggling by Bedouin in South Sinai' by Emanuel Marx (2008).

This case illustrates the changing fortunes of the smuggling operations of South Sinai Bedouin (Marx, 2008: 29):

> The Bedouin are a link in the international drug traffic delivering hashish and other drugs to the inhabitants of the Nile Valley. The full-scale entry of the South Sinai Bedouin into drug smuggling began around 1950, and in less than two decades smuggling grew into a major industry. At its zenith it provided about 30% of the aggregate income of the Bedouin population. Then smuggling stopped almost overnight, for during the 15 years of Israeli occupation, from 1967 to 1982, the crossing from the Sinai Peninsula into mainland Egypt was too dangerous for the operators. During my fieldwork in South Sinai, which overlapped with the Israeli occupation, most of the Bedouin were working as migrant labourers and a handful entered the budding local tourist industry, so that the loss of income from smuggling did not cause them economic hardship. But the leaders of the smuggling gangs remained at home, and it was quite easy to meet them. They appeared to be inactive, but I soon realized that they were working hard at keeping the smuggling organizations alive: they fostered the ties with members of their former gangs and looked after their mountain retreats. They were convinced that the political and economic situation would sooner or later change, and that drug smuggling would once again become feasible. Other Bedouin too acted to forestall an uncertain future: they maintained orchards and small flocks, which at that time yielded no income, as an economic reserve. They would fall back on it when migrant labour would no longer be plentiful.
>
> Conditions in Sinai changed again when it reverted to Egyptian rule in 1982. The State developed hotel tourism as the major industry. The hotels employed only a small number of Bedouin men, and the formerly thriving Bedouin guest

lodges lost some of their customers. Therefore many Bedouin returned to migrant labour, and also increased their flocks and cultivated their orchards more intensively. The hashish trade too revived very quickly, this time with a difference: now the Bedouin smugglers not only conveyed drugs to mainland Egypt, but also sold them to international tourists and to fellow Bedouin. The drug dealers and other men were gradually becoming smokers.

In terms of the Y model, the desired situation was always to run hashish smuggling into Egypt, thereby making money for the Bedouin population. In terms of the current situation, it changed dramatically during Israeli occupation, thereby requiring entrepreneurial adaptation to the new situation.

8. Knowledge management in criminal entrepreneurship

The purpose of this chapter is to apply the resource-based theory of the enterprise to criminal entrepreneurship in criminal business enterprises to shed new light on organized crime in an entrepreneurship and innovation perspective. This chapter makes a contribution to existing theory. Using a resource-based theory approach, this chapter attempts to develop new means of conceptualizing organized crime. It is timely in as much as this is a growing area of concern for researchers active in entrepreneurship.

Knowledge is an important and often the most important organizational resource. Unlike other inert organizational resources, the application of existing knowledge has the potential to generate new knowledge. Not only can knowledge be replenished in use, it can also be combined and recombined to generate new knowledge. Once created, knowledge can be articulated, shared, stored and re-contextualized to yield options for the future. For all of these reasons, knowledge has the potential to be applied across time and space to yield increasing returns (Garud and Kumaraswamy, 2005).

The strategic management of organizational knowledge is a key factor that can help organizations to sustain competitive advantage in volatile environments. Organizations are turning to knowledge management initiatives and technologies to leverage their knowledge resources. Knowledge management can be defined as a systemic and organizationally specified process for acquiring, organizing and communicating knowledge of employees so that other employees may make use of it to be more effective and productive in their work (Kankanhalli et al., 2005).

Knowledge management is also important in inter-organizational relationships. Inter-organizational relationships have been recognized to provide two distinct potential benefits: short-term operational efficiency and longer-term new knowledge creation. For example, the need for continual value innovation is driving supply chains to evolve from a purely transactional focus to leveraging inter-organizational partnerships for sharing information and, ultimately, market knowledge creation. Supply chain partners are engaging in interlinked processes that enable rich (broad ranging, high quality and privileged) information sharing, and building information technology infrastructures that allow them to process information obtained from their partners to create new knowledge (Malhotra et al., 2005).

CHARACTERISTICS OF KNOWLEDGE

Knowledge is a renewable, reusable and accumulating resource of value to the organization when applied in the production of products and services. Knowledge cannot as such be stored in computers; it can only be stored in the human brain. Knowledge is what a knower knows; there is no knowledge without someone knowing it.

The need for a knower in knowledge existence raises the question as to how knowledge can exist outside the heads of individuals. Although knowledge cannot originate outside the heads of individuals, it can be argued that knowledge can be represented in and often embedded in organizational processes, routines and networks, and sometimes in document repositories. However, knowledge is seldom complete outside of an individual.

In this book, knowledge is defined as information combined with experience, context, interpretation, reflection, intuition and creativity. Information becomes knowledge once it is processed in the mind of an individual. This knowledge then becomes information again once it is articulated or communicated to others in the form of text, computer output, spoken or written words or other means. Six characteristics of knowledge can distinguish it from information: knowledge is a human act, knowledge is the residue of thinking, knowledge is created in the present moment, knowledge belongs to communities, knowledge circulates through communities in many ways, and new knowledge is created at the boundaries of old. This definition and these characteristics of knowledge are based on current research (e.g. Poston and Speier, 2005; Ryu et al., 2005; Sambamurthy and Subramani, 2005; Tanriverdi, 2005; Wasko and Faraj, 2005).

Today, any discussion of knowledge quickly leads to the issue of how knowledge is defined. A pragmatic definition defines the topic as the most valuable form of content in a continuum starting at data, encompassing information and ending at knowledge. Typically, data are classified, summarized, transferred or corrected in order to add value, and become information within a certain context. This conversion is relatively mechanical and has long been facilitated by storage, processing and communication technologies. These technologies add place, time and form utility to the data. In doing so, the information serves to inform or reduce uncertainty within the problem domain. Therefore, information is united with the context; that is, it only has utility within the context (Grover and Davenport, 2001).

Knowledge has the highest value, the most human contribution, the greatest relevance to decisions and actions, and the greatest dependence on a specific situation or context. It is also the most difficult of content types to manage because it originates and is applied in the minds of human beings. People who are knowledgeable not only have information, but also have the ability to integrate and frame the information within the context of their experience, expertise and judgment. In doing so, they can create new information that expands the state of possibilities, and in turn allows for further interaction with experience, expertise and judgment. Therefore, in an organizational context, all new knowledge stems from people. Some knowledge is incorporated in organizational artefacts like processes, structures and technology. However, institutionalized knowledge often inhibits competition in a dynamic context, unless adaptability of people and processes (higher order learning) is built into the institutional mechanisms themselves.

Our concern with distinctions between information and knowledge is based on real differences as well as technology implications. Real differences between information and knowledge do exist, although for most practical purposes these differences are of no interest at all. Information technology implications are concerned with the argument that computers can only manipulate electronic information, not electronic knowledge. Business systems are loaded with information but are without knowledge.

Davenport and Prusak (1998) define knowledge as a fluid mix of framed experience, values, contextual information and expert insights that provides a framework for evaluating and incorporating new experiences and information. It originates and is applied in the minds of knowers. In organizations, it often becomes embedded not only in documents or repositories but also in organizational routines, processes, practices and norms. Distinctions are often made between data, information, knowledge and wisdom:

- *Data* are letters and numbers without meaning. Data are independent, isolated measurements, characters, numerical characters and symbols.
- *Information* is data that are included in a context that makes sense. For example, 40 degrees can have different meanings depending on the context. There can be a medical, geographical or technical context. If a person has 40 degrees celsius in fever, that is quite serious. If a city is located 40 degrees north, we know that it is far

south of Norway. If an angle is 40 degrees, we know what it looks like. Information is data that make sense because it can be understood correctly. People turn data into information by organizing it into some unit of analysis, for example dollars, dates or customers. Information is data endowed with relevance and purpose.

- *Knowledge* is information combined with experience, context, interpretation and reflection. Knowledge is a renewable resource that can be used over and over, and that accumulates in an organization through use and combination with employees' experience. Humans have knowledge; knowledge cannot exist outside the heads of individuals in the company. Information becomes knowledge when it enters the human brain. This knowledge transforms into information again when it is articulated and communicated to others. Information is an explicit representation of knowledge; it is in itself no knowledge. Knowledge can both be truths and lies, perspectives and concepts, judgments and expectations. Knowledge is used to receive information by analysing, understanding and evaluating; by combining, prioritizing and decision making; and by planning, implementing and controlling.

- *Wisdom* is knowledge combined with learning, insights and judgmental abilities. Wisdom is more difficult to explain than knowledge, since the levels of context become even more personal, and thus the higher-level nature of wisdom renders it more obscure than knowledge. While knowledge is mainly sufficiently generalized solutions, wisdom is best thought of as sufficiently generalized approaches and values that can be applied in numerous and varied situations. Wisdom cannot be created like data and information, and it cannot be shared with others like knowledge. Because the context is so personal, it becomes almost exclusive to our own minds and incompatible with the minds of others without extensive transaction. This transaction requires not only a base of knowledge and opportunities for experiences that help create wisdom, but also the processes of introspection, retrospection, interpretation and contemplation. We can value wisdom in others, but we can only create it ourselves.

It has been argued that expert systems using artificial intelligence are able to do knowledge work. The chess-playing computer called Deep Blue by IBM is frequently cited as an example. Deep Blue can compete with the best human players because chess, though complex, is a closed system of unchanging and codifiable rules. The size of the board never varies, the rules are unambiguous, the moves of the pieces are clearly defined, and there is absolute agreement about what it means to win or lose (Davenport and Prusak, 1998). Deep Blue is no knowledge worker; the computer only performs a series of computations at extremely high speed.

While knowledge workers develop knowledge, organizations learn. Therefore, the learning organization has become a term frequently used. The learning organization is similar to knowledge development. While knowledge development is taking place at the individual level, organizational learning is taking place at the firm level. Organizational learning occurs when the firm is able to exploit individual competence in new and innovative ways. Organizational learning also occurs when the collective memory – including local language, common history and routines – expands. Organizational learning causes growth in the intellectual capital. Learning is a continuous, never-ending process of knowledge creation. A learning organization is a place where people are constantly driven to discover what has caused the current situation and how they can change the present. To maintain competitive advantage, an organization's investment decisions related to knowledge creation are likely to be strategic in nature (Chen and Edgington, 2005).

Alavi and Leidner (2001) make the case that the hierarchy of data–information–knowledge can be of a different nature. Specifically, they claim that knowledge can be the basis for information, rather than information the basis for knowledge. Knowledge must exist before information can be formulated and before data can be measured to form information. As such, raw data do not exist – the thought or knowledge processes that led to its identification and collection have already influenced even the most elementary piece of data. It is argued that knowledge exists which, when articulated, verbalized and structured, becomes information which, when assigned a fixed representation and standard interpretation, becomes data (Alavi and Leidner, 2001: 109):

> Critical to this argument is the fact that knowledge does not exist outside an agent (a knower): it is indelibly shaped by one's needs as well as one's initial stock of knowledge. Knowledge is thus the result of cognitive processing triggered by the inflow of new stimuli. Consistent with this view, we posit that information is converted to knowledge once it is processed in the mind of individuals and the knowledge becomes information once it is articulated and presented in the form of text, graphics, words, or other symbolic forms. A significant implication of this view of knowledge is that for individuals to arrive at the same understanding of data or information, they must share a certain knowledge base. Another important implication of this definition of knowledge is that systems designed to support knowledge in organizations may not appear radically different from other forms of information systems, but will be geared toward enabling users to assign meaning to information and to capture some of their knowledge in information and/or data.

KNOWLEDGE VALUE LEVEL

It is not difficult to agree with this reasoning. In fact, our hierarchy from data via information to knowledge is not so much a road or direction, as it is a way of suggesting resource value levels. Knowledge is a more valuable resource to the organization than information, and information is a more valuable resource than data. This is illustrated in Figure 8.1. The figure illustrates that it is less the knowledge existing at any given time per se than the organization's ability effectively to apply the existing knowledge to develop new knowledge and to take action that forms the basis for achieving long-term competitive advantage from knowledge-based assets.

According to Grover and Davenport (2001), knowledge processes lie somewhere between information and the organization's source of revenue, its products and services. This process can be generically represented in three sub-processes: knowledge generation, knowledge codification and knowledge transfer/realization. Knowledge generation includes all processes involved in the acquisition and development of knowledge. Knowledge codification involves the conversion of knowledge into accessible and applicable formats. Knowledge transfer includes the movement of knowledge from its point of generation or codified form to the point of use.

One of the reasons that knowledge is such a difficult concept is because this process is recursive, expanding and often discontinuous. According to Grover and Davenport (2001), many cycles of generation, codification and transfer are concurrently occurring in businesses. These cycles feed on each other. Knowledge interacts with information to increase the state space

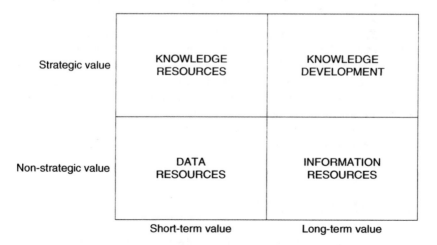

Figure 8.1   Value levels of resources in the organization

of possibilities and provide new information, which can then facilitate generation of new knowledge. The knowledge process acts on information to create new information that allows for greater possibilities to fulfil old or possibly new organizational needs. This process is often discontinuous, where new needs and their fulfilment mechanism could be created.

In our resource-based perspective of knowledge, data are raw numbers and facts, information is processed data, and knowledge is information combined with human thoughts. Knowledge is the result of cognitive processing triggered by the inflow of new stimuli. Information is converted to knowledge once it is processed in the mind of individuals, and the knowledge becomes information once it is articulated and presented to others. A significant implication of this view of knowledge is that for individuals to arrive at the same understanding of information, they must share the same knowledge framework.

In Figure 8.1, we can imagine that data are assigned meaning and become information, that information is understood and interpreted by individuals and becomes knowledge, and that knowledge is applied and develops into new knowledge. We can also imagine the opposite route. Knowledge develops in the minds of individuals. This knowledge development causes an increase in knowledge resources. When the new knowledge is articulated, verbalized and structured, it becomes information and causes an increase in information resources. When information is assigned a fixed representation and standard interpretation, it becomes data and causes an increase in data resources.

There are alternatives to our perspective of knowledge as a resource in the organization. Alavi and Leidner (2001) list the following alternatives: knowledge is a state of mind, knowledge is an object to be stored, knowledge is a process of applying expertise, knowledge is a condition of access to information, and knowledge is the potential to influence action.

This book applies the resource-based theory of the organization, where the knowledge-based perspective identifies the primary role of the organization as integrating the specialist knowledge resident in individuals into goods and services. The task of management is to establish the coordination necessary for this knowledge integration. The knowledge-based perspective serves as a platform for a view of the organization as a dynamic system of knowledge production and application.

IDENTIFICATION OF KNOWLEDGE NEEDS

To classify knowledge as a resource, there has to be a need for that knowledge. Hence, identification of knowledge needs in an organization

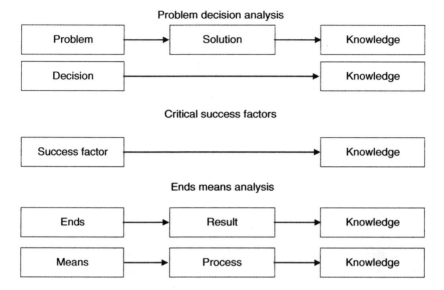

Figure 8.2   Methods to identify knowledge needs

is important. Three supplementary methods exist to identify needs for knowledge, as illustrated in Figure 8.2:

- *Problem decision analysis.* This method aims at identifying and specifying problems that knowledge workers have, solutions they can find, decisions they have to make, and what knowledge they need to solve problems and make decisions. For a lawyer, the problem can be an insurance claim by a client, the decision can be how to approach the insurance company, and the knowledge need can be outcomes of similar cases handled by the law firm.
- *Critical success factors.* This method aims at identifying and specifying what factors cause success. Success can be at firm level, individual level or individual case level. For a lawyer, critical success factors at the individual case level can be quality of legal advice and service level of advice delivery. Critical knowledge in this case includes legal knowledge as well as procedural knowledge.
- *Ends means analysis.* This method aims at identifying and specifying external demands and expectations to goods and services from the firm. For a lawyer, the client expectation might be that she or he wins the case. The end is winning the case. Knowledge needs associated with winning a case include legal, procedural and analytical knowledge of successful cases in the past. The means for winning a case

might be access to resources of various kinds, such as client documents and client funds. Knowledge needs associated with means include historical records and analysis of legal client practice.

KNOWLEDGE CATEGORIES

Many researchers have tried to define categories and dimensions of knowledge. A common distinction is made between explicit and tacit knowledge. *Explicit knowledge* can be expressed in words and numbers and shared in the form of data, scientific formulae, specifications, manuals and the like. This kind of knowledge can be readily transmitted between individuals both formally and systematically. *Tacit knowledge* is on the other hand highly personal and hard to formalize, making it difficult to communicate or share with others. Subjective insights, intuitions and hunches fall into this category of knowledge. Tacit knowledge is deeply rooted in an individual's actions and experience as well as in the ideals, values or emotions he or she embraces. Tacit knowledge is embedded in the human brain and cannot be expressed easily while explicit knowledge can be easily codified. Both types of knowledge are important but Western firms have focused largely on managing explicit knowledge (Grover and Davenport, 2001).

Tacitness may be considered as a variable, with the degree of tacitness being a function of the extent to which the knowledge is or can be codified and abstracted. Knowledge may dynamically shift between tacit and explicit over time, although some knowledge always will remain tacit. Nonaka et al. (2000) have suggested that knowledge creation is a spiralling process of interactions between explicit and tacit knowledge. This spiralling process consists of socialization, externalization, combination and internalization, as we will see later in this chapter.

The concept of tacit knowledge corresponds closely to the concept of knowledge with a low level of codification. Codification is the degree to which knowledge is fully documented or expressed in writing at the time of transfer between two persons. The complexity of knowledge increases with lower levels of codification. A similar distinction which scholars frequently make is between practical, experience-based knowledge and the theoretical knowledge derived from reflection and abstraction from that experience.

A distinction is sometimes made between codification and personalization. This distinction is related to the tacit versus explicit concept. It involves an organization's approach to knowledge transfer. Companies using codification approaches rely primarily on repositories of explicit knowledge. Personalization approaches imply that the primary mode of knowledge transfer is direct interaction among people. Both are necessary in most organizations, but an increased focus on one approach or the other at any given time within a specific organization may be appropriate (Grover and Davenport, 2001).

Explicit knowledge is sometimes called articulable knowledge (Hitt et al., 2001). Articulable knowledge can be codified and thus can be written and easily transferred. Tacit knowledge is not articulable and therefore cannot be easily transferred. Tacit knowledge is often embedded in uncodified routines and in a firm's social context. More specifically, it is partially embedded in individual skills and partially embedded in collaborative working relationships within the firm. Tacit knowledge is integral to professional skills. As a result, tacit knowledge is often unique, difficult to imitate and uncertain. It has a higher probability of creating strategic value than articulable knowledge.

Distinctions can be made between core, advanced and innovative knowledge. These knowledge categories indicate different levels of knowledge sophistication. Core knowledge is that minimum scope and level of knowledge required for daily operations, while advanced knowledge enables a firm to be competitively viable, and innovative knowledge is the knowledge that enables the firm to lead its industry and competitors:

- *Core knowledge* is the basic knowledge required to stay in business. This is the type of knowledge that can create efficiency barriers for entry of new companies, as new competitors are not up to speed in basic business processes. Since core knowledge is present at all existing competitors, the firm must have this knowledge even though it will provide the firm with no advantage that distinguishes it from its competitors. Core knowledge is that minimum scope and level of knowledge required just to play the game. Having that level of knowledge and capability will not assure the long-term competitive viability of the firm, but does present a basic industry knowledge barrier to entry. Core knowledge tends to be commonly held by members of an industry and therefore provides little advantage other than over nonmembers (Zack, 1999).

  In a law firm, examples of core knowledge include knowledge of the law, knowledge of the courts, knowledge of clients and knowledge of procedures. For a student in a business school, core knowledge includes knowledge of what subjects to study this term and where the lectures take place.

  According to Tiwana (2002), core knowledge is the basic level of knowledge required just to play the game. This is the type of knowledge that creates a barrier for entry of new companies. Since this level of knowledge is expected of all competitors, you must have it even though it will provide your company with no advantage that distinguishes it from its competitors. Let's take two examples: one from the consumer electronics (hard product) business and one from Internet programming (soft product). To enter the modem manufacturing market, a new company must have extensive knowledge of these aspects: a suitable circuit design, all electronic parts that go into a modem, fabricating surface mount (SMD) chip boards, how to write operating system drivers for modems, and familiarity with computer telephony standards. Similarly, a company developing websites for, say, florists, needs server-hosting capabilities, Internet programming skills, graphic design skills, clearly identified target markets and necessary software. In either case, just about any competitor in those businesses is assumed to have this knowledge in order to compete in their respective markets; such essential knowledge therefore provides no advantage over other market players.

- *Advanced knowledge* is what makes the firm competitively visible and active. Such knowledge allows the firm to differentiate its products and services from that of a competitor through the application of superior knowledge in certain areas. Such knowledge allows the firm to compete head on with its competitors in the same market and for the same set of customers. Advanced knowledge enables a firm to be competitively viable. The firm may have generally the same level, scope or quality of knowledge as its competitors although the specific knowledge content will often vary among competitors, enabling knowledge differentiation. Firms may choose to compete on knowledge head on in the same strategic position, hoping to know more than a competitor. Alternatively, they may choose to compete for that position by differentiating their knowledge (Zack, 1999).

In a law firm, examples of advanced knowledge include knowledge of law applications, knowledge of important court rulings and knowledge of successful procedural case handling. For a student in a business school, advanced knowledge includes knowledge of important articles and books which are compulsory literature in subjects that term.

According to Tiwana (2002), advanced knowledge is what makes your company competitively viable. Such knowledge allows your company to differentiate its product from that of a competitor through the application of superior knowledge in certain areas. In the case of a company trying to compete in modem manufacturing markets, superior or user-friendly software or an additional capability in modems (such as warning online users of incoming telephone calls) represents such knowledge. In case of the website development firm, such knowledge might be about international flower markets and collaborative relationships in Dutch flower auctions that the company can use to improve websites delivered to its customers.

- *Innovative knowledge* allows a firm to lead its entire industry to an extent that clearly differentiates it from competition. Such knowledge allows a firm to change the rules of the game by introducing new business practices. Such knowledge enables a firm to expand its market share by winning new customers and by increasing service levels to existing customers. Innovative knowledge enables an enterprise to reach and stay at the leading edge in its industry. Innovative knowledge often enables a firm to change the rules of the game itself (Zack, 1999).

In a law firm, examples of innovative knowledge include knowledge of standardizing repetitive legal cases, knowledge of successful settlements and knowledge of modern information technology to track and store vast amounts of information from various sources. For a student in business school, innovative knowledge includes knowledge of important topics within subjects, links between subjects, typical exam questions and knowledge of business cases where theory can be applied.

According to Tiwana (2002), innovative knowledge allows a company to lead its entire industry to an extent that clearly differentiates it from competition. Innovative knowledge allows a company to change the rules of the game. Patented technology is an applicable example of changing the rules. Innovative knowledge cannot always be protected by patents, as the lawsuit between Microsoft and Apple in the 1980s should serve to remind us. Apple sued Microsoft for copying the look and feel of its graphical user interface (GUI). The Supreme Court ruled that things like look and feel cannot be patented; they can only be copyrighted. Microsoft won the case, since it copied the look and feel but used entirely different code to create it in the first place.

Many more categories and dimensions of knowledge have been suggested by researchers. The problem with most of these classifications is that they do not seem to satisfy three important criteria for classification. The first requirement is that a classification should always be complete; there should be no category missing. The second requirement is that each category should be different from all other categories; that is, there should be no overlap between categories. The final requirement is that each category should be at the same level; there should be no category including another category. Consider the following categories suggested by researchers: formal knowledge, instrumental knowledge, informal knowledge, tacit knowledge, meta knowledge and context-independent knowledge. These categories seem to violate some of the classification rules. For example, there seems to be an overlap between informal knowledge and tacit knowledge. Maybe Long and Fahey's (2000) classification into human knowledge, social knowledge and structured knowledge satisfies our requirements:

- *Human knowledge.* This constitutes the know-what, know-how and know-why of individuals. Human knowledge is manifested in individual skills (e.g. how to interview law firm clients) or expertise (e.g. why this case is similar to a previous case). Individual knowledge usually combines explicit and tacit knowledge. This type of knowledge may be located in the body, such as knowing how to touch type on a PC or how to ride a bicycle. This type of knowledge may be cognitive; that is, largely conceptual and abstract.
- *Social knowledge.* This kind of knowledge exists only in relationships between individuals or within groups. For example, high-performing teams of tax lawyers share certain collective knowledge that is more than the sum of the individual knowledge of the team's members. Social or collective knowledge is mainly tacit knowledge, shared by team members, and develops only as a result of team members working together. Its presence is reflected by an ability to collaborate effectively.
- *Structured knowledge.* This is embedded in an organization's systems, processes, tools, routines and practices. Knowledge in this form is explicit and often rule based. A key distinction between structured knowledge and the first two types of knowledge is that structured knowledge is assumed to exist independently of individual knowers. It is, instead, an organizational resource. However, to be complete, this knowledge has to be in the heads of individuals.

Two dimensions have been introduced to classify knowledge. The first dimension is concerned with whether an individual knows. The second dimension is concerned with whether an individual knows whether he or she knows. This is illustrated in Figure 8.3. I can either have the knowledge (I do know) or not have the knowledge (I don't know). I can either be aware of it (I know it) or not be aware of it (I don't know it).

Some researchers have argued that the real tacit knowledge is found in the upper right quadrant. In this dimension, I do know, but I don't know that I know. Tacit knowledge in this sense is also called hidden knowledge or non-accessible knowledge. In this book, we do not use this extremely

	I know it	I don't know it
I do know	I know that I know	I don't know that I know
I don't know	I know that I don't know	I don't know that I don't know

Figure 8.3   Dimensions of individual knowledge

limited definition of tacit knowledge. We define tacit knowledge as personal and difficult, but not impossible, to communicate.

Classification of knowledge into categories and dimensions may depend on industry. For example, there are likely to be different knowledge categories in a bank compared with a law firm. At the same time, there will be certain generic knowledge categories such as market intelligence and technology understanding in most companies independently of industry. When classifying knowledge in a firm, it is important to do the analysis without the organization chart. If you classify knowledge into technology knowledge, production knowledge, marketing knowledge and financial knowledge, it may be because the firm according to the organization chart consists of a development department, production department, marketing department and financial department. It might be more useful to introduce new knowledge categories such as product knowledge, which includes knowledge of development, production, marketing and finance. By identifying cross-sectional knowledge categories and dimensions, solutions for improved knowledge flows in the organization will emerge.

A law firm is a good example. A law firm is organized according to legal disciplines. Some lawyers work in the tax department while others work in the department for mergers and acquisitions. The types of knowledge involved in the practise of law can be categorized as administrative, declarative, procedural and analytical knowledge (Edwards and Mahling, 1997):

- *Administrative knowledge* includes all the nuts and bolts information about firm operations, such as hourly billing rates for lawyers, client names and matters, staff payroll data and client invoice data.
- *Declarative knowledge* is knowledge of the law, the legal principles contained in statutes, court opinions and other sources of primary legal authority; law students spend most of their time at law school acquiring this kind of knowledge.
- *Procedural knowledge* involves knowledge of the mechanisms of complying with the law's requirements in a particular situation: how documents are used to transfer an asset from company A to company B, or which forms must be filed where to create a new corporation. Declarative knowledge is sometimes labelled know-that and know-what while procedural knowledge is labelled know-how.
- *Analytical knowledge* pertains to the conclusions reached about the course of action a particular client should follow in a particular situation. Analytical knowledge results, in essence, from analysing declarative knowledge (i.e. substantive law principles) as it applies to a particular fact setting.

Classification of knowledge into categories and dimensions has important limitations. For example, the classification into explicit and tacit knowledge may create static views of knowledge. However, knowledge development and sharing are dynamic processes, and these dynamic processes cause tacit knowledge to become explicit and explicit knowledge to become tacit over time. Tacit and explicit knowledge depend on each other, and they influence each other. In this perspective, Alavi and Leidner (2001) stress that arguing whether tacit or explicit knowledge is the more valuable may not be important at all. The two knowledge categories are not dichotomous states of knowledge but mutually dependent and reinforcing qualities of knowledge: tacit knowledge forms the background necessary for assigning the structure to develop and interpret explicit knowledge.

According to Alavi and Leidner (2001), the linkage of tacit and explicit knowledge suggests that only individuals with a requisite level of shared knowledge are able to exchange knowledge. They suggest the existence of a shared knowledge space that is required in order for individual A to understand individual B's knowledge. The knowledge space is the underlying overlap in knowledge base of A and B. This overlap is typically tacit knowledge. It may be argued that the greater the shared knowledge space, the less the context needed for individuals to share knowledge within the group and, hence, the higher the value of explicit knowledge. For example, in a law firm lawyers in the maritime law department may have a large knowledge space so that even a very limited piece of explicit knowledge can be of great value to them. Alavi and Leidner (2001: 112) discuss knowledge space in the following way:

> Whether tacit or explicit knowledge is the more valuable may indeed miss the point. The two are not dichotomous states of knowledge, but mutually dependent and reinforcing qualities of knowledge: tacit knowledge forms the background necessary for assigning the structure to develop and interpret explicit knowledge. The inextricable linkage of tacit and explicit knowledge suggests that only individuals with a requisite level of shared knowledge can truly exchange knowledge: if tacit knowledge is necessary to the understanding of explicit knowledge, then in order for Individual B to understand Individual A's knowledge, there must be some overlap in their underlying knowledge bases (a shared knowledge space). However, it is precisely in applying technology to increase 'weak ties' in organizations, and thereby increase the breadth of knowledge sharing, that IT holds promise. Yet, absent a shared knowledge space, the real impact of IT on knowledge exchange is questionable. This is a paradox that IT researchers have somewhat eschewed, and that organizational researchers have used to question the application of IT to knowledge management. To add to the paradox, the very essence of the knowledge management challenge is to amalgamate knowledge across groups for which IT can play a major role. What is most at issue is the amount of contextual information necessary for one person or group's knowledge to be readily understood by another.
>
> It may be argued that the greater the shared knowledge space, the less the context needed for individuals to share knowledge within the group and, hence, the higher the value of explicit knowledge and the greater the value of IT applied to knowledge management. On the other hand, the smaller the existing shared knowledge space in a group, the greater the need for contextual information, the less relevant will be explicit knowledge, and hence the less applicable will be IT to knowledge management.

Some researchers are interested in the total knowledge within a company while others are interested in individual knowledge. Dixon (2000) was interested in the knowledge that knowledge workers develop together in the organization. Employees gain this knowledge from doing the organization's tasks. This knowledge is called common knowledge to differentiate it from book knowledge or lists of regulations or databases of customer information. Some examples of common knowledge are what medical doctors in a hospital have learned about how to carry out certain kinds of surgery, what an organization has learned about how to introduce a new drug into the diabetes market, how to reduce cost on consulting projects, and how to control the amount of analysis in maritime law cases. These examples all include the how-to rather than the know-what of school learning. Moreover, it is know-how that is unique to a specific company. In the law firm example, procedural knowledge was classified as know-how.

CRIME KNOWLEDGE

Knowledge is a resource in organized crime. This chapter has made a contribution to existing theory. Using a resource-based theory approach, we have attempted to develop new means of conceptualizing organized crime. It is timely in as much as this is a growing area of concern for researchers active in entrepreneurship. However, the developments made in this book need to be further explored in future research to make a significant contribution. As an early exploration into the possible fit between resource-based theories of the firm and criminal entrepreneurship, the book does suggest some linkages that might profitably be researched.

The essence of the resource-based theory of the enterprise lies in its emphasis on the internal resources available to the enterprise, rather than on the external opportunities and threats dictated by industry conditions. Enterprises are considered to be highly heterogeneous, and the bundles of resources available to each enterprise are different. This is both because enterprises have different initial resource endowments and because managerial decisions affect resource accumulation and the direction of enterprise growth as well as resource utilization.

Organized criminals apply their criminal entrepreneurship in resource allocation decisions. The business enterprise model of organized crime focuses on how economic considerations, rather than hierarchical or ethnic considerations, lie at the base of the formation and success of organized crime groups. Regardless of ethnicity or hierarchy, the enterprise model labels economic concerns as the primary cause of organized criminal behaviour. A study of illicit drug sales in the southwest USA found that the drug markets consisted of small organizations rather than massive, centralized bureaucracies, that were competitive rather than monopolistic in nature. A study of bookmaking, loan sharking and numbers gambling in New York City found them not monopolies in the classic sense or subject to control by some external organization (Albanese, 2004). Instead, economic forces arising from the illegality of the product tended to fragment the market, making it difficult to control or centralize these illegal activities on a large scale.

When studying robberies of cash-in-transit vans, Gill (2001) found that criminal entrepreneurs quickly need to acquire knowledge and develop expertise, since they have a lot to lose in terms of freedom and injuries. A knowledge of people and how to relate to them, the ability to lead, the ability to establish a presence, the skill to stimulate confidence in and from others, being able to work alone as well as part of a team and generally being professional are critical to the success of cash-in-transit robbers.

Illegal entrepreneurship knowledge might also be applied to legal business development. In a study by Aidis and Praag (2004), illegal entrepreneurship experience was found to be associated with business motivation. This is in line with human capital theory that maintains that knowledge provides individuals with increases in their cognitive abilities, leading to more productive and efficient potential activity.

Aidis and Praag (2004) found that the skills developed through illegal business activities under socialist systems in Eastern Europe were not acquired with the expectation that they would ultimately be useful in a completely different setting of transition to market economy. Nevertheless, such prior experience in the black or grey market provides valuable human capital for entrepreneurs in a market-oriented setting, thereby changing the perception of the 'unofficial' or 'black' economy. Illegal entrepreneurship experience within centrally planned economies is a unique and historical phenomenon.

THE CASE OF TERRORIST NETWORKS

This case is based on the research article 'Similarities between terrorist networks in antiquity and present-day cyberterrorist networks' by Matusitz (2008).

While terrorism is no typical illegal business, since it is lacking profit as the main motivation, it still needs to finance its criminal activities. A classic terrorist organization was the Zealots (Matusitz, 2008: 185):

> The Zealots were a Jewish extremist group of the first century A.D. involved in fierce terrorist acts during the Roman Empire; they not only refused that Jews pay taxes to Rome; they also aimed to defeat the authority of the Roman emperor and overthrow his government. The Zealots held out against Rome for 6 years before choosing mass suicide over surrender in Masada in 73 A.D., when the second Temple was burned down and the Jewish state ceased to exist. They were convinced that political change could come only through 'propaganda of the deed'. Their violence and fanaticism were reflected in their willingness to use any weapon to strike Roman soldiers (who had by military force occupied the Holy Land and the City of David), Jewish 'collaborators' who favored these Romans (i.e., the Pharisees), and Jewish moderates in Palestine who had succumbed to Hellenistic influences. This is why they adopted terrorism as their main form of struggle. Their most basic motive was that all means were justified to attain political and religious liberation. The Zealots encouraged citizens to take a dagger and become involved in the act of committing murders, on their own, against the Romans. Some terrorist acts were also executed by lonely individuals such as Herostrat, the citizen of Ephesus, who burned the local temple.

Today, one of the most well-known terrorist organizations is Al Qaeda, which was founded by Usama bin Laden. While the Zealots were fighting the Roman empire, Al Qaeda is fighting US world dominance.

In conjunction with several other Islamic militant leaders, bin Laden issued two fatwa – in 1996 and then again in 1998 – that Muslims should force the United States and its allies to withdraw their military forces from the Arabian peninsula by attacking American military and civilian targets.

THE CASE OF INTERVIEWING FINNISH CRIMINAL ENTREPRENEURS

This case is based on the research article 'Depth-interviewing Finnish professional criminals' by Junninen (2008).

The transnational types of crimes that Finns typically commit include smuggling of goods such as spirits, tobacco and drugs, trafficking in prostitutes and organizing their work, handling stolen goods and money laundering. The persons selected by Junninen (2008) for interviewing were still committing or had recently committed these types of crimes.

When selecting study method, Junninen (2008) considered what would be the best way of obtaining reliable information on research questions: how, why and in which areas of crime have Finnish professional criminals been organized in the 1990s, and what are the participants like. Qualitative thematic interviews were chosen to be able to measure attitudes, values, family relations and so on within their context. Such interviews can produce in-depth information about the group's level of organization and the professionalism of the participants.

The data required for identifying suitable informants were collected from both public and non-public sources. Public sources included TV, radio, newspapers, magazines, books and justice documents, and non-public sources included police, customs, border guards and tax authority data files. Junninen (2008: 62) selected 21 interviewees based on the following criteria:

1) Were most active in committing selected crimes in the 1990s,
2) Represented equally all selected crime areas,
3) Represented equally the different Finnish professional criminal groups active in the studied crime areas,
4) A larger number of acceptable persons were selected in order to have a reserve of informants in case somebody would eventually become unavailable (refusal, death or other reason).

Two of the selected persons in Junninen's (2008) reserve were killed in the course of the 3.5 months' fieldwork. All interviewees were male. Ten of them were serving prison sentences in Finland. Eleven were free and living mainly in Finland, with some staying part of the year abroad. Only two of the contacted persons refused an interview.

Finding each interviewee was not difficult for Junninen. Persons in prison had time to speak. Persons outside sometimes rescheduled interviews due to their business matters. Interviews were conducted in prison cells and visiting areas, and in public coffee places or restaurants. Topics in each interview included group structure, crimes, personal feelings, external threats to the group, the group's relationships to other Finnish groups, the group's international relationships and personal details.

In the thematic interview framework chosen by Junninen (2008), the informant is the main character and the one who wants to tell the interviewer what he knows. When using thematic interviews, the interviewer does not have exactly formulated questions, but rather a list of themes to be discussed. Each theme is introduced in a general way in the interview. During the conversation, the interview can become as in-depth as the research question requires and the informant is willing to allow.

Junninen's (2008) analysis of research material included 50 hours of recorded interviews. The tapes were transcribed to 600 pages of text. Text analysis was applied to find personal information and relevant crimes linked to each informant from the large quantity of material. Text analysis in terms of content analysis can be applied to texts that have been gathered in different ways.

THE CASE OF INTERVIEWING NORWEGIAN ALCOHOL SMUGGLERS

This case is based on the research article 'Never a final design: interviewing Norwegian alcohol smugglers' by Johansen (2008).

A typology of respondents was encountered by Johansen (2008) in interview-based research on the illegal alcohol market in Norway. Six distinct types were identified:

- The *social talker* is a story teller who likes to talk. A fascinating story is appreciated, both when they socialize with each other and when they meet police detectives who they are relating to during police investigations. The social talker tells anecdotes, where smuggling for them is a kind of lifestyle, with social talking as an important and pleasant element.
- The *expert witness* takes an analytical approach, with perspectives on market mechanisms, supply and demand, product quality and networking. Critical comments are made and gossip about other

smugglers is communicated as such. The way of talking is similar to that of lawyers, journalists and professors. The expert witness has analytical talent and substantial information about what is going on in the smuggling business.

- The *flasher* has a big ego and likes to talk much more than to listen. Flashers are easily contacted but they are very subjective in their stories, never relating the successes of their competitors. Some flashers have a reluctant relationship to the truth to improve their own image. Even before court it happens that a flasher admits a spectacular crime that the criminal never committed. Reputation means more than the court sentence in terms of months or years in prison.
- The *manipulator* is determined to cover his back by controlling information. The manipulator is lying to confuse and to protect himself from arrest, robbers and competitors. He may claim that he is taking a break from crime, while in reality being quite active. He may claim that he never met 'Mr. Hansen', although the two have been in business together for many years.
- The *paranoid* has gone almost mad after stressful years on the run or in prison or followed by competitors. He sees enemies everywhere. The paranoid is unwilling to talk, and he is quite unreliable in terms of appointments for interviews. He typically seldom shows up, even if the researcher got in contact with him through one of his closest associates.
- The *politician* defends his smuggling business by arguing that the tax on alcohol is extremely high and unfair. This type is not a typical smuggler.

Social talkers and expert witnesses were the most common among Johansen's (2008) informants, followed by flashers, who sometimes also have a touch of social talker.

Conclusion

Most of the entrepreneurship literature seems to engage in a positive enthusiasm about the role of the entrepreneur. This book has demonstrated the role of the entrepreneur in criminal business. Criminal entrepreneurship can develop in legal organisations, as illustrated by stages of financial crime by business organisations as well as stages of organised crime by business organisations. Criminal entrepreneurs make careers which may start in gangs of friends at one extreme or in established mafia organisations at the other extreme.

This book has illustrated how so many issues for entrepreneurs and entrepreneurship are similar in legal and illegal business. Entrepreneurial judgment in decision making, for example, is just as important in both situations. Leadership roles may vary and so may project management, but we can still apply the same kind of frameworks to understand entrepreneurship.

Also, value configurations in terms of value chain, value shop and value network require different attention to efficiency, effectiveness and knowledge management. In the value shop, for example, problems of money laundering or corruption are solved by applying knowledge. An entrepreneur has to behave differently depending on the value configuration he or she is to establish.

Our understanding of entrepreneurship and organised crime through entrepreneurs in illegal business should be interesting to everyone who is studying entrepreneurship. In addition, law enforcement all over the world should be interested in gaining new insights into organised crime and criminal organisations that are initiated and managed by entrepreneurs. This book has made a significant contribution in that respect.

Much of the research into entrepreneurship and organised crime in terms of entrepreneurs in illegal business has, for obvious reasons, avoided interviewing members of the criminal community. Recently, some exceptions have emerged. For example, Rawlinson (2008) interviewed organised criminals in Russia. One of the criminals she interviewed was Oleg. Oleg and his commercial partners ran the prostitution ring in one of St Petersburg's major hotels and at one point a favourite with foreign businessmen. They paid protection money to one of the city's large criminal groups.

Rawlinson (2008: 16) describes her approach to interviewing Oleg:

I made initial contact by becoming a regular feature in one of the bars in the hotel. After a while Oleg and his friend began to regard me as a curiosity rather than a threat. The three of us engaged in conversation one evening, and when Oleg realised I was there to study rather than inform, he opened the doors to his activities and agreed to be interviewed. The openness of our exchange, under the gaze of the bar staff, the clients, including foreign businessmen, and those who ran the protection racket in the hotel, pointed out by Oleg, gave a guarantee of safety. I agreed to meet Oleg the next week in his 'office' in the hotel.

Oleg's two-roomed office comprised a small lounge with an even smaller bedroom in which his 'girls' worked. I refused to be cajoled into watching them with their punters, and assured Oleg that I trusted they were, as he kept insisting, the best in the city. Of the girls I spoke to alone, none of them complained about exploitation by their pimps. Nonetheless, their situation, as a Western woman, made me ill at ease. When, prior to the interview Oleg showed me the 'working bedroom' with its slightly sweaty aroma, it was difficult not to feel hostile towards my prospective respondent.

Oleg originally agreed to be taped, but once Rawlinson (2008) switched on the recorder, he became hesitant and uncertain. A culture in Russia pervades that interviewing can be synonymous with interrogation. Oleg's fear was directed at the security services that arbitrarily pick up individuals and take away their passports. Oleg's awkwardness, anger and fear, expressed through body language, told a different story from the verbal arrogance which preceded the interview. In the interview, Oleg justified his criminal activities by describing society as a system riddled with corruption, violence and exploitation.

Siegel (2008a) argues that open interviews and unplanned conversations with criminals are an important part of ethnographic research in criminology. She conducted anthropological fieldwork interviews among criminal entrepreneurs in Russia. Anthropological fieldwork interviews take place in a social situation in which researcher and informant communicate in an informal context, usually in the natural setting of the informant. Such interviews are different from structured and semi-structured interviews applied in management research.

The trust of Siegel's (2008a: 26) informants was vital in building relationships and gathering valuable information:

> While my efforts to get access and to build trust appeared to be going along smoothly, and important contacts were established, expectations were created on the side of the respondents. The main question to arise at this phase was: why do people talk? The answer was that they were mostly driven by self-interest. When they provided me with important information, these respondents expected something in return, for example revenge. They wanted to publish the 'truth' about their business rivals, allegedly involved in illegal activities or connected to criminal organizations. In these cases, when their purpose became clear to me, I had to be especially careful with my facts, and check them even more thoroughly

than in other cases, in order not to ruin the reputation of persons involved and to avoid becoming a tool in the hands of informants with an agenda.

Fieldwork among criminal entrepreneurs is considered dangerous by many researchers. However, Siegel (2008a) never saw her informants as dangerous criminals. By presenting and representing the role of researcher with a scientific and neutral attitude, criminals become a source of important information about criminal entrepreneurship.

Antonopoulos (2008) interviewed three retired Kurdish cigarette smugglers in a town in the North East of England. These individual entrepreneurs were one pusher and two street-sellers. The interviews provided information about a cigarette-smuggling network operating in Greece in 2002 and 2003. Greece is a source, transit and destination country in which prices of cigarettes are relatively low. Greece is the top smoking country worldwide in terms of per capita cigarette consumption.

The network in which the three Kurds were involved was heterogeneous as it involved Greeks, Russians, Ukrainians, Armenians, Georgians, Kurds, Bulgarians, Albanians and Romanians. There were several roles in the network (Antonopoulos, 2008: 71):

- *Wholesaler*. The wholesaler has a 'managerial' position in the whole business.
- *Procurer*. The procurer buys large quantities of cigarettes from Greek tobacco companies with the intention to export and sell them in Bulgaria.
- *Pusher*. The pusher is responsible for introducing the smuggled cigarettes to the market via street-sellers.
- *Street-seller*. This individual is often a woman from the former Soviet Union.
- *Scouter*. This person is basically in-and-around the street-selling areas to warn street-sellers about the presence of the police in the area.
- *House guard*. The house guard has the responsibility of guarding the house, rooms, etc. at the central business district and transitional zone in Athens that are used as storing places for boxes of cigarettes before they are distributed to the street-sellers or sold to some customers directly.
- *Shop owner*. The legitimate shop owner owns a shop in or around the street-selling area and 'operates' as a quick 'refuelling' point for street-sellers and/or a place of quickly 'hiding' the smuggled cigarettes when police are very close to the street-selling point.
- *Thief*. This is a person who steals cigarettes destined for the legal cigarette market and who forwards them to pushers.
- *Driver*. A car driver has the responsibility of transporting quantities of cigarettes into Greece.
- *Protector*. This is an individual who engages in the protection of the interests of the cigarette smuggling business from Albanian and Russian extortion gangs.
- *Corrupt official*. A corrupt public official might be customs officers, police officers and coast guards, who either allow the importation of smuggled

cigarettes in the country or 'turn a blind eye' to storing places for large quantities of smuggled cigarettes.

According to Antonopoulos (2008), there are basically three ways of obtaining cigarettes for the black market: either stealing cigarettes from legal warehouses, importation of smuggled cigarettes from Ukraine and Russia by ship, or importation of smuggled cigarettes from Bulgaria by truck.

This book has been concerned with entrepreneurship and organised crime, focusing on entrepreneurs in illegal business. Throughout the text, comparisons have been made between legal and illegal entrepreneurs. Many similarities have been proposed and confirmed. Also, differences have been exploited. A final difference, which is sometimes suggested, is related to time perspective. It is suggested that entrepreneurs who want to make quick and easy money tend to choose the criminal route, while more patient and thorough entrepreneurs choose the legal route. While an intriguing idea, there is to our knowledge no empirical study of this hypothesis. The argument is that it takes more time and effort to become rich along the legal path than the illegal path.

However, the opposite might be argued. If you were to travel to Amsterdam to buy some cocaine and then sell it in your home town, you may run into all sorts of problems. First, the dealers in Amsterdam, typically supervised by Hells Angels Holland, do not know you and will be suspicious. Probably, they will not deal with you at all. To be able to buy narcotics from wholesalers in Amsterdam, you need to have established yourself within a criminal network. That takes time. When you finally become approved as a customer, you buy your stuff and travel home. If not before, on the streets in your home town you run into more trouble. An ethnic group such as Somalians or Moroccans may be in charge of cocaine distribution. They certainly do not like your competition. They will not compete with you on price. They will use other competitive weapons against you, such as threats and violence. It will take a long time for you to find yourself a position within the distribution chain in your local market. In addition to these problems, other problems such as financing your operations and recruiting associates will also take time. Hence, it is not obvious on a general basis that illegal entrepreneurs can make money faster than legal entrepreneurs.

The criminal entrepreneur has certainly emerged on the world scene. The criminal entrepreneur is often a transnational opportunist, an individual who operates globally and with complete disregard not only for national laws, but also for national borders and boundaries. Criminals today find entrepreneurial opportunities in a global economy. Criminal entrepreneurs see cross-border operations as beneficial in terms of both increased profits and as an aid to minimize their risk of detection, arrest and prosecution by law enforcement authorities on either side of a border.

This book has made a contribution to entrepreneurship research by presenting and discussing criminal entrepreneurship – the 'bad' kind of entrepreneurship in an economy. According to Davidsson (2008), there is progress in entrepreneurship research, and there is conceptual development that attracts attention such as the concept of criminal entrepreneur introduced in this book. While entrepreneurship is a societal phenomenon, it might be carried out in practice both positively and negatively for society.

References

Abadinsky, H. (2007). *Organised Crime*, Eighth Edition, Thomson Wadsworth, Belmont, CA.

Abramova, I. (2007). The funding of traditional organised crime in Russia, *Economic Affairs*, March, 18–21.

Aidis, R. and Van Praag, M. (2004). *Illegal Entrepreneurship Experience*, Tinbergen Institute Discussion paper TI 2004–105/3, Erasmus University, The Netherlands.

Albanese, J.S. (2004). *Organised Crime in our Times*, Fourth Edition, LexisNexis, Anderson Publishing, Cincinnati, OH.

Alavi, M. and Leidner, D.E. (2001). Knowledge management and knowledge management systems: Conceptual foundations and research issues, *MIS Quarterly*, 25 (1), 107–36.

Allum, F. (2007). Doing It for Themselves or Standing in for Their Men? Women in the Neapolitan Camorra (1950–2003). In: Fiandaca, G. (ed.), *Women and the Mafia – Female Roles in Organised Crime Structures*, Studies of Organised Crime, Springer, New York, pp. 9–18.

Alvarez, S.A. and Barney, J.B. (2007). The entrepreneurial theory of the firm, *Journal of Management Studies*, 44 (7), 1058–63.

Amoruso, D. (2007a). Terrence 'Terry' Adams, *Gangsters Inc.*, posted 5 April, http://gangstersinc.tripod.com/TerryAdams.html.

Amoruso, D. (2007b). Curtis 'Cocky' Warren, *Gangsters Inc.*, posted 16 August, http://gangstersinc.tripod.com/CurtisWarren.html.

Amoruso, D. (2007c). Tam 'The Licensee' McGraw, *Gangsters Inc.*, posted 15 August 2007, http://gangstersinc.tripod.com/McGraw.html.

Andersen, J.A. (2002). Organisational design: Two lessons to learn before reorganising, *International Journal of Organisation Theory and Behaviour*, 5 (3/4), 343–58.

Anderson, A. (1995). Organised crime, mafia and governments. In: Fiorentini, G. and Peltzman, S. (eds), *The Economics of Organised Crime*, Cambridge University Press, Cambridge, England, pp. 33–54.

Anderson, A.R. and Jack, S.L. (2008). Role typologies for enterprising education: The professional artisan?, *Journal of Small Business and Enterprise Development*, 15 (2), 259–73.

Anderson, S.W., Glenn, D. and Sedatole, K.L. (2000). Sourcing parts of complex products: Evidence on transaction costs, high-powered incentives and ex-post opportunism, *Accounting, Organisations and Society*, 25 (5), 723–49.

Andreassen, T. (2008). Priset for lang og utro tjeneste (Prized for long and unfaithful service), *Aftenposten* (daily newspaper), Monday 30 June, pp. 6–7.

Antonopoulos, G.A. (2008). Interviewing retired cigarette smugglers, *Trends in Organized Crime*, 11, 70–81.

Artto, K., Kujala, J., Dietrich, P. and Martinsuo, M. (2008). What is project strategy?, *International Journal of Project Management*, 26, 4–12.

Audretsch, D.B. and Keilbach, M. (2007). The theory of knowledge spillover entrepreneurship, *Journal of Management Studies*, 44 (7), 1242–54.

Auteri, M. and Wagner, R. (2007). The organisational architecture of nonprofit governance: Economic calculation within an ecology of enterprises, *Public Organisation Review*, 7, 57–68.

Beare, M.E. (2000). Structures, strategies and tactics of transnational criminal organisations: Critical issues for enforcement. Paper presented at the *Transnational Crime Conference* convened by the Australian Institute of Criminology in association with the Australian Federal Police and Australian Customs Service and held in Canberra, 9–10 March 2000.

Beare, M.E. (2007). The devil made me do it: Business partners in crime, *Journal of Financial Crime*, 14 (1), 34–48.

Becucci, S. (2008). New Players in an Old Game: The Sex Market in Italy. In: Siegel, D. and Nelen, H. (eds), *Organized Crime: Culture, Markets and Policies*, Springer, New York, pp. 57–69.

Bergeron, D.M. (2007). The potential paradox of organisational citizenship behaviour: Good citizens at what cost?, *Academy of Management Review*, 32 (4), 1078–95.

Bezlov, T. and Gounev, P. (2008). The Vehicle Theft Market in Bulgaria. In: Siegel, D. and Nelen, H. (eds), *Organized Crime: Culture, Markets and Policies*, Springer, New York, pp. 71–82.

Borgers, M.J. and Moors, J.A. (2007). Targeting the proceeds of crime: Bottlenecks in international cooperation, *European Journal of Crime, Criminal Law and Criminal Justice*, 1–22.

Bryan, L.L. and Joyce, C.I. (2007). Better strategy through organisational design, *McKinsey Quarterly*, 2, www.mckinseyquarterly.com.

Carpo (2006). *Situation Report on Organised and Economic Crime in South-eastern Europe*, Carpo Regional Project, European Commission, Department of Crime Problems, 67075 Strasbourg Cedex, France.

Carpo (2007). Update on the 2006 situation report on organised and economic crime in South-eastern Europe, *Trends in Organised Crime*, 10, 102–21.

Casson, M. and Godley, A. (2007). Revisiting the emergence of the modern business enterprise: Entrepreneurship and the Singer global distribution system, *Journal of Management Studies*, 44 (7), 1064–77.

Casson, P.D. and Nisar, T.M. (2007). Entrepreneurship and organisational design: investor specialization, *Management Decision*, 45 (5), 883–96.

Chaikin, D. (2000). Tracking the proceeds of organised crime – the Marcos case. Paper presented at the *Transnational Crime Conference* convened by the Australian Institute of Criminology in association with the Australian Federal Police and Australian Customs Service and held in Canberra, 9–10 March 2000.

Chang, J.J., Lu, H.C. and Chen, M. (2005). Organised crime or individual crime? Endogenous size of a criminal organisation and the optimal law enforcement, *Economic Inquiry*, 43 (3), 661–75.

Chawla, S. and Pietschmann, T. (2005). Drug Trafficking as a Transnational Crime. In: Reichel, P. (ed.), *Handbook of Transnational Crime and Justice*, Sage Publications, London, pp. 160–80.

Chen, A.N.K. and Edgington, T.M. (2005). Assessing value in organizational knowledge creation: Considerations for knowledge workers, *MIS Quarterly*, 29 (2), 279–309.

Coase, R.H. (1937). The nature of the firm, *Economica*, 4 (16), 386–405.

Commission (2004). *The 9/11 Commission Report*, final report of the national commission on terrorist attacks upon the United States, Claitor's Publishing Division, LA.

Council of Europe (2002). *Crime Analysis: Organised Crime – Best Practice Survey No. 4*, Economic Crime Division, Department of Crime Problems, Directorate General I – Legal Affairs, Council of Europe, Strasbourg, France.

Council (2007). Council Conclusions setting the EU priorities for the fight against organised crime based on the 2007 organised crime threat assessment, *Council of the European Union*, 1048 Brussels, Belgium.

Dana, L.P., Etemad, H. and Wright, R.W. (2008). Toward a paradigm of symbiotic entrepreneurship, *International Journal of Entrepreneurship and Small Business*, 5 (2), 109–26.

Das, T.K. and Teng, B.S. (2002). Alliance constellations: A social exchange perspective, *Academy of Management Review*, 27 (3), 445–56.

Davenport, T.H. and Prusak, L. (1998). *Working Knowledge*, Harvard Business School Press, Boston, MA.

Davidsson, P. (2008). *The Entrepreneurship Research Challenge*, Edward Elgar Publishing, Cheltenham, UK.

Dean, G. and Gottschalk, P. (2007). *Knowledge Management in Policing and Law Enforcement: Foundations, Structures and Applications*, Oxford: Oxford University Press.

Dickie, J. (2006). *Cosa Nostra – Historien om den sicilianske mafiaen (Cosa Nostra – The History of the Sicilian Mafia)*, Spartacus Forlag, Oslo, Norway.

Dickson, P.H., Solomon, G.T. and Weaver, K.M. (2008). Entrepreneurial selection and success: Does education matter?, *Journal of Small Business and Enterprise Development*, 15 (2), 239–58.

DiModica, P. (2007). Hunt for business: Grow now or be eaten! Proven management methods to grow your business, *Cost Engineering*, 49 (8), 36–7.

Dixon, N.M. (2000). *Common Knowledge*, Harvard Business School Press, Boston, MA.

Donk, D.P. van and Molloy, E. (2008). From organising as projects to projects as organisations, *International Journal of Project Management*, 26, 129–37.

Doumeingts, G., Müller, J., Morel, G. and Vallespir, B. (2007). Preface. In: Doumeingts, G., Müller, J., Morel, G. and Vallespir, B. (eds), *Enterprise Interoperability: New Challenges and Approaches*, Springer Verlag, London, UK.

Drejer, A., Christensen, K.S. and Ulhoi, J.P. (2004). Understanding intrapreneurship by means of state-of-the-art knowledge management and organisational learning theory. *International Journal of Management and Enterprise Development*, 1 (2), 102–19.

Duyne, P.C. van (2007). Crime Finances and State of the Art. Case for Concern? In: Duyne, P.C. van, Maljevic, A., Dijck, M. van, Lampe, K. von and Harvey, J. (eds), *Crime Business and Crime Money in Europe – The Dirty Linen of Illicit Enterprise*, Wolf Legal Publishers, Nijmegen, The Netherlands, pp. 69–95.

Duyne, P.C. van, Lampe, K. von and Newell, J. (2003). *Criminal Finances and Organising Crime in Europe*, Wolf Legal Publishers, Nijmegen, the Netherlands.

Duyne, P.C. van, Lampe, K. von, Dijck, M. van and Newell, J. (2005). *The Organised Crime Economy: Managing Crime Markets in Europe*, Wolf Legal Publishers, Nijmegen, the Netherlands.

Earl, M.J. (2000). Evolving the e-business, *Business Strategy Review*, 11 (2), 33–8.

Edwards, D.L. and Mahling, D.E. (1997). Toward knowledge management systems in the legal domain, *Proceedings of the International ACM SIGGROUP Conference on Supporting Group Work Group '97*, The Association of Computing Machinery ACM, pp. 158–66.

Eisenhardt, K.M. (1985). Control: Organisational and economic approaches, *Management Science*, 31(2), 134–49.

Eisenhardt, K.M. and Martin, J.A. (2000). Dynamic capabilities: What are they?, *Strategic Management Journal*, 21, 1105–21.

Elvins, M. (2003). Europe's Response to Transnational Organised Crime. In: Edwards, A. and Gill, P. (eds), *Crime: Perspectives on Global Security*, Routledge, London, pp. 29–41.

Ethiraj, S.K. and Levinthal, D. (2004). Bounded rationality and the search for organisational architecture: An evolutionary perspective on the design of organisations and their evolvability, *Administrative Science Quarterly*, 49, 404–37.

Europol (2006). *OCTA: EU Organised Crime Threat Assessment 2006*, European Police Office, Hag, the Netherlands.

FBI (2008). *Department of Justice Launches New Law Enforcement Strategy to Combat Increasing Threat of International Organised Crime*, Press Release 23 April Federal Bureau of Investigation, www.fbi.gov. 'Overview of the Law Enforcement Strategy to Combat International Organised Crime', U.S. Departement of Justice, Washington, DC.

Felsen, D. and Kalaitzidis, A. (2005). A Historical Overview of Transnational Crime. In: Reichel, P. (ed.), *Handbook of Transnational Crime and Justice*, Sage Publications, London, pp. 3–19.

Felson, M. (2006). The ecosystem for organized crime. Antilla Lecture given in Helsinki, Finland on 5 October by Marcus Felson, Rutgers University, New Jersey, USA.

Finckenauer, J.O. (2005). Problems of definition: What is organised crime?, *Trends in Organised Crime*, 8 (3), 63–83.

Finckenauer, J.O. and Chin, Ko-lin (2006). Asian transnational organised crime and its impact on the United States: Developing a transnational crime research agenda, *Trends in Organised Crime*, 10 (2), 18–109.

Fiss, P.C. (2007). A set-theoretical approach to organisational configurations, *Academy of Management Review*, 32 (4), 1180–98.

Foss, K., Foss, N.J., Klein, P.G. and Klein, S.K. (2007). The entrepreneurial organisation of heterogeneous capital, *Journal of Management Studies*, 44 (7), 1165–86.

Frame (1995). *Managing Projects in Organisations*. Jossey-Bass Publishers, San Francisco.

Frankfort-Nachmias, C. and Nachmias, D. (2002). *Research Methods in the Social Sciences*, Fifth Edition Arnold, London.

Frossard, D. (2007). Women in Organised Crime in Brazil. In: Fiandaca, G. (ed.), *Women and the Mafia – Female Roles in Organised Crime Structures*, Studies of Organised Crime, Springer, New York, pp. 181–204.

Garud, R. and Kumaraswamy, A. (2005). Vicious and virtuous circles in the management of knowledge: The case of Infosys Technologies, *MIS Quarterly*, 29 (1), 9–33.

Gilinskiy, Y. (2006). Crime in contemporary Russia, *European Journal of Criminology*, 3 (3), 259–92.

Gill, M. (2001). The craft of robbers of cash-in-transit vans: Crime facilitators and the entrepreneurial approach, *International Journal of the Sociology of Law*, 29, 277–91.

Gottschalk, P. (2007). *Knowledge Management in Law Enforcement: Technologies and Techniques*, Idea Group Publishing, Hershey, PA.

Gottschalk, P. and Solli-Sæther, H. (2006). Maturity model for IT outsourcing relationships, *Industrial Management & Data Systems*, 105 (6), 685–702.

Gottschalk, P. and Tolloczko, P. (2007). Maturity model for mapping crime in law enforcement, *Electronic Government, an International Journal*, 4 (1), 59–67.

Gross, E. (1978). Organisational crime: A theoretical perspective, *Studies in Symbolic Interaction*, 1, 55–85.

Grotenhuis, F. and Kamminga, P. (2008). Continuity and change in alliances, joint ventures, and mergers and acquisitions: A matter of cooperation or domination?, *International Journal of Entrepreneurship and Small Business*, 5 (2), 170–78.

Groth, L. (1999). *Future Organisational Design*, Wiley Series in Information Systems, John Wiley & Sons, Chichester, England.

Grover, V. and Davenport, T.H. (2001). General perspectives on knowledge management: Fostering a research agenda, *Journal of Management Information Systems*, 18 (1), 5–21.

Hagan, F.E. (2006). 'Organised Crime' and 'organised crime': Indeterminate problems of definition, *Trends in Organised Crime*, 9 (4), 127–37.

Hann, J. and Weber, R. (1996), Information systems planning: A model and empirical tests, *Management Science*, 42 (7), 1043–64.

Hinttu, S., Forsman, M. and Kock, S. (2004). A Network Perspective of International Entrepreneurship. In: Dana, L. (ed.), *Handbook of Research on International Entrepreneurship*, Edward Elgar Publishing, Cheltenham, UK, pp. 715–31.

Hitt, M.A., Bierman, L., Shumizu, K. and Kochhar, R. (2001). Direct and moderating effects of human capital on strategy and performance in professional service firms: A resource-based perspective, *Academy of Management Journal*, 44 (1), 13–28.

Hofstede, G., Neuijen, B., Ohayv, D.D. and Sanders, G. (1990). Measuring organisational cultures: A qualitative and quantitative study across twenty cases, *Administrative Science Quarterly*, 35 (2), 286–316.

Housel, T. and Bell, A.H. (2001). *Measuring and Managing Knowledge*, McGraw-Hill Irwin, New York.

Huovinen, J. and Tihula, S. (2008). Entrepreneurial learning in the context of portfolio entrepreneurship, *International Journal of Entrepreneurial Behaviour & Research*, 14 (3), 152–71.

Independent (2007), 'Global trail of abuse led to arrest of five suspects', *Independent*, November 11, 2007.

Jacobides, M.G. and Winter, S.G. (2007). Entrepreneurship and firm boundaries: The theory of a firm, *Journal of Management Studies*, 44 (7), 1213–41.

Jayasinghe, K., Thomas, D. and Wickramasinghe, D. (2008). Bounded emotionality in entrepreneurship: An alternative framework, *International Journal of Entrepreneurial Behaviour & Research*, 14 (4), 242–58.

Johansen, P.O. (2005). Organised Crime, Norwegian Style. In: Duyne, P.C. van, Lampe, K. von, Dijck, M. van and Newell, J. (eds), *The Organised Crime Economy: Managing Crime Markets in Europe*, Wolf Legal Publishers, Nijmegen, the Netherlands, pp. 189–208.

Johansen, P.O. (2007). The Come-back Boys of the Illegal Markets. In: Duyne, P.C. van, Majevic, A., Dijck, M. van, Lampe, K. von and Harvey, J. (eds), *Crime Business and Crime Money in Europe. The Dirty Linen of Illegal Enterprise*, Wolf Legal Publishers, Nijmegen, the Netherlands, pp. 209–26.

Johansen, P.O. (2008). Never a final design: Interviewing Norwegian alcohol smugglers, *Trends in Organized Crime*, 11, 5–11.

Johnson, G. and Scholes, K. (2002). *Exploring Corporate Strategy*, Harlow, Essex, Pearson Education, Prentice Hall.

Joyce, E. (2005). Expanding the International Regime on Money Laundering in Response to Transnational Organised Crime, Terrorism, and Corruption. In: Reichel, P. (ed.), *Handbook of Transnational Crime and Justice*, Sage Publications, London, pp. 79–97.

Junninen, M. (2008). Depth-interviewing Finnish professional criminals, *Trends in Organized Crime*, 11, 59–69.

Kankanhalli, A., Tan, B.C.Y. and Wei, K.K. (2005). Contributing knowledge to electronic knowledge repositories: An empirical investigation, *MIS Quarterly*, 29 (1), 113–43.

Kaplan, D.E. and Dubro, A. (1986). *Yakuza – The Explosive Account of Japan's Criminal Underworld*, Addison-Wesley Publishing Company, Reading, MA.

Karlsen, J.T., Gottschalk, P., Glomseth, R. and Fahsing, I.A. (2007). Managing police investigations by projects, *International Journal of Innovation and Learning*, 4 (4), 391–410.

Kazanjian, R.K. (1988). Relation of dominant problems to stages of growth in technology-based new ventures, *Academy of Management Journal*, 31 (2), 257–79.

Kazanjian, R.K. and Drazin, R. (1989). An empirical test of a stage of growth progression model, *Management Science*, 35 (12), 1489–1503.

Kenney, M. (2007). The architecture of drug trafficking: Network forms of organisation in the Colombian cocaine trade, *Global Crime*, 8 (3), 233–59.

Ketchen, D.J., Combs, J.G., Russell, C.J., Shook, C., Dean, M.A., Runge, J., Lohrke, F.T., Naumann, S.E., Haptonstahl, D.W., Baker, R., Beckstein, B.A., Handler, C., Honig, H. and Lamoureux, S. (1997). Organisational configurations and performance: A meta-analysis, *Academy of Management Journal*, 40 (1), 223–40.

King, W.R. and Teo, T.S.H. (1997). Integration between business planning and information systems planning: Validating a stage hypothesis, *Decision Sciences*, 28 (2), 279–307.

Kivivuori, J. (2007). Crime by proxy, *British Journal of Criminology*, 47, 817–33.

Klerks, P. (2007). Methodological aspects of the Dutch National Threat Assessment, *Trends in Organised Crime*, 10, 91–101.

Kor, Y.Y., Mahoney, J.T. and Michael, S.C. (2007). Resources, capabilities and entrepreneurial perceptions, *Journal of Management Studies*, 44 (7), 1187–1212.

Kropp, F., Lindsay, N.J. and Shoham, A. (2008). Entrepreneurial orientation and international entrepreneurial business venture startup, *International Journal of Entrepreneurial Behaviour & Research*, 14 (2), 102–17.

Kugler, M., Verdier, T. and Zenou, Y. (2005). Organised crime, corruption and punishment, *Journal of Public Economics*, 89, 1639–63.

Lampe, K. von (2005). Organised Crime in Europe. In: Reichel, P. (ed.), *Handbook of Transnational Crime and Justice*, Sage Publications, London, pp. 403–17.

Lampe, K. von (2007). Criminals are not Alone. Some Observations on the Social Microcosm of Illegal Entrepreneurs. In: Duyne, P.C. van, Majevic, A., Dijck, M.

van, Lampe, K. von and Harvey, J. (eds), *Crime Business and Crime Money in Europe. The Dirty Linen of Illegal Enterprise*. Wolf Legal Publishers, Nijmegen, the Netherlands, pp. 131–56.

Lampe, K. von and Johansen, P.O. (2003). *Criminal Networks and Trust*, third annual meeting of the European Society of Criminology, Helsinki, Finland, 29 August.

Lange, D. (2008). A multidimensional conceptualization of organizational corruption control, *Academy of Management Review*, 33 (3), 710–29.

Langlois, R.N. (2007). The entrepreneurial theory of the firm and the theory of the entrepreneurial firm, *Journal of Management Studies*, 44 (7), 1107–24.

Lemieux, V. (2003). *Criminal Networks*, Royal Canadian Mounted Police, Ottawa, Canada.

Levi, M. (2004). *Towards a European Organised Crime Strategy?* PHS-Forskning 2004:2, Norwegian Police University College, Oslo, Norway.

Levitt, S.D. and Dubner, S.J. (2005). *Freakonomics: A Rogue Economist Explores the Hidden Side of Everything*, Allen Lane Publishing, London, UK.

Liddick, D. (1999). The enterprise 'model' of organised crime: Assessing theoretical propositions, *Justice Quarterly*, 16 (2), 404–30.

Lindkvist, L. (2008). Project organisation: Exploring its adaptation properties, *International Journal of Project Management*, 26, 13–20.

Loasby, B.J. (2007). A cognitive perspective on entrepreneurship and the firm, *Journal of Management Studies*, 44 (7), 1078–1106.

Long, D.W. and Fahey, L. (2000). Diagnosing cultural barriers to knowledge management, *Academy of Management Executive*, 14 (4), 113–27.

Longrigg, C. (2007). Women in Organised Crime in the United States. In: Fiandaca, G. (ed.), *Women and the Mafia – Female Roles in Organised Crime Structures*, Studies of Organised Crime, Springer, New York, pp. 235–84.

Low, A. (2008). Economic outcomes of female immigrant entrepreneurship, *International Journal of Entrepreneurship and Small Business*, 5 (3/4), 224–40.

Luo, Y. (2002). Contract, cooperation, and performance in international joint ventures, *Strategic Management Journal*, 23 (10), 903–19.

Lyman, M.D. and Potter, G.W. (2007). *Organised crime*, Fourth Edition, Pearson Prentice Hall, Upper Saddle River, NJ.

Madsen, H., Neergaard, H. and Ulhøi, J.P. (2008). Factors influencing the establishment of knowledge-intensive ventures, *International Journal of Entrepreneurial Behaviour & Research*, 14 (2), 70–84.

Malhotra, A., Gosain, S. and El Sawy, O.A. (2005). Absorptive capacity configurations in supply chains: Gearing for partner-enabled market knowledge creation, *MIS Quarterly*, 29 (1), 145–87.

Markovska, A. (2007). The Bitter Pill of a Corrupt Heritage: Corruption in Ukraine and Developments in the Pharmaceutical Industry. In: Duyne, P.C. van, Majevic, A., Dijck, M. van, Lampe, K. von and Harvey, J. (eds), *Crime Business and Crime Money in Europe. The Dirty Linen of Illegal Enterprise*, Wolf Legal Publishers, Nijmegen, the Netherlands, pp. 227–46.

Markovski, S. and Hall, P. (2007). Public sector entrepreneurship and the production of defence, *Public Finance and Management*, 7 (3), 260–94.

Martin, K.D., Cullen, J.B., Johnson, J.L. and Parbotteeah, K.P. (2007). Deciding to bribe: A cross-level analysis of firm and home country influences on bribery activity, *Academy of Management Journal*, 50 (6), 1401–22.

Martin, R. (2007). How successful leaders think, *Harvard Business Review*, June, 2–8.

Marx, E. (2008). Hashish Smuggling by Bedouin in South Sinai. In: Siegel, D. and Nelen, H. (eds), *Organized Crime: Culture, Markets and Policies*, Springer, New York, pp. 29–37.

Mason, J. and Lefrere, P. (2003). Trust, collaboration, e-learning and organisational transformation, *International Journal of Training and Development*, 7 (4), 259–70.

Matthews, J. (2005). Learning to grow a business, *University of Auckland Business Review*, Autumn, 84–8.

Matusitz, J. (2008). Similarities between terrorist networks in antiquity and present-day cyberterrorist networks, *Trends in Organized Crime*, 11, 183–99.

Maylor, H. (2005). *Project Management*, Third Edition, Prentice Hall, Pearson Education, Harlow, England.

McKenna, M. (2005). Singapore's hand in Golden Triangle, *Singapore Window*, 23 November, www.singapore-window.org.

Mintzberg, H. (1979). *The Structuring of Organisations*, Prentice-Hall, Englewood Cliffs, NJ.

Mintzberg, H. (1994). Rounding on the managers' job, *Sloan Management Review*, 36 (1), 11–26.

Misangyi, V.F., Weaver, G.R. and Elms, H. (2008). Ending corruption: The interplay among institutional logics, resources, and institutional entrepreneurs, *Academy of Management Review*, 33 (3), 750–70.

Moussavou, J. (2006). Organisational architecture and decision-making, *Journal of Portfolio Management*, Autumn, 103–11.

Newell, J.L. (2003). Political Corruption in Italy. In: Duyne, P.C. van, Lampe, K. von and Newell, J. (eds), *Criminal Finances and Organising Crime in Europe*, Wolf Legal Publishers, Nijmegen, the Netherlands, pp. 191–212.

Nicola, A.D. (2005). Trafficking in Human Beings and Smuggling of Migrants. In: Reichel, P. (ed.), *Handbook of Transnational Crime and Justice*, Sage Publications, London, pp. 181–203.

Nolan, R.L. (1979). Managing the crises in data processing, *Harvard Business Review*, March–April, 115–26.

Nonaka, I., Toyama, R. and Konno, N. (2000). SECI, ba and leadership: A unified model of dynamic knowledge creation, *Long Range Planning*, 33 (1), 5–34.

OCTA (2007). *EU Organised Crime Threat Assessment 2007*, Europol, the Hague, Netherlands, http://www.europol.europa.eu.

Paoli, L. (2001). The 'invisible hand of the market': The illegal drugs trade in Germany, Italy and Russia, *Third Colloquium on Cross-border Crime*, Police Academy, Bratislava, Slovak Republic, October, pp. 19–38.

Perkowski, F. (2007). Five ways to grow your business, *Official Board Markets*, 6 October, 26–30.

Pettus, M.L. (2001). The resourced-based view as a development growth process: Evidence from the deregulated trucking industry, *Academy of Management Journal*, 44 (4), 878–96.

Pfarrer, M.D., DeCelles, K.A., Smith, K.G. and Taylor, M.S. (2008). After the fall: Reintegrating the corrupt organization, *Academy of Management Review*, 33 (3), 730–49.

Pinto, J., Leana, C.R. and Pil, F.K. (2008). Corrupt organizations or organizations of corrupt individuals? Two types of organization-level corruption, *Academy of Management Review*, 33 (3), 685–709.

Porter, M.E. (1985). *Competitive advantage: Creating and sustaining competitive performance*, New York: The Free Press.

Porter, M.E. (2001). Strategy and the internet, *Harvard Business Review*, March, 63–78.

Poston, R.S. and Speier, C. (2005). Effective use of knowledge management systems: A process model of content ratings and credibility indicators, *MIS Quarterly*, 29 (2), 221–44.

Quinn, J. and Koch, D.S. (2003). The nature of criminality within one-percent motorcycle clubs, *Deviant Behaviour: An Interdisciplinary Journal*, 24, 281–305.

Rao, S.S. and Metts, G. (2003). Electronic commerce development in small and medium sized enterprises: A stage model and its implications, *Business Process Management*, 9 (1), 11–32.

Rawlinson, P. (2008). Look who's talking: Interviewing Russian criminals, *Trends in Organized Crime*, 11, 12–20.

Reavley, M.A. and Lituchy, T.R. (2008). Successful women entrepreneurs: A six-country analysis of self-reported determinants of success – more than just dollars and cents, *International Journal of Entrepreneurship and Small Business*, 5 (3/4), 272–96.

Reggi, V. (2007). Counterfeit medicines: An intent to deceive, *International Journal of Risk & Safety in Medicine*, 19, 105–8.

Riffe, D. and Freitag, A. (1997). A content analysis of content analyses: Twenty-five years of journalism quarterly, *Journalism Mass Communication Quarterly*, 74 (2), 873–82.

Rivkin, J.W. and Siggelkow, N. (2003). Balancing search and stability: Interdependencies among elements of organisational design, *Management Science*, 49 (3), 290–311.

Ruggiero, V. (2000). *Crime and Markets – Essays in Anti-criminology*, Oxford University Press, Oxford, England.

Ryu, C., Kim, Y.J., Chaudhury, A. and Rao, H.R. (2005). Knowledge acquisition via three learning processes in enterprise information portals: Learning-by-investment, learning-by-doing, and learning-from-others, *MIS Quarterly*, 29 (2), 245–78.

Sambamurthy, V. and Subramani, M. (2005). Special issue on information technologies and knowledge management, *MIS Quarterly*, 29 (1), 1–7 and 29 (2), 193–5.

Schein, E.H. (1990). Organisational culture, *American Psychologist*, 45 (2), 109–19.

Schneider, S. (2004). Organised crime, money laundering, and the real estate market in Canada, *Journal of Property Research*, 21 (2), 99–118.

Schulte-Bockholt, A. (2001). A neo-marxist explanation of organised crime, *Critical Criminology*, 10, 225–42.

Seet, P.S., Ahmad, N.H. and Seet, L.C. (2008). Singapore's female entrepreneurs – are they different?, *International Journal of Entrepreneurship and Small Business*, 5 (3/4), 257–71.

Shelley, L.I., Picarelli, J.T., Irby, A., Hart, D.M., Craig-Hart, P.A., Williams, P., Simon, S., Abdullaev, N., Stanislawski, B. and Covill, L. (2005). *Methods and Motives: Exploring Links between Transnational Organised Crime & International Terrorism*, Document No. 211207, US Department of Justice, Washington, USA.

Siegel, D. (2008a). Conversations with Russian mafiosi, *Trends in Organized Crime*, 11, 21–9.

Siegel, D. (2008b). Diamonds and Organized Crime: *The Case of Antwerp*: In: Siegel, D. and Nelen, H. (eds), *Organized Crime: Culture, Markets and Policies*, Springer, New York, pp. 85–96.

Small, K. and Taylor, B. (2006). State and local law enforcement response to transnational crime, *Trends in Organised Crime*, 10 (2), 5–17.

Solinge, T.B. van (2008). Eco-crime: The Tropical Timber Trade. In: Siegel, D. and Nelen, H. (eds), *Organized Crime: Culture, Markets and Policies*, Springer, New York, pp. 97–111.

Stabell, C.B. and Fjeldstad, Ø.D. (1998). Configuring value for competitive advantage: On chains, shops, and networks. *Strategic Management Journal*, 19, 413–37.

Steffensmeier, D.J. and Ulmer, J.T. (2005). *Confessions Of A Dying Thief: Understanding Criminal Careers and Illegal Enterprise*, New Lines in Criminology, New Brunswick, NJ: Aldine/Transaction Publishers.

Symeonidou-Kastanidou, E. (2007). Towards a new definition of organised crime in the European Union, *European Journal of Crime, Criminal Law and Criminal Justice*, 83–103.

Takeyh, R. and Gvosdev, N. (2002). Do terrorist networks need a home?, *Washington Quarterly*, 25 (3), 97–108.

Tang, J. (2008). Environmental munificence for entrepreneurs: Entrepreneurial alertness and commitment, *International Journal of Entrepreneurial Behaviour & Research*, 14 (3), 128–51.

Tanriverdi, H. (2005). Information technology relatedness, knowledge management capability, and performance of multibusiness firms, *MIS Quarterly*, 29 (2), 311–34.

Teece, D.J., Pisano, G. and Shuen, A. (1997). Dynamic capabilities and strategic management, *Strategic Management Journal*, 18 (7), 509–33.

Tendo, S. (2007). *Yakuza Moon: Memoirs of a Gangster's Daughter*, Kodansha International, Tokyo.

Thomas, A. and Mancino, A. (2007). The relationship between entrepreneurial characteristics, firms' positioning and local development, *Entrepreneurship and Innovation*, 8 (2), 105–14.

Thorne, K. (2005). Designing virtual organisations? Themes and trends in political and organisational discourses, *Journal of Management Development*, 24 (7), 580–607.

Tiwana, A. (2002). *The Knowledge Management Toolkit – Practical Techniques for Building a Knowledge Management System*, Second Edition, Prentice Hall, Upper Saddle River, NJ.

Tunander, O. (2007). Afghansk opiumskrig (Afghan opium war), *Aftenposten*, (Norwegian newspaper) 26 November, p. 5.

United Nations (2002). *Results of a Pilot Survey of Forty Selected Organised Criminal Groups in Sixteen Countries*, New York: United Nations, Office of Drugs and Crime.

Varese, F. (2006). *The Structure of Criminal Connections: The Russian–Italian Mafia Network*, Oxford University Press, Oxford, England.

Veiga, J., Lubatkin, M., Calori, R. and Very, P. (2000). Measuring organisational culture clashes: A two-nation post-hoc analysis of a cultural compatibility index, *Human Relations*, 53 (4), 539–57.

Vita, R., Sciascia, S. and Alberti, F. (2008). Managing resources for corporate entrepreneurship: The case of Naturis, *Entrepreneurship and Innovation*, 9 (1), 63–8.

Ward, J. and Peppard, J. (2002), *Strategic Planning for Information Systems*, London: Wiley.

Wasko, M.M., and Faraj, S. (2005). Why should I share? Examining social capital and knowledge contribution in electronic networks of practice, *MIS Quarterly*, 29 (1), 35–57.

Weenink, A. and Laan, F. (2007). The search for the Russian Mafia, *Trends in Organised Crime*, 10, 57–76.

Westcott, K. (2007). The challenge of breaking the Mafia, *BBC News*, http://news.bbc.co.uk/2/hi/europe/7078954.stm.

White, R. (2007). *Anti-Gang Strategies and Interventions*, Australian Research Alliance for Children & Youth, University of Tasmania, Australia, www.aracy.org.au.

Williams, C.C. (2006). *The Hidden Enterprise Culture – Entrepreneurship in the Underground Economy*, Edward Elgar Publishing, Cheltenham, UK.

Williamson, O.E. (1979). Transaction-cost economics: The governance of contractual relations, *Journal of Law and Economics*, 22, 233–61.

Witt, U. (2007). Firms as realizations of entrepreneurial visions, *Journal of Management Studies*, 44 (7), 1125–40.

Wright, A. (2006). *Organised Crime*, Willan Publishing, Cullompton, England.

Yusuf, A. (2005). Workforce diversity in small enterprises: Implications on firm performance, *International Journal of Management and Enterprise Development*, 2 (2), 240–56.

Zack, M.H. (1999). Developing a knowledge strategy, *California Management Review*, 41 (3), 125–45.

Zaitch, D. (2002). *Trafficking Cocaine – Colombian Drug Entrepreneurs in the Netherlands*, Studies of Organized Crime, Kluwer Law International, the Hague, the Netherlands.

Zaluar, A. (2001). Violence in Rio de Janeiro: Styles of leisure, drug use, and trafficking, *International Social Science Journal*, 169, September, 369–78.

Zander, I. (2007). Do you see what I mean? An entrepreneurship perspective on the nature and boundaries of the firm, *Journal of Management Studies*, 44 (7), 1141–64.

Zhang, Y. and Rajagopalan, N. (2003). Explaining new CEO origin: Firm versus industry antecedents, *Academy of Management Journal*, 46 (3), 327–38.

Zhang, Y. and Rajagopalan, N. (2004). When the known devil is better than an unknown god: An empirical study of the antecedents and consequences of relay CEO successions, *Academy of Management Journal*, 47 (4), 483–500.

Index

9/11 attacks 70
acceptability, in organisational
    structure 104, 105
acquisitions *see* mergers and
    acquisitions
activity-based criminal organisations
    26, 27, 29, 30–31, 34, 35
Adams, Terrence 17–18, 32, 57–8, 130
adhocatic projects 72
administrative knowledge 177–8
advanced knowledge 173, 174–5
Afghanistan, drugs trade 59, 80
agency business 45–6
    see also federal business
        organisations
agent stage, in criminal–legal
    partnerships 51–2
Ahmidan, Jamal 58
Al Qaeda 39, 181–2
Albania, organised crime groups 96
alcohol smuggling, case study 29, 87–8,
    183–4
alliance business 46–7, 119, 120–21
American mafia 8, 132–3
analytical knowledge 177, 178
armed robbery 135–7
arms trade 58, 76–7, 90
artefacts, as organisational culture 33
articulable knowledge *see* explicit
    knowledge
artificial intelligence 167–8
authority lines *see* centralization;
    decentralization; hierarchy; unit
    grouping
auto theft 115–16

bank robberies 29, 59
Bedouin, drugs trade 162–3
behavioural formalization, and
    organisational structure 100, 102
Bin Laden, Usama 70

Black Disciples 24
black economy 161
Bout, Victor 58
Brazil, criminal organisations in 28
bribery *see* corruption
Bulgaria, vehicle theft 115–16
bureaucratic–economic structures 103
bureaucratic projects 71
business analysis 146, 147, 150–53
business conception 10, 126
business direction, analysis of 151
business organisations *see* criminal
    business organisations; legal
    business organisations
business processes
    development of 127–9
    and information systems 149, 154–60
    knowledge categories 176, 177–8
    see also interoperability
business strategy 141–5, 153–60

Camorra mafia 48, 58, 69, 131–2
capital *see* entrepreneurial capital;
    human capital; social capital
car theft 115–16
cash-in-transit vans, robbery 160, 180
centralization 101
    see also decentralization; hierarchy
chief executive officers 57–61
    see also top management
cigarette smuggling 14, 90, 187–8
Clerkenwell Crime Syndicate 17–18
co-offending 14
co-operation, and organisational
    culture 107
cocaine, value chain 79–80
codification of knowledge 172–3
collaboration *see* alliance business;
    co-operation; networks
collective knowledge 176
common knowledge 179

competition
  analysis of 151
  in criminal organisations 98, 107,
    108
competitive advantage
  and dynamic capabilities 135
  and knowledge 125, 173–5
  and market development 121
  and resources 123, 124
competitive imperfections, and market
    development 54–5
conflict diamonds 43
conflict timber 76–7
Contini, Edoardo 58
control systems *see* planning and
    control systems
core knowledge 173–4
Corleonesi mafia 36, 37
corruption
  and criminal organisations 35, 48–9,
    92, 93–4, 95
  in federal/hybrid business
    organisations 40, 42
  and market development 16
  in the police force 45, 137–8
  in political leaders 42, 44–5, 58,
    76–7, 82
  as value shop 82–4
Cosa Nostra 28, 34–7, 48, 59, 69
Costa, Arlete da 131
crime, proceeds of *see* proceeds of
    crime
crime strategy 160–61
criminal business organisations
  stages of growth models 38–43
  see also organised financial crime
criminal careers 22–4, 135–9, 161–2
criminal entrepreneurship
  case studies 17–18, 49–50, 111–15,
    131–2, 135–9
  characteristics 11–15
  and legal business 50–53, 93
  research strategies 182–3, 186–7
  social microcosm 14
  see also women, as entrepreneurs
criminal finances *see* entrepreneurial
    capital; financial management;
    money laundering; organised
    financial crime
criminal gangs, stages of growth 22–4

criminal knowledge 180–81
criminal organisations
  characteristics 92–9
  compared to legal organisations
    96–9, 101, 102, 104–5
  competition in 98, 107, 108
  corruption in *see* corruption
  entrepreneurial theory 8, 9–10
  evolution in *see* evolution; stages of
    growth models
  family roles 8, 12, 17, 35, 69, 107
  interoperability in 133–5
  management *see* management
  markets *see* market development
  networks in *see* networks
  political influence 58, 92, 94
  rationality in 7
  stages of growth *see* stages of
    growth
  structure *see* organisational structure
  transnational 52–3, 89, 93, 95–6
  values *see* organisational culture;
    value configurations
  violence in 65, 92, 94, 107, 135–9
  virtual 39
  see also criminal business
    organisations; criminal gangs;
    organised crime; organised
    financial crime
criminal projects
  characteristics 66–9
  in the drugs trade 103
  leader selection 69–70
  management 70–72
  phases 67–8
critical success factors, in knowledge
    management 171
culture *see* organisational culture
customer needs
  solutions for 120–21
  see also value configurations, value
    shops

data
  and knowledge 165, 166, 168–70
  see also explicit knowledge
De Beers 43
debt collection (violent) *see* torpedo
decentralization 8, 101, 102
  see also networks

decision making 55, 101, 129–31
declarative knowledge 178
Deep Blue (chess program) 167–8
Denaro, Matteo Messina 36, 37
design parameters
  for business processes 128–9
  for information management
    systems 147
  for organisational structure 99–101,
    102, 105–6
diamond smuggling 43
diversification 98–9, 121
divisionalized projects 71
dominant problems, and stages of
  growth 21
drugs trade
  case studies 17–18, 24–5, 137, 162–3
  family orientation 107
  leaders 57–8, 59–60, 72–6
  leadership style 65
  and markets 54–5, 117, 122–3
  and networks 123, 127
  organisational structure 103, 109
  and partner organisations 52
  process 188
  stages of growth model 28, 29–30, 31
  as value chain 79–81
  as a value shop 90
Durante, Georgia 132–3
dynamic capabilities 125, 135

e-business 20, 149
eco-crime 76–7, 90
economic–bureaucratic structures 103
economic crime 89
  see also arms trade; diamond
    smuggling; drugs trade; money
    laundering; organised financial
    crime; trafficking
economy, in organisational structure
  104, 105
education *see* entrepreneurial
  education; indoctrination;
  learning-by-doing; learning
  organisations; training
ends means analysis, in knowledge
  management 171–2
Enron 47
enterprise paradigm, of organised
  crime 7, 61–2

entrepreneurial capital 15–16, 122
entrepreneurial education 109–111
entrepreneurial judgment 55
entrepreneurial leadership 55–6, 65
entrepreneurial management 56–7
  see also chief executive officers
entrepreneurial orientation 14–15
entrepreneurial strategy 118–19, 140
  see also strategic management
entrepreneurial structures 6–7
  see also organisational structure
entrepreneurial theory, of criminal
  organisations 8, 9–10
entrepreneurial vision 10, 126
entrepreneurship
  definitions 5, 9–11, 117, 123
  innovation levels 12
  and organisational performance
    11–12
  personality traits 13
  see also criminal entrepreneurship
environmental analysis 152
espionage, leadership style 65
European Union, Schengen system
  53
evolution
  in criminal organisations 8–10, 56
  of e-business 20
  see also stages of growth models
executive *see* chief executive officers;
  top management
expert systems 167–8
expert witnesses 183–4
explicit knowledge 172–3, 176, 178–9
  see also data
external knowledge analysis 153

failed states, benefits for criminal
  entrepreneurs 39
family roles 8, 12, 17, 35, 69, 107
federal business organisations 40, 42
  see also agency business
Ferris, Paul 137–8
financial crime *see* organised financial
  crime
financial management 107–8
  see also entrepreneurial capital;
    money laundering
Finland, case studies 182–3
flashers 184

flexibility, in organisational structure 104, 105

gangs *see* criminal gangs
gate-keeping role *see* monitor role
Goodwin, Sam 161–2
Greece, cigarette smuggling 187–8
group orientation, in criminal organisations 107
Guttman scales 20

Han, Lo Hsing 29–30, 58
heads of state *see* political leaders
Heavenly Alliance (Taiwan) 85–6, 120
Hells Angels 24, 33, 41, 47–8, 70
heroin, value chain 80–81
hierarchy, in criminal organisations 6–7, 33, 35, 87, 92, 95, 106, 108–9
Holleeder, Willem ('The Nose') 25
horizontal decentralization 101, 102
human capital
   in criminal entrepreneurship 10, 57
   knowledge resources 31, 35, 165–6, 172–3
   see also talent
human knowledge 176
hybrid business organisations 40, 41, 42
   see also network business

ideology *see* organisational culture
independent-network structures 103
indoctrination, and organisational structure 100, 102
information, and knowledge 165–7, 168–70
information management strategy
   principles 141–3
   strategic alignment 153–60
   Y model 145–8
      case study 162–3
      describing current situation 145–6, 147, 148–50
      describing desired situation 146, 147, 150–53
   see also interoperability; knowledge management
information technology
   assessment of 155, 157, 159

executive, role of 155, 156, 157–9
   growth model 20
innovation levels 12
innovative knowledge 173, 175
intangible assets 121
   see also knowledge; talent
integration, in business processes 128, 154–60
integrative thinkers 129
inter-organisational relationships, and knowledge management 164–5
internal knowledge analysis 153
international organised crime
   definition 5
   see also transnational criminal organisations
Internet, and strategic planning 145
interoperability, in criminal organisations 133–5
intrapraneurship, definition 140
Italy
   sex trade 139
   see also Camorra mafia; Corleonesi mafia; Cosa Nostra

Jahre, Anders 49–50
Japan
   Yakuza 22, 122–3
   Yamaguchi Gumi 59
Jay-Z 24
job specialization 93, 99–100, 102
joint ventures 120
judgment *see* decision making; entrepreneurial judgment

Karamanski, Ivo 58–9, 116
Karzai, Ahjed Wali 59
knowledge
   analysis of 153
   asymmetry, in entrepreneurship 10
   categories 172–9
   see also tacit knowledge
   characteristics 165–8
   and competitive advantage 125, 173–5
   criminal 180–81
   value 164, 169–70
   see also data; information; value configurations, value shops

knowledge-based criminal
  organisations 26, 27, 29–30, 31,
  34, 35
knowledge management
  codification 172–3
  definition 164
  identification of needs 170–72
  and inter-organisational
    relationships 164–5
  and shared knowledge space 178–9
  strategy 143
  see also information management
    strategy
knowledge processes 169–70
Korea, drug trade 122–3

law enforcement *see* police
leaders
  arms trade 58
  drugs trade 57–8, 59–60, 72–6
  entrepreneurial 55–6, 65
  roles 62–4, 69
  selection 60–61, 69–70
  of terrorist groups 58, 70
  see also decision making; political
    leaders; top management
learning-by-doing 110
learning organisations 168
legal business organisations 40
  see also federal business
    organisations; hybrid business
    organisations
legal–criminal partnerships 51–2, 93
legal organisations
  compared to criminal organisations
    96–9, 101, 102, 104–5
  rationality in 7
liaison functions, and organisational
  structure 101, 102
liaison role 63–4, 65, 69
Liberia, timber trade 76–7
Lo Piccolo, Salvatore 36–7

McGraw, Terry (Tam, Thomas) 59,
  130–31, 135–9
Madrid bombing 58
mafia *see* American mafia; Camorra
  mafia; Corleonesi mafia; Cosa
  Nostra; Russian mafia
mafia business 46, 48

Mallorca, Russian mafia group 6
management
  of criminal projects 70–72
  financial *see* financial management
  and information systems *see*
    information management
    strategy; knowledge
    management
  of resources *see* resources,
    management
  structures 108–9
  use of violence 107
  see also business processes; decision
    making; entrepreneurial
    management; project
    management; strategic
    management
manipulators 184
Marcos, Ferdinand 42, 44–5, 82
market development
  case study 122–3
  and competitive imperfections 54–5
  and corruption 16
  drugs trade 54–5, 117, 122–3
  factors in 122
  identification of markets 126
  methods 120–21
  strategy 143, 151
Marzola's Studio 9, 90–91
Mazza, Anna 131–2
means ends analysis, in knowledge
  management 171–2
medical sector, corruption in 16
Mello, Suely Correia de 131
mergers and acquisitions 119
Mexico, drugs trade 60
mission, definition 142
Mohammed, Khalid Sheikh 70
money laundering 6, 15–16, 44, 81–2
  see also proceeds of crime
monitor role 63, 64, 65, 69
motivation
  and entrepreneurship 13
  see also personnel leaders
motorcycle clubs *see* Hells Angels

narcotics *see* drugs trade
Netherlands
  and international cooperation on the
    proceeds of crime 41

Russian mafia activities 90
Verhagen Group 28, 47, 109
network business 46, 47–8
    see also hybrid business
        organisations
networks
    and cigarette smuggling 187–8
    and the drugs trade 123, 127
    as organisational structures 7–8, 14,
        35, 93, 103, 109, 127
    see also inter-organisational
        relationships; interoperability;
        liaison role; spokespersons;
        symbiotic entrepreneurship;
        value configurations, value
        networks
Norway
    case studies 29, 49–50, 87–8, 183–4
    Statoil 40

objectives, definition 143
Oleg (case study) 185–6
opiates *see* heroin
opportunism 126–7
opportunity-based criminal
    organisations 26–7
organisational architecture 103–5
organisational change *see* evolution;
    stages of growth models
organisational culture 56, 96, 106–8
    see also value-based criminal
        organisations
organisational learning 168
organisational performance
    and entrepreneurship 11–12
    see also performance criteria
organisational structure 95
    contingency factors 101–2
    decentralization in 8, 101, 102
    definitions 96
    design parameters 99–101, 102,
        105–6
    drugs trade 103, 109
    entrepreneurial 6–7
    hierarchies 6–7, 33, 35, 87, 92, 95,
        106, 108–9
    legal compared to illegal 97, 101,
        102, 104–5
    networks 93, 127
    organisational architecture 103–5

organisational configuration 102
    parasite 45–6, 47
    police 99–101
    see also interoperability
organised crime
    definitions 4–7, 38, 39, 94
    enterprise paradigm 7, 61–2
    networks 87, 109
    see also criminal organisations
Organised Crime Continuum 21–2
organised financial crime
    stages of growth models 43–9
        case study 49–50
    see also corruption; economic crime;
        money laundering
organised tax fraud 50

paedophilia 9, 90–91
paranoids 184
parasite organisational structures 45–6,
    47
partner stage, in criminal–legal
    partnerships 51, 52
partnerships *see* alliance business;
    inter-organisational relationships;
    joint ventures; legal–criminal
    partnerships
people smuggling *see* trafficking
performance criteria, for IT 155, 157
personality, and entrepreneurship
    13
personalization of knowledge 172–3
personnel leaders 62, 63, 64, 69
PEST/PESTLE analysis 152
Petrov, Gennadijus 6
Philippines *see* Marcos, Ferdinand
pimps 139
planning and control systems, and
    organisational structure 101,
    102
police
    corruption in 45, 137–8
    organisational structure 99–101
political influence, of criminal
    organisations 58, 92, 94
political leaders, corruption in 42,
    44–5, 58, 76–7, 82
politicians 184
problem decision analysis, in
    knowledge management 171

problem solving *see* decision making; solution managers; value configurations, value shops
procedural knowledge 177, 178, 179
proceeds of crime
  international cooperation in 41–2
  see also money laundering
processes *see* business processes; knowledge processes
product development 117, 121, 125, 135
product diversification 98–9, 121
product portfolio analysis 151–2
professional projects 71–2
project management 70–72
prostitution *see* sex trade; trafficking
Provenzano, Bernardo 36, 37, 59

rationality
  in entrepreneurship 13
  in organisations 7
recruitment 122
relay succession of CEOs 60–61
reliability, in organisational structure 104, 105
reputation, in organised crime 94, 95
resource-based criminal organisations *see* knowledge-based criminal organisations
resource-based strategy, definition 141
resource stage, in criminal–legal partnerships 51
resources
  allocators 62, 63, 64, 69
  control of 55
  and dynamic capabilities 135
  management 123–7, 180
  for market development 121, 122
  see also human capital; intangible assets; knowledge; social capital
robbery 29, 59, 135–7, 160, 180
  see also car theft; thief-takers
rule-based criminal organisations *see* activity-based criminal organisations
Russia, sex trade 185–6
Russian mafia 6, 36, 52, 84, 88–90

Schengen system 53
sex trade
  case studies 85–6, 139, 185–6
  see also trafficking
shared knowledge space 178–9
Sicilian mafia *see* Cosa Nostra
Siemens 42
simple projects 71
simplicity, in organisational structure 103–4, 105
smuggling *see* alcohol smuggling; cigarette smuggling; diamond smuggling; drugs trade; trafficking
social capital 10
  see also networks
social knowledge 176
social microcosm *see* networks
social talkers 183, 184
solution managers 63–4, 69
specialization *see* job specialization
spokespersons 62–3, 64, 69
stages of growth models
  characteristics 19–21
  for criminal careers 22–5
  for criminal organisations 25–6, 30
    activity-based 26, 27, 29, 30–31, 34, 35
    benchmark variables 34, 35
    business 38–43
    examples 28–30, 31, 32, 34–7, 49–50
    financial 43–50
    knowledge-based 26, 27, 29–30, 31, 34, 35
    opportunity-based 26–7
    Organised Crime Continuum 21–2
    strategy-based 26, 27–8, 30, 32, 34, 35
    value-based 30, 32–4, 35, 37
states *see* failed states; political leaders
Statoil 40
strategic alliances *see* alliance business
strategic management 118–19, 140–41, 149
  see also business strategy; crime strategy; entrepreneurial strategy; information management strategy; knowledge management; resource-based strategy

strategic partnerships *see*
    alliance business; symbiotic
    entrepreneurship
strategy-based criminal organisations
    26, 27–8, 30, 32, 34, 35
structure *see* entrepreneurial structures;
    organisational structure
structured knowledge 176
success factors
    in decision making 129–31
    in knowledge management 171
succession, in CEOs 60–61
SWOT analysis 27–8, 150
symbiotic entrepreneurship 119

tacit knowledge 57, 172–3, 176–7,
    178–9
Taiwan, Heavenly Alliance 85–6,
    120
talent, and market development 122
tax fraud 50
Taylor, Charles 76–7
Tendo, Shoko 22
terrorist groups 39, 58, 65, 70, 181–2
thief-takers 24, 111–12
top management
    and IT planning 155, 156, 157–9
    see also chief executive officers
torpedo, leadership style 65
Toska, David 29
trafficking 85–6, 90, 96, 120, 128,
    129
training, and organisational structure
    100, 102
transaction costs 56, 97, 98, 99, 126–7,
    134–5
transnational criminal organisations
    52–3, 89, 92, 93, 95–6
triggers, for IT development 155, 157
tropical timber trade 76–7
Tsukasa, Shinobu 59

Ukraine
    corruption in 16
    Marzola's Studio 9, 90–91
underground work 161
unit grouping, in organisational
    structure 100, 102

unit size, and organisational structure
    101, 102
United Nations Convention on
    Transnational Organised Crime
    95–6
United States, 9/11 attacks 70
user participation, in IT planning 155,
    158

value-based criminal organisations 30,
    32–4, 35, 37
value configurations 78–9
    and information systems 149
    value chains 78, 79–81, 86–8
    value networks 78, 84–7, 90–91
    value shops 27, 42, 78, 81–4, 86–7,
    88–90
value creation, and criminal
    entrepreneurship 12–13, 69
values *see* organisational culture
vehicle theft 115–16
Verhagen Group 28, 47, 109
vertical decentralization 101, 102
violence, in organised crime 65, 92, 94,
    107, 135–9
virtual criminal organisations 39
vision 10, 126, 142

Warren, Curtis (Cocky) 59–60, 72–6,
    130
weapons trade 58, 76–7, 90
Wild, Jonathan 111–15
wisdom, definition 167
women
    as entrepreneurs 131–3
    roles 69
    see also family roles; sex trade;
    trafficking

X model of business analysis 150

Y model *see* information management
    strategy, Y model
Yakuza (Japan) 22, 122–3
Yamaguchi Gumi (Japan) 59

Zambada-Garcia, Ismael 54–5, 60
Zealots 181